CW01430519

# An Introductory Outline Of The Practice Of Shipbuilding, Etc.

## John Fincham

In the interest of creating a more extensive selection of rare historical book reprints, we have chosen to reproduce this title even though it may possibly have occasional imperfections such as missing and blurred pages, missing text, poor pictures, markings, dark backgrounds and other reproduction issues beyond our control. Because this work is culturally important, we have made it available as a part of our commitment to protecting, preserving and promoting the world's literature. Thank you for your understanding.

AN

# INTRODUCTORY OUTLINE

OF

## THE PRACTICE OF

# SHIP-BUILDING,

*&c. &c.*

SECOND EDITION.

BY JOHN FINCHAM,

SUPERINTENDENT OF THE SCHOOL OF NAVAL ARCHITECTURE IN
PORTSMOUTH DOCK YARD.

*PORTSEA:*

PRINTED BY WILLIAM WOODWARD, ON THE HARD.

1825.

TO THE

# REVEREND JAMES INMAN, D.D.

PROFESSOR OF THE ROYAL NAVAL COLLEGE AND SCHOOL OF
NAVAL ARCHITECTURE IN PORTSMOUTH
DOCK YARD.

---

REVEREND SIR,

IF the instruction given in these establishments, on the subject of Ship-building, should be at all facilitated by the following short Outline, it is owing to the influence of your counsel and support. I embrace, therefore, this opportunity of acknowledging it; as well as the assistance and encouragement you have always afforded me; and of expressing the sentiments of esteem and respect with which I am,

Reverend Sir,

Your most obedient Servant,

· JOHN FINCHAM.

*School of Naval Architecture,*
*Portsmouth Dock-Yard, Dec. 17, 1821.*

# ADVERTISEMENT.

—◦◦◦—

The Author of this Introductory Outline of the Construction of a Ship, in the execution of his duty, has to instruct the Students at the School of Naval Architecture at Portsmouth, in the Practice of Ship Building ; he also gives occasional explanations on the same subject to the Students at the Royal Naval College. He has printed the following Outline under the hope that it will prove useful to both Establishments ; to the former, as affording some little assistance in overcoming the first steps in the practical part of their profession ; and to the latter, as containing probably sufficient for their present information.

In the first part, he has explained the general connexion of the several principal parts of a ship, from the keel upwards. Secondly, he has entered somewhat more at large into the description of the different timbers which compose the various parts, and the manner in which they are put together and fastened, both in the old and new modes of building. And lastly, he has added a short Vocabulary of the principal English terms used in ship-building, together with the corresponding terms in other languages, which last he has thought may prove useful to officers on foreign stations.

# ADVERTISEMENT

## SECOND EDITION.

---

THE want of some work to introduce the students of the School of Naval Architecture, in a regular way, into the first branches of Ship-Building, was the cause of this Outline being written. The assistance the first edition has given the Author in surmounting the difficulties of his profession, and the means it has afforded, of leading many of the young gentlemen of the Royal Naval College, intended for the sea service, to attend to the subject, have induced him to print a second edition; in which such alterations have been made as experience has suggested.

An elementary work that affords the young ship-builder the means of acquiring a correct understanding of the technicalities of his profession, and that leads him at the same time progressively to a knowledge of the disposition and manner of combining the several parts of a ship, in such a way as to enable him to form an accurate and comprehensive idea of the whole structure, cannot fail of being useful : since if he has no other means of acquiring a knowledge of ship-building than that which is possessed by the working mechanic, he could only become acquainted with the practical rules of the art, by repeatedly performing the same, or similar manual operations ; and for want of being enabled to combine what he may learn from practice, with the general principles upon which the subject rests, he would be very deficient in a complete knowledge of his profession.

A general description of the principal component parts of the structure of a ship, must be also of considerable use to an officer of the navy.

To be thoroughly acquainted with the various branches of naval tactics, and all matters relating to seamanship, is certainly of primary importance ; and more immediately calculated to make him distinguished in his profession : but since his comfort, his safety, his success in enterprize, depend more or less on the ship in which he navigates, he must feel that a correct information respecting the nature and properties of the fabric, in the qualities of which he is so much interested, would be a valuable addition to his nautical knowledge. It will enable him in many circumstances in which he may be called to act, to exercise his own judgement and skill instead of trusting entirely to another ; and especially when the safety of the ship, the lives of the crew, or the accomplishment of an object, which it may be, is of the first importance to his country or his own honour, is in question.

In this second edition, some corrections have been made ; and the arrangement has been altered. It has likewise been considered more convenient to have the part on mast-making in a separate work ; since it required to be arranged under different heads, and to be extended beyond the prescribed limits of this Outline.

In the Vocabulary, several articles have been added, and others corrected and enlarged, which it is hoped will render it more useful as a reference.

# CONTENTS.

—••◉•◦—

xii

AN

# INTRODUCTORY OUTLINE

## OF THE PRACTICE OF

# SHIP - BUILDING,

### &c. &c.

———

## General Remarks on the Construction of a Ship.

To delineate correctly the form of a well-con-structed body upon the mould-loft floor, that the structure may be erected in exact accordance with the design, is of the first importance; but however well the body may be constructed, and its parts adjusted on correct principles, and however well the form may be maintained in building, still, if the combination of its parts be not adequate to give the requisite support, the structure is no sooner borne by the elements in which it is destined to float, than it becomes a distorted machine, and the niceness of adjustment in its formation, and exactness in the erection, is in part rendered useless*.

In giving to the various parts that enter into the construction of a ship, their true disposition and proportion, we are not guided by rules so certain

---

* Ships have been known to break their sheer in launching, from 8 to 12 inches; and old ships, as much as from 18 inches to 2 feet

B

as in structures erected to continue upon an immoveable basis, or as in those machines that are known to be acted upon by constant forces.

As many of the forces that act on a ship are continually varying, both in direction and degree, it is exceedingly difficult to determine them, so as to give proportionate strength to the different parts of a ship, to resist them: investigation therefore, with a view to forming a suitable combination, is generally limited to comparison, and a close observation of effects produced on the system by continued action, and under different circumstances; and from facts thus obtained, proper conclusions are drawn, and a suitable application is made, both of strength and rigidity.

From the vertical pressure of the water on different portions of the body not being equal to the superincumbent weights, and from the continual change of support in a sea, arise, in weak ships, certain effects, as an extension, compression, and dropping longitudinally, of the parts at the extremities; and from varied pressures exerted by the fluid when the ship is inclined, action of the weights, tension of the shrouds that support the masts, &c. a continued alteration of form, transversely, when the body is rolling. These strains cause, on the parts that are the most acted upon, a distortion, or a disruption; and it is by observations made on the degrees of these disruptions on different ships, that suitable degrees of strength and stiffness may be given, according to the stress to which the different parts of the structure are subject; and the compactness of the system, under violent impulses be prevented from being destroyed.

The body of a ship, or, as it is commonly named, the hull, has two principal distinguishing parts, the one which is immersed, called the bottom or quick work ; and the supernatant part, called the upper or dead work; these have their appropriate forms which are given principally by timbers placed longitudinally and transversely.

The longitudinal form is determined by timbers called the keel (Fig. 1 and 11, *p*), stem (Fig. 2 and 11, *m*, *n*, *o*), and stern post (Fig. 6, 7, 8, and 11, *c*). The stem, which is at the foremost extremity, is supported in its combination with the keel, which is the lowest part of the structure, by other timbers lying in its concave part, called the apron (Fig. 2*x*, 3*g*, and 11 *R*), and stemson (Fig. 11, *T*): the apron and stemson unite with timbers called the deadwood (Fig. 11, *M*, *N*, and *f*) and keelson (Fig. 11, *G*), which timbers give support to the keel: the stern-post, which is at the aftermost extremity, is supported by timbers called inner stern post (Fig. 11, *h*) and stemson (Fig. 11, *d*) ; and these timbers likewise form a junction with the keelson, deadwood, and keel, so that a mutual connexion is kept up by them to preserve the longitudinal form.

Transversely, the form is given and an union formed by assemblages of timbers placed vertically, called frames. The lowest timbers of the frames, called floors (Fig. 12 and 13, *a*) are connected with deadwood, and lie between the keel and keelson, extending equally on each side; the other timbers of the frames, called futtocks and top timbers (Fig. 12 and 13) keep up a connexion from the keel to the timbers that form the upper boundary of the structure, called gunwales (Fig. 22 and 25, *h*) and plank sheers.

The longitudinal form is further maintained, and connexion preserved, by exterior and interior linings, called planking (Fig. 22 and 23), and interior binders, called shelf-pieces (Fig. 26 and 27, *a*), united to the frames. The exterior lining or planking (Fig. 22 and 23, *tvx*), which is connected with, and covers the whole surface of the frame, is made water-tight, to preserve the buoyancy of the body. The two sides are connected and sustained at their proper distance apart by timbers lying horizontally, called beams (Fig. 22 and 23, *s*), firmly united to the sides of the ship. Platforms, called decks, are laid on the beams, on which the guns and other necessary furniture of the ship are placed; and which afford cabins for the accommodation of the officers and ship's company.

The height of the lowest deck on which guns are placed is determined by keeping it sufficiently above water to fight the leeward guns in a fresh breeze. This height varies in different classes of ships; the average height is about six feet above the line of floatation when the ship is upright.

In three-deck ships, the different decks for the batteries are distinguished by the lower deck, middle deck, upper deck, quarter deck, forecastle, and round house, in general called poop. Below the lower gun deck is the orlop; the midship part of this platform is for stowing the cables; the extremities for store rooms and cabins for the accommodation of several of the officers. Two-deck ships have the same, except the middle deck. Frigates have only the upper deck, quarter deck, and forecastle as batteries; the lower deck is for the accommodation of the ship's company: below the lower deck, in the larger class of frigates, in midships, is the orlop, for stowing the cables; at each extremity, separate from the orlop, are the fore and after platforms, for the different store rooms; between the after platform and orlop is the after hold; and between the orlop

and fore platform is the fore hold: the after hold is
for stowing part of the provisions; the fore and the
main hold, which is under the orlop, is for stowing
the water.

The smaller frigates have no orlop, in which
case the cables are generally stored in the main hold.
Flush deck vessels, as corvettes, brigs, and cutters,
have only one deck as a battery, the upper deck:
and one deck for accommodation and stores, the
lower deck.

The beams are so disposed on the different decks,
that their sides may form the hatchways and ladderways, which are the communications from one deck
to another, and to the hold; and to give support
to pieces fixed to them, called mast partners, for
wedging and securing the masts. The riding bitts,
for securing the cables when the ship is at anchor,
and all other bitts, are also fastened to the beams.
There is one beam placed under every port, and one
between every two ports; and the beams are so
placed on the different decks as to be immediately
over one another, in order that pillars may be placed
between them, to convey to the upper decks the support given the lower beams by pillars on the keelson.

The beams are secured to the side by large timbers, called shelf pieces (Fig. 26, a), on which the
beams lie, and to other large timbers called waterways
(Fig. 26, c), lying on the ends of the beams, both
well fastened to the ship's side. Chocks under the
beams, and iron plates bolted to the side and to the
beams, give additional security.

Below the lower deck, in two-deck ships and
upwards, upon the inside planking, were formerly
placed interior frames, in the full part of the body,
extending from the keelson upwards to the lower

deck beams, called bends of riders (Fig. 22, *a, c, b, d*); the lowest timber, called the floor rider (*a*), extended equally on each side the middle; the other timbers, according to their position with this, were called, first (*c*), second (*b*), and third (*d*) futtock riders. These timbers were for supporting the body against the upward pressure of the fluid, and when the ship takes the ground.

These riders are now discontinued; diagonal frames (Fig. 27, *m, n, x, y*), which has been lately introduced on the inside of the frame timbers, forming a system of braces (*x*) and trusses (*y*), rendering them useless. The diagonal framing was adopted to prevent ships breaking longitudinally, called hogging, which is occasioned by the unequal vertical pressures of the weights downwards, and the water upwards, in different parts of the ship's length; the weights towards the extremities being always much greater than the vertical pressure of the water on the corresponding part of the body*. In two and

---

* The form given to the bodies of ships is such, that although the whole vertical pressure of the fluid is equal to the weight of the ship; yet the vertical pressure on every portion of the body, is not equal to the superincumbent weights, which is seen by the following table of weights and vertical pressures on a ship of 74 guns, of the second class.

### ON THE FORE BODY.

| Feet. | Feet. | Weights. Tons. | Vertical Pressure. Tons. | Moments of Weight. Tons. | Moments of Pressure. Tons. |
|---|---|---|---|---|---|
| From ⊙ to | 20,85 | 511,7 | 467,2 | 11390,9 | 7166,4 |
| 20 - | 37,60 | 437,6 | 363,0 | 14171,4 | 15572,4 |
| 37,60 | 54,35 | 262,2 | 330,0 | 11976,9 | 15146,4 |
| 54,35 | 71,10 | 226,2 | 250,6 | 12560,8 | 10729,0 |
| 71,10 | extremity | 148,6 | 93,4 | 5715,1 | 4812,6 |
| Total on the fore body | | 1586,3 | 1504,2 | 55815,1 | 53426,8 |

three-decked ships the diagonal framing is formed of wood, the principal timbers of the frame being laid so as to act as braces, and short timbers abutting on them and on longitudinal pieces, placed between the braces, to act as trusses. In frigates, iron braces are used instead of wood, with thick plank scoring over them, laid longitudinally.

The openings between the timbers are now filled in and caulked*, from the orlop deck clamp downwards, to give security in case of any accident to the plank of the bottom, to prevent accumulation of dirt, which may be the means of the decay of the timbers and the injury of the health of the crew, and to prevent the ship hogging.

## ON THE AFTER BODY.

| Feet. | Feet. | Weights. Tons. | Vertical Pressure. Tons. | Moments of Weight. Tons. | Moments of Pressure. Tons. |
|---|---|---|---|---|---|
| From ⊙ to | 18,23 | 369,5 | 405,4 | 3038,2 | 3674,6 |
| 18,23 | 34,98 | 289,4 | 356,8 | 7364,4 | 9419,4 |
| 34,98 | 51,73 | 234,2 | 317,0 | 9916,6 | 19663,8 |
| 51,73 | 68,48 | 230,2 | 249,0 | 13780,4 | 14801,4 |
| 68,48 | extremity | 278,0 | 153,8 | 21719,5 | 11829,4 |
| Total on the after body... | | 1401,3 | 1482,0 | 55819,1 | 53418,6 |
| on the fore body ... | | 1586,3 | 1504,2 | | |
| Weight of the hull and all it contains } | | 2987,3 | 2986,2 | | |

The consequence of this unequal distribution of the weights with the pressure of the fluid is, that the body will endeavour to assume a form, by the rising of the middle part and falling of the extremities, to equalize the pressures; this can only be prevented entirely by rendering the body perfectly rigid, but as this can never be the case, the extremities will fail more or less according to the materials, and the manner in which the parts are combined; this falling is called hogging.

* Caulking is the operation of forcing oakum into the seams, rents, and butts, by means of a mallet and iron; this operation is the same as the force of the wedge, when acted on by impact, to close all the smaller rents, and to make the different parts as one body, in opposing the passage of the water (see Caulking).

# DESCRIPTION OF THE DIFFERENT PARTS OF A SHIP.

1. Ships are in general built upon inclined surfaces, called slips; whose inclination to the horizon is about 4°. In the middle of the slip are placed short pieces of timber, called blocks, about five feet asunder and four feet long, with their upper surface in general to an inclination with the horizon of $\frac{1}{4}$ of an inch to a foot longitudinally, and lying horizontally in a transverse direction. This inclination need not be a standard under all circumstances, for the ship would be less strained, when there is depth of water to float before she sends, if the blocks were laid to such an inclination, that the light water line might be horizontal; or when there is shallow water, were the blocks laid to as great an inclination as possible; for by that means the after part of the body will sooner receive support from the fluid.

### *The Keel* (Fig. 1 and 11, *P*).

2. The keel is the first timber laid, and forms the lower boundary of the longitudinal section. It is one of the principals in the fabric, and forms a basis for raising the superstructure. It is kept in a direct position upon the blocks, while building, by short treenails called nogs, driven into these blocks, on each side of it.

3. The keel is of elm, which is found to be sufficiently durable under water. It is of a parallel

breadth or siding, excepting towards the extremities, where it is reduced from two to three inches; in the proportion of $\frac{1}{4}$ inch in a foot on each side.

4. As the keel cannot be obtained in one piece, as to length, several pieces are united together lengthways, by what is called a side or vertical coak scarph (Fig. 1, *mn*); the scarphs being in length about three times the depth of the keel. The coaks (Fig. 1, *xc*) are for the support of the bolts, especially to resist the strain when the butts of the scarphs are being caulked; they are one-half the length of the scarph, and their breadth one-third its depth. The corresponding parts that are taken out to receive the coaks are called sunk coaks, while the coaks themselves are distinguished by being called raised coaks; the raised coak is upon the lip (Fig. 1, *o*) or thin part of the scarph, and the sunk (Fig. 1, *x*) coak taken out to correspond in the thick part. Sometimes circular coaks have been introduced into a plane scarph; but as these coaks do not form a stop water, nor give such good support in the event of sagging taking place, they are not so much to be recommended.

5. The scarphs are bolted with from six to eight bolts; eight, from frigates upwards, and six to smaller vessels: half of the bolts are driven from each lip side, with a ring upon the head, and clenched upon a ring on the opposite side.

6. The French and most other nations have flat or horizontal scarphs; but as these scarphs tend to weaken the keel, in the direction in which it is most subject to strain, more than the side scarphs, the English mode is preferable; for the keel

bends vertically, which brings a tension on the upper
or lower fibres, according as hogging or sagging
takes place, which fibres are cut off, in a greater
number in these scarphs, to let in the lips; and
when sagging takes place there is a tendency to open
the joint at the lower lip; this opening will cause
the scarphs to leak, except a stopwater be placed at
the intersection of the joint of the scarph with the
outer edge of the garboard seam*, or by increasing
the length of the scarphs.

7. The English or vertical scarphs have their
upper and lower joints caulked with the same number of threads of oakum as the plank of the bottom;
and when the upper joint is caulked, a batten ¼ of
an inch thick, and about three inches wide, is let in
over it, and its edges likewise caulked. The great
pressure of the fluid upon the keel requires that
every attention should be paid to keep them from
leaking.

8. Out of the side, at the upper edge of the
keel, a groove (Fig. 1, x) called a rabbet, is taken
out to receive the edge of the lower strake of the
exterior planking; this rabbet is taken out to an
equilateral triangle, each side being equal to the
thickness of the plank; and after the ship is in a
state of forwardness to require it, the upper part or
what is called the back rabbet, is made to conform
to the body. The lower edge of the after part of the
rabbet of the keel is taken out nearly square to the
fine part of the body, immediately above the rabbet.

---

* The garboard seam is the joint between the lower edge of the
garboard or lower strake of the plank of the bottom and the keel
(see Seam).

In building ships, a temporary keel is generally laid till the ship is far advanced, to prevent the premature decay of the keel.

### The Stem (Fig. 2, 3, and 11, *mno*).

9. The stem is a circular timber connected with the foremost extremity of the keel, and forms the foremost boundary of the timbers that compose the frame. The exterior planking* terminates in rabbets taken out of the sides of the stem.

10. The rabbet is taken out, either upon the after edge or in the middle of the side of the stem; it is formed as the rabbet of the keel, and conforms to it where the stem and keel unite.

11. The stem is of oak timber, with the range of fibre following its curvature as near as possible, especially in the wake of the scarphs; its breadth or siding is given at the head (where it is the largest, to give a firmer bed to the bowsprit), at the lower side of the lower check†, and at the keel, to which it corresponds.

As it is impracticable to provide it in one piece, in consequence of its length and curvature, it is composed of two or three pieces (Fig. 2 and 3, *m* upper, *n* middle, and *o* lower) united together by a flat and coak scarf (Fig. 2, *c*); the length of the scarphs and coaks bearing the same relation to the stem as those of the keel do to the keel.

---

* See Planking.

† Cheeks are knees brought on each side of the knee of the head for supporting it, and at the same time forming ornamental mouldings, which terminate at the figure with scrolls (*see Head*).

The scarph that unites the stem to the keel is a vertical coak scarph, similar to the scarphs of the keel It lets into the fore part of the foremost piece of keel, called the boxen (Fig. 2, *x*) of the fore foot (Fig. 2 and 5, *b*) ; the fore end of the fore foot being formed so as to give an abutment to the gripe (Fig. 5, *d*). This scarph is consequently called the boxen scarph

This method of uniting the keel to the stem, though generally adopted, is inferior to the plan that has been introduced at times by the English ship-builder, and more generally used by the French and other nations ; that is, to have the foremost piece of keel formed with a knee, or to partake of the curvature of the lower part of the stem, and to scarph to it with a flat scarph (Fig. 3, *x*). This latter plan is superior both as to strength and safety, when the ship takes the ground ; for through the curvature of the lower pieces of the stem in the present plan, the grain is generally very short at the upper part of the lip of the scarph, which is the only part that is united to the long grained wood in the forefoot, which must evidently make it weak ; while the boxen that is left for the gripe (Fig. 5, *b*) may become a complete barrier, in the event of the ship taking the ground, to her being moved ahead, when the gripe is knocked off, until the forefoot is gone ; which can only be carried away by some sudden stroke upon the ground, and not by any force used on board : whereas by making an abutment for the gripe, by forming the upper part of the false keel to the stem (Fig. 4, *b*), when the gripe is carried away, the false keel will readily go too, and free the ship.

### The Apron (Fig. 2*x*, 3*g*, and 11 *R*).

12. The apron is a timber conforming in shape,

and fixed in the concave part of the stem, extending from the head to some distance below the lower scarph ; it is for aiding the scarphs and maintaining its shape. The scarphs therefore which are flat, and plain scarphs (Fig. 2, *g*), are placed between those of the stem, called giving shift to them.

13. The apron is of oak ; and when the rabbet is on the after edge of the stem, it is of a parallel breadth or siding, nearly equal to the stem at the head ; but when the rabbet is in the middle, it is made to correspond to the siding of the stem its whole length.

14. Before the apron is fixed to the stem, one bolt is driven through each lip of the scarphs of the stem, from the lip side, and clenched upon the stem ; and when the apron is fixed, the remaining bolts of the scarph are driven through, and clenched upon it, which unites the stem and apron together sufficiently until the knee of the head bolts are driven (Fig. 11, *DABC*, shewn by dotted lines). One bolt in each scarph is omitted, a knee of the head bolt passing through the scarph rendering it unnecessary.

### The Knight-Heads (Fig. 15, c).

15. The knight-heads are timbers placed on each side of the apron when the rabbet is on the after edge of the stem ; but when in the middle, they are placed partly on the stem, and partly on the apron. These timbers give support to the bowsprit, and render more secure the foremost extremities of the exterior planking, called the wooden

c 3

ends; they extend a sufficient height above the bowsprit to receive a chock over it (Fig. 15, *r*), and sometimes above the chock to form a timber head (*s*), and at other times to receive the planking for forecastle barricading: they extend downwards, if practicable, below the deck. When the diameter of the bowsprit exceeds the siding of the stem at the head too much, so that the knight-heads would be cut considerably to allow the bowsprit to pass between them, which will take place in small frigates and all upwards, a piece is then introduced between the apron and stem and knight-heads, called a stem-piece, to give them more spread (Fig. 15, *v*).

16. The knight-heads and stem-pieces are of oak; and are made conformable to the scantlings of the frame, in and out, except the upper ends, where there is an additional substance, called the boxen; equal to the thickness of the interior and exterior planking, in the wake of the bowsprit, extending from about one foot above to a foot below: this wood is left to prevent joints in the hole for the bowsprit.

17. The knight-heads and stem-pieces are bolted to the stem: when the body is not too acute, the bolts pass through both and the stem; but when too acute to pass through both, the bolts are driven from each side through one knight-head and stem only.

18. In addition to the bolts, several circular coaks are placed in the stem-piece and stem, and knight-heads and stem-piece.

### The Stern Frame (Fig. 6 and 8).

19. The stern frame is an assemblage of oak timbers united together, forming the after part of the ship. It is composed of the stern post, inner post, transoms, and fashion pieces. They are secured together before the frame is placed in its proper situation.

### The Stern Post (Fig. 6, 7, 8, and 11, C).

20. The stern post is a straight timber of oak, united to the after extremity of the keel, forming the after boundary of the timbers of the frame. The rudder is hung to the after side of this timber; and in corvettes, brigs, cutters, and all flush deck vessels, its upper end extends of sufficient height to receive a brace above the upper deck*; but in larger ships, the upper end terminates so as to allow the tiller to work over it (Fig. 6, y) clear of the lower side of the upper deck beams (Fig. 6, z). This timber is of a parallel breadth or siding, from the head to the lower side of the deck transom (Fig. 8, q), if any; if not, to the lower side of the wing transom (Fig. 8, m), from which place it tapers to the lower end, where it corresponds with the keel.

21. The lower end of the stern post is united to the keel, in general, by two tenons (Fig. 6, dd), and a dovetail plate (Fig. 9, ab) on each side. The tenons, which are to prevent the lower end of the

---

* Braces are straps of mixed metal, or iron above water, which are secured to the stern post and plank of the bottom, for hanging the rudder to (see Rudder).

stern post from working out of its position, are about one-fourth the depth of the keel in length, one-third the breadth of the keel thick or athwartships, and about twice their thickness wide, or fore and aft; between these tenons the wood is left of the same breadth with them, about ¼ of an inch down, and to correspond with it, a groove is taken out of the keel so as to form a stop for caulking the abutment of the post. The dovetail plates (Fig. 9, *ab*), which assist in fastening the keel and stern post together, are of mixed metal\*, and let in so that their outer surfaces may correspond with the outer surface of the keel and stern post, through which they are bolted with six bolts. The plates are let in immediately opposite each other, so as for the bolts to pass through both plates.

22. On each side of the stern post, a groove or rabbet is taken out to form an abutment (terminating at the line *bb*, Fig. 6) for the wooding ends: it is therefore taken out in depth equal to the thickness of the plank of the bottom.

23. The stern post is of oak; and when practicable, has the top end of the tree worked uppermost.

*The Inner Post* (Fig. 6, 11, *h*).

24. At the fore side of the stern post is placed an oak timber of equal siding, called the inner post (Fig. 6 and 11, *h*), for aiding in the security of the wooding ends, and for letting the transom

---

\* Mixed metal is a compound of copper and zinc, mixed with grain tin, to give it sufficient rigidity.

into\*. The upper end of this timber forms an abutment under the deck or wing transom, and its lower end tenons into the keel with one tenon (Fig. 6, z) of the same dimensions as those of the stern post.

## The Transoms (Fig. 6 and 8, mnqg).

25. The transoms are transverse timbers, connected and placed square with the stern post. The upper one is called the wing transom, which forms the basis of the upper stern. The after sides of all the transoms below the wing transom, and the wing transom to a short distance below the upper edge, partakes of the form of the body, and receives the fastening of the exterior planking. A short parallel distance below the upper edge of the after side, is called the margin (Fig. 8, a), at the lower part of which the planking ends. A rail called the tuck rail, is fixed on the margin, forming an abutment and finish to the ends of the plank. The next principal transom below is called the deck transom (q), it corresponds in height, and supports the after extremity of the lower deck, and has its upper surface of the same round-up; this transom is always left as wide as possible for fastening the ends of the deck; between these two transoms, which are governed as

* If the inner post was not introduced on the fore side of the main post, it would be necessary, to prevent the fastening of the heeding ends coming in the same range of fibre, to have the main post considerably wider before the rabbet, which would be attended with disadvantages. When transoms were used, a score was taken out of the inner post, the depth up and down of the transom, and likewise a score out of the transom, sufficiently on to let the transom aft to the rabbet or bearding; and of a width to allow a facing to be taken out of the side of the inner post, from one inch to one inch and a half from the inner part of the score, to the bearding or rabbet.

to their situations, one or more transoms are placed, according to the distance between them, called filling transoms (*n*); the remaining transoms (*gggg*) are distinguished by numbers according to their order below the deck transom.

26. The whole of the transoms are of oak; and are scored (Fig. 6, *kkk*), and faced (Fig. 6, *iii*) upon the stern and inner post, to which they are bolted, with one bolt passing through each, driven from the fore side of the transom and clenched upon the after part of the post.

## The Fashion Pieces (Fig. 6 and 8, *f*)

27. The fashion pieces are timbers having their outer surfaces corresponding to the form of the body, which face over the ends of the transoms, and are secured to them by one bolt in the end of each. The sides of the fashion pieces are in a vertical plane, but oblique to the plane of elevation.

28. The fashion pieces (Fig. 6 and 8, *f*) are from one to three in number on each side. The foremost one extending above the wing transom, a sufficient height to form a scarph for a top timber, and to bolt the heel of the side counter timber (Fig. 6 and 7, *ccc*); the second one forms an abutment under the deck transom; and if three, the after one abuts under the third transom below the deck. The whole of them have their lower ends resting upon a stepping formed in the deadwood, to which they are bolted with one bolt that passes through each fashion piece and its opposite.

29. Through the expense and difficulty of providing timber suited for transoms, the whole of them of late, except the wing transom, have been substituted by timbers similar to the fashion pieces (Fig. 7, *ttt*), which form an abutment under the wing transom, and are continued to the stern post.

## On the Round-Aft and Square Tuck
### (Fig. 10, *badc*).

30. The round aft and square tucks are stern frames of a different construction from that just described; and are used in sharp vessels, as brigantines, cutters, and generally yachts and ships built of fir. This frame is composed of the stern post, inner post, fashion pieces (*a*) or tuck timbers, and a transom (*b*). The outsides of the fashion pieces are turned to the form of the body; and the exterior planking ends in rabbets taken out of the fore parts of their outer sides. When the after side of the fashion pieces are in a transverse inclined plane, the vessel is said to have a square tuck; when the after sides form part of the surface of a cylinder, a round-aft tuck.

31. The square or round-aft tuck has the transom (Fig. 10, *b*) determined as to height, and fixed to the stern post the same as the wing transom (25), but has its after side in the same surface as the fashion pieces, either straight or cylindrical.

32. The fashion pieces (Fig. 10, *a*) lap over the post in a rabbet taken out, nearly to the thickness of the plank of the bottom, to give sufficient caulking on each side, and meet at the middle on the

fore side. They halve\* (Fig. 10, *m*) upon the transom, and are bolted to it with four bolts at each end, driven from the aft side, and clenched on the fore; they are likewise united together where they meet at the middle line by a dovetail plate (Fig. 10); two of the bolts that pass through the plate are placed so as to pass through the stern post and clench on the aft side; the remaining bolts, which are two on each side, pass through the plate and fashion pieces only.

33. When the fashion pieces are bolted, the inner post is let over them, and has two bolts to pass through it, the fashion piece, and stern post, above and below the dovetail plate.

34. The transoms and fashion pieces are of oak; and on the aft side between them the space is filled in with oak plank, equal in thickness to the plank of the bottom (Fig. 10, *c*).

### The Deadwood (Fig. 11, *MN, f*)

35. The deadwood is an assemblage of oak timber, with its lower parts coinciding with the upper edge of the keel, and extending from the apron to the inner post, for the seating of the floors, and giving the form of the body in the acute parts.

36. At each extremity, the sharpness or fullness of the body determines the height necessary to be given to the deadwood, which is made up by placing

---

\* To halve two pieces together is to take equal portions off from each, at the places where they unite, that their two surfaces may be fair with each other.

several pieces one upon the other (*fff*). It forms the fine part of the body as high as the stepping or bearding line, which gives the height at which the timbers afore and abaft the floors step, in a rabbet on the deadwood.

37. In disposing (technically called shifting) the deadwood, the several heights are made to form an abutment against the floors as they shorten (Fig. 11, *x*); the upper piece forward abutting against the foremost floor, and abaft against the after floor, and the upper part making a fair curve with the upper part of the floors. The scarphs (Fig. 11, *e*) are shifted in the several pieces that unite lengthways, so as to be placed at some distance from those of the keel, and that their upper lips may come under a floor to prevent short grained wood, when the score is taken out. The several pieces that unite lengthways are scarphed together by flat scarphs; and the several heights (*fff N R*) of deadwood are fastened to each other and to the keel by two or three treenails in each piece, until the keelson bolts are driven. The after end of each height has a tenon into the inner post.

38. When the stepping for the heels of the timbers is not worked out of the deadwood, as in the new system of building, a piece to the form of the bearding line (Fig. 13, *p*) is brought in the side of the deadwood, and treenailed and dowelled to it*.

---

* When the ship has a rise of floor and considerable floor hollow, pieces are brought under the heels of the timbers, and to the form of the body, to take away the small chocks (Fig. 11, *y*) that must necessarily be brought on, to aid the conversion; these pieces, instead of being brought to a sharp at the lower and upper edges, should be formed in a rabbet (as shewn by Fig. 13, *c*) square to the body, both into the deadwood and under the

39. In the after deadwood, a knee (Fig. 11, *K*) is frequently introduced for uniting the deadwood to the stern post, from the upper side of which several of the deadwood bolts are driven ; for if all the bolts, as shewn by the dotted lines, were driven from the upper side of the sternson and keelson, the bolts on the inside would be unnecessarily close together, from the boundary of the keel and stern post (Fig. 11, *Pc*) being much greater than of the keelson and sternson (Fig. 11, *gd*) from the bolt in the after floor, which is vertical, and the bolt in the lower transom, which is horizontal.

40. The deadwood in French ships partakes but little of the form of the body, not being of much more than sufficient height for stepping the timbers, which tenon into it in the acute parts. The after deadwood is formed by a knee *(courbe d'etambot)* and one piece *(massif de l'arrière)* that over-runs the after scarph of the keel, and the fore deadwood is formed by a piece *(massif de l'avant)* that scarphs to the apron *(contre etrave)*, the apron giving shift to the lower scarph of the stem, and the deadwood over-running the foremost scarph of the keel. The knee is bolted to the after end of the keel, and lower end of the stern post independent of the

---

timbers, that the caulking of the frame may be good, and for properly fastening the garboard and other strakes that may come upon them. Forward, the stepping pieces have been made to form an abutment for the stem-pieces or knight-heads ; and aft, a similar rabbet to that taken out of the deadwood, has been taken out of the stern and inner post for the post timbers, which is then bolted and coaked similar to the knight-heads, that there may be the better security for the hooding ends. Aft, or where the body is acute, two or three breadths of these pieces are worked one above the other, to prevent having chocks upon the heels of the timbers in this place.

timbers; other bolts pass through the timbers and deadwood and into the keel, and horizontally through the timbers, knee, and stern post, and forelock upon the foreside of one of the timbers.

41. Though there is little working, when afloat, in the neighbourhood of the deadwood, or little other strain than a compression, yet the manner of disposing it in French and ships of most other nations, except the English, is little calculated to resist any force whatever; without considering the casualties of taking the ground, and knocking off any of the planks of the bottom, when the water would have a free passage into the ship; which is not the case in the English manner of disposing of the deadwood, being a complete stop in the sharp parts of the body, while the timbers are filled in and caulked in the full parts. *Oct 21st, 1827*

THE FRAME (Fig. 12 and 13).

42. The frame of a ship is composed of timbers placed vertically, which give the form of the ship. These timbers are secured together in independent assemblages, called frames or bends. It is divided into the square frame, which is placed transversely, and the cant frame, which is placed obliquely to the longitudinal vertical plane. The timbers of the frame are distinguished by the names, floor; first, second, third, and fourth futtocks; and long and short top timbers.

*The Floors* (Fig. 12 and 13, *ab*).

43. The floors are timbers that score over and lay across the deadwood, which bisects them, and

together with the keel are those timbers which will have to sustain the body when it takes the ground, and becomes inclined; they should therefore extend in the fullest part of the body, beyond the point which would come in contact with the supporting surface. These timbers extend in general forward, as far as the fore mast; and aft, as far as the square body extends, or as the acuteness of the body will admit of timbers being obtained with sufficient curvature to form them.

44. The floors of ships, commonly extended out from the keel to one-fourth the breadth on each side, and at this place the rise of the floor was usually determined. When they are nearly horizontal from the rabbet of the keel, the ship is said to have a flat floor; and when the flatness extends a considerable distance longitudinally, she is said to have a long floor; and as the floors rise above an horizontal line, from the rabbet, the ship is said to have a rising or sharp floor.

The scores (Fig. 11, *p*) of the floors are taken out of them, at the middle, to a width less than the siding of the deadwood; and a score and facing (Fig. 11, *OK x*) taken out of the deadwood to correspond, to preserve them in their position; the depth of the score is governed by the depth of the floor, and the height of the deadwood at its station, leaving at least, when the score is taken out, as much wood above it as the floor is wide or sided. The distance from the upper edge of the keel to the upper part of the floors, at the middle, is called the cutting down; and the line bounding the upper part of the floors, and upper part of the deadwood before and abaft the floors, is called the cutting down line.

## The Frame Timbers (Fig. 12).

45. The timbers of the frame are so disposed, that they give shift to each other; the upper and lower ends of the timbers, which are called the heads and heels, coming near the middle of the adjoining timbers of the frame. The first futtock (*b*) abuts against the deadwood, and extends from five to seven feet above the floor-head; the second (*c*) abuts on the floor-head, and extends from four to six feet above the first; the third (*d*) abuts upon the first, and extends from four to six feet above the second; the fourth (*e*) abuts on the second, and extends to the top of the side, excepting in two-deck ships and upwards, when a short top-timber (*g*) is scarphed to it with a flat scarph, if a port timber*, about two feet above the gun deck upper sill; but if it be not a port timber, the scarph, which is then a side scarph, is brought in the same line with the ports. The flat scarph is two feet in length, and fastened generally with two treenails; though it is sometimes fastened with two bolts and two dowels: the side scarph is about three feet six inches long, having two dowels in it, and fastened with three bolts. The long top-timber (*f*) abuts on the third head.

46. The frames are distinguished into frames and filling frames: every other one is a frame, and the intermediate one a filling frame. The frames mostly extend from the keel to the top side, whereas the filling frames are frequently cut off by the ports.

---

* The port timbers are the timbers that form the sides of the ports, and in general have an excess of siding from one inch to one inch and half.

D

47. The several futtocks are united together in frames before they are put in place, by first bolting the second futtock to the first, which agrees in form from the floor to the first head; these timbers are then turned over, and the third is bolted to the second, the third agreeing in form from the first to the second head; the same progressive manner is pursued until the whole of the timbers are connected into frames, and each over-launching part bolted with two or three bolts.

48. The timbers are united together at their abutments by angular pieces, called chocks (Fig. 12, *i*), which are treenailed to the heads and heels of the timbers. These chocks are trimmed, and kept out of their place till the progress of the work requires them to be put in. The first futtocks are secured together, over the deadwood, by pieces of timber, called cross-chocks, scarphing with the lower ends of every two opposite first futtocks, and fastened to each by two treenails.

49. The middle of the opening between the timbers of the frame is called the joint; and the distance between the joints of two frames is called the room and space. The moulds by which the timbers are turned to their proper form are made to the form of the body at the joint, but from the shortness of the openings between the timbers, the error is of no consequence in practice.

50. The frames are distinguished, those before the greatest transverse section, by *letters*, and those abaft by *figures*; beginning from this section, which is called dead-flat, and distinguished thus ⊕ : but

should there be several sections of the same area, which is frequently the case in full ships, those before are called A and B, &c. flats, and those abaft 1 and 2, &c. flats, and are marked thus (1), (2), (A), (B); (Fig. 13). *Nov = 1827*

51. When the whole of the timbers are united into frames and filling frames, every frame is got up and secured in its proper position, by bolting the first futtock to the floors, and fixing the frames to their proper breadth by pieces lying horizontally across, that form a temporary security until the beams are in place. The breadth of the ship at the different stations is marked on the cross-spalls, and the frames are brought to agree with these marks, by which they are brought to their proper form.

52. The frames when up are placed in their true position, by making the plane of their sides athwartships and perpendicular to the keel, and the middle of the cross-spall, which is always marked upon it, in a vertical line with the middle line of the keel. The filling frames are next got up, and kept within the others by some temporary means until the frames are secured.

53. The frames are secured in their position, until the exterior planking is brought on, by pieces of fir timber, extending the length of the square body, called ribbands; and at the extremities, by pieces formed to the curve of the body, called harpins, placed one about three feet out from the keel, one about eighteen inches below the floor-head, and one in the middle between each head and heel; others are likewise placed about twelve inches below

each port, and at the top breadth and top side*. They are got up, and nailed to the frames with one nail in each timber ; and several of them shored †, to support the ship while the different works are going on. The filling frames are then got into their true position, and the ribbands and harpins nailed to them.

### The Cant Frame (Fig. 15, e, e).

54. In the fore part of the body the plane of the sides of the frame is vertical, but inclined forward, and in the after part inclined aft, to prevent an unnecessary expense of timber, which would be the case if the timbers were placed square in the sharp parts of the body. Instead of floors and second futtocks in the cant frames, large timbers, called double futtocks (Fig. 15, o, o, o), are used ; double futtocks, being substituted in a frame for the floor and second futtocks. The stations of the cant timbers are marked on the harpins, by which they are brought to their proper place.

### The Hawse-Pieces (Fig. 15, d, x).

55. The space from the foremost cant frame to the knight-head is filled with timbers, called hawse-

---

* The top side is the upper extremity of the timbers of the frame, before the fore drift, and abaft the main drift. The line that bounds the heads of the timbers between the drifts, or the uppermost line that can be carried the whole length of the ship, parallel to the sheer, without being broken off by the drifts, is called the top timber line ; this line terminates the frame between the drifts.

† Shores are props placed under the ribbands, and at different parts of the frame, or against the sides and bottom, to support the ship while building.

pieces (*d*), having the plane of their sides nearly fore and aft, and forming their abutments against the fore side of the foremost cant timber.; though sometimes part of them form their abutments upon cant timbers (Fig. 15, *e*), left short for that purpose. In disposing these timbers, one (*d'*) is cut off by each hawse-hole, and is about three inches less in breadth than the size of the hawse-hole; there is frequently one placed between the foremost hole and knight-head, two between the holes; and abaft, there are as many as the space requires.

56. Of late, instead of having the common hawse-pieces, the cant frames are continued to the knight-heads (Fig. 15, *x*), and take the common stepping, the plane of their sides gradually approaching a fore and aft line; where this is the case, there is still a single timber (*x'*) so placed as to be cut off by each hawse-hole.

### The After Timbers.

57. At the after extremity, the frames gradually cant from the after square frame to the fashion-piece (27), when there is a stern frame. But when the ship is constructed with a round stern[*], the frames and filling frames (Fig. 16) are continued aft to the timbers that are fixed on each side of the stern post (20), called the post timbers (Fig. 16, *a*); these timbers are brought upon two fillings (*ob*), six inches in thickness, that are united to the side of

---

[*] The round stern is a new mode of constructing the stern or after extremity of the ship, designed to make them more effective at this part in time of battle, by giving a greater latitude to the training of the guns.

the post, with their after side coinciding with the rabbet, and extending from a chock (c), that abuts on the stepping, to the top of the side. The post timbers are bolted through the fillings and post, the bolts passing through both timbers and fillings; and have likewise several circular coaks in them and the fillings, and likewise in the post.

58. The plane of the sides of the timbers that compose the round stern cants more and more from the after square frame to the post timber; the timbers that form the sides of the ports that make the lights incline inwards, their directions meeting in a point in the middle line above the stern.

*Small Timber Frame* (Fig. 13).

59. To make the difficulty less in providing the timbers of the frame, and to reduce the expense, a frame composed of timbers much shorter and of less siding than otherwise given, has been adopted. By reducing the length of the timbers, the curvature is considerably diminished, which gives great advantage in procuring them. The expense is diminished by using smaller timber, considering the total quantity the same, since the price of timber increases in a greater proportion than the dimensions*.

60. By this method two or three more futtocks are introduced into the frames, and instead of having the heads and heels connected by chocks, they abut square upon each other, with a circular coak in their ends (Fig. 13).

---

* With this frame, timber that before would only answer for the frames of frigates, is brought into use for ships of the line (see *Quarterly Review*, vol. 22, page 46).

61. In point of strength, this frame may be considered without its connexion with the other parts of the structure to be weaker than the common*, except when the forces act in the direction lengthways upon the timbers, and bring the pressure directly upon their abutments; for when the forces occasioned by the action of the weights and reaction of the fluid have a tendency to work the butts by their revolving about either edge, the coaks are not of sufficient length, nor the wood sufficiently incompressible to resist them.

62. For if we consider the weight of the guns and pressure of the fluid, &c. to be forces tending to press the side of the ship out and in alternately, as the body is inclined by the force of the wind, or in rolling, it is evident that the center of motion must be the outer or inner part of the timbers at their abutments, and the only resistance to motion is the force the coaks oppose to describing a circular arc round the said center. If therefore the coak is short, it is evident that it will lie so much in the direction of the arc, that its resistance to motion (except it be fitted extremely tight, and the wood incompressible) will be inconsiderable.

---

* By an experiment made on the frame of two ships, one on the common (45), and the other on the new principle of building (59), it was found that the latter exceeded the other in strength very considerably (see *Quarterly Review*, vol. 22, page 47). This may arise in part from the workmanship, as the strength of the common frame depends greatly on the manner in which it is put together, occasioned by the faying, and the abutment of the chocks being close. Whereas the new frame having but a simple abutment, and the certainty of the circular coak being close, has the advantage in an experiment of this description; but however this may be, the system that is most simple, and depends the least upon the workmen, where considerable works are carrying on, must have the superiority.

63. In comparing the efficacy of the dowels with that of the chocks, according to the latter principle, the timber being acted upon as the one coaked, the tendency to motion on the inclined side will be round the outer part of the timber, and the resistance will be proportional to the distance of the treenail (48) from it, which is much greater than that of the coaks: it must therefore be concluded that this is the strongest method under such forces, and with such support. On the side raised out, the motion takes place round the inner part of the abutment of the chock, and there is a tendency to separate the heel of the timber from the chock at the abutment of the timbers, but this is resisted as before by the treenails.

64. The two frames have been considered exclusively of their connexion with any other part of the structure. But as the exterior and interior planking, and other parts in conjunction form the principle in combining the timbers in both principles, their support must be regarded; for the frame without its connexion with the other parts of the structure can only be considered as a number of separate assemblages (42), and as forming no adequate strength to the mass of materials*. In the new principle, with the square butts, before a derangement can take place, the timbers must rise on the side opposite to that round which the motion takes place, but this will be opposed by the in and out fastenings, and resisted by the planks, edge to edge,

---

* The strength of an assemblage of pieces can be considered only in degrees, as the parts are combined, and they are brought to act in mass.

throughout the structure, while the coaks prevent any lateral motion; whereas the timbers with the chocks having a tendency to work in the direction of the fastening, more by the lips being thrown off, than to rise on the opposite side to the center of motion. The timbers therefore abutting square, must give a better security to the planking, and with its fastenings no motion can take place, either upon the outer or inner part of the abutments, without destroying the fastenings to the timbers in conjunction; or, if in working the motion takes place round any part that is firmly fixed, the coak must be destroyed before a derangement can take place, which is impossible under the common forces they are subject to. *Feb. 8th 1827*—

### *The Counter Timbers* (Fig. 8, *o, o, o*).

65. The upper part of the stern, above the wing transom, is formed by timbers, called side ($x$) and midship (*o*) counter-timbers. They form the sides of the stern lights, and receive the ring and eye bolts, by which the guns are worked, when used at the stern. The stations of these timbers are given on the wing transom, according to the number and size of the stern lights; and their directions are determined so that, if produced, they would meet in a point above the stern.

66. The lower end of the side counter-timber (Fig. 8, *x*) partakes of the form of the side; it forms an abutment upon the wing transom and against the aft side of the fashion-piece, and it is bolted with one bolt, that passes through the fashion-pieces and the after cant frame; two or three others are placed

above it, and made to pass through the short filling timbers which are fixed upon it, and the after cant frame: all these bolts are forelocked*. The side counter-timber is frequently in two pieces length-ways; the lower piece extends as high up as it can be conveniently got, and has a piece scarphed on its upper end with a side scarph, fastened with two circular coaks and three bolts.

67. The lower part of the after side of the counter-timbers is formed into two curves, concave the after side; the lower curve (Fig. 6, *v*), which springs from the aft side of the wing transom, is called the lower counter; the upper curve (*u*), which springs from the upper part of the lower counter, is called the upper or second counter; above the upper part of the second counter, the timber is straight. The angular points (Fig. 6, *rr*) formed by the lower and second counter, and second counter and upper part of the timber, are called the lower and upper knuckles, or knuckles of lower and upper counter.

### The Midship Counter.

68. Timbers, which are sometimes called the stern timbers, have their lower ends dovetailed into the wing transom, the dovetails being in *length* the depth of the margin, and their ends being let in and faced upon the transom, from one to two inches. But when the ship has a square or round-aft tuck, the timbers tenon and face into the transom. The

---

* To forelock the bolts, is to secure their points from drawing out of the wood, by having a mortise in them, and a thin wedge of iron driven through it.

after part of the tenon is the thickness of the
counter-plank from the after edge of the transom;
it is fore and aft about ⅟₇ the breadth of the transom,
and in breadth so as to be one inch within the timber on each side, and in length about four inches;
the timber lets wholly into the transom, one inch
from the after part of the tenon to about three inches
from the fore edge of the transom.    The midship
counter-timbers have an iron strap over each of
their heels on the fore side, extending down the
transom, and bolted through the transom and
timber.

## Upon the Keelson (Fig 11, G).

69. The keelson (G) is a timber in the interior
of the ship, placed immediately over the keel, lying
upon the upper part of the floors as far as they
extend, and afore and abaft them upon the deadwood.    It is for uniting in one mass the keel, deadwood, and floors, that a compact union may be
formed throughout the system.

70. This timber is in several pieces, scarphed
together lengthways, formerly with a flat and hook
scarph (s); but now, instead of a hook, the scarphs
have two or more circular coaks in them, and are
sufficiently long to receive two bolts in each.

71. The keelson is bolted at the floors, or
cross-timbers, if a made floor, as far as they extend,
with one bolt in each, which passes through the
deadwood and keel, and is clenched upon the under
side; afore and abaft the floors, they are placed, one
abaft, within six inches of the after end of the keel,
passing through the lower end of the stern and inner

post; and one forward, within six inches of the fore end of the keel, passing through the thick part of the scarph of the stem: between these bolts, and those that pass through the foremost and aftermost floors, the bolts are placed at equal distances; they are upon the keelson about 18 inches apart, and upon the under side of the keel according to the space. In the upper lip of each scarph, two short bolts are driven, in general.

72. The keelson formerly was scored over the floors, by taking the cross-chocks down one inch below their upper surfaces to the breadth of the keelson; but now, a circular coak is placed in each cross-chock when the floors are not made, but when made, one is placed in the half-floor. Where it lies upon the deadwood, the coaks are about three feet apart. This timber is of oak, though sometimes foreign wood is used for the purpose.*

### On the Stemson (Fig. H).

73. The stemson (T) is a timber at the foremost extremity inside, united to the fore end of the keelson, and extending upwards to the upper deck, with its fore side contiguous to the apron (12); it is for giving support to the stem and apron. This timber is scarphed to the fore end of the keelson with a flat scarph, which has two or more circular coaks in it. It is fastened, with the knee of the head bolts, as low down as they extend, below which the bolts are placed in it, at the same distance apart as the keelson bolts; they pass through the stem, and are driven from the outside or in, as can be done

---

* At present, timber from the Brazils and Africa is frequently employed for this purpose.

with the least inconvenience, and clenched upon the opposite side.

The stemson is of oak. It has frequently several circular coaks placed in it and the apron, where they fay together.

### Sternson (Fig. 11, d).

74. The sternson (d) is a timber placed at the after extremity in the interior, scarphing to the after end of the keelson, and extending up to the lower deck, with its after side, where there are transoms, faying against them; if none, it is brought against the inner post: it is for better preserving the union of the after timbers. This timber is scarphed to the after end of the keelson with a flat scarph, having circular coaks, the same as the stemson; and it is bolted all the way up when there are no transoms, with the bolts at the same distance apart upon the inside, as the keelson, bringing one of them on the outside, within six inches of the lower end of the stern post; the others, at equal distances upon the aft side to the upper bolt, which is driven nearly horizontal. If there are transoms, one bolt is driven through each.

75. The sternson is of oak: and sometimes has three or four circular coaks in the inner post; when there are transoms, it has one coak in each.

76. When the keel and deadwood, stem, apron, and knight-heads, stern-frame, floors, and the whole of the frames, with the hawse-pieces, counter-timbers, and keelson, stemson and sternson, are in their places, and the frame secured and shored, the

38

ship is said to be in frame; and in this state she remains to season, from six to twelve months or more. The keelson, stemson, and sternson, are frequently blocked off from their places, to allow a circulation of air to pass upon their faying surface, and upon the surface they would be in contact with; and they remain so until it becomes necessary, in carrying on the different work, to remove the temporary keel, which most large ships are built upon*, and place the permanent one, for driving the bolts.

*Upon the Planking.* (Fig. 17 to 27).

77. Planking is the covering of the outer and inner surface of the frame (45) with strakes or breadths of plank, which extend in ranges lengthways. The outer plank terminates abaft, below the wing transom in the rabbet of the stern post on the wing transom at the margin (25), and above the wing transom at the after edge of the side counter timber (65); and forward in the rabbet of the stem. The inside plank terminates aft, below the lower deck, at the fashion-piece (43); and above, at the wing-transom or side counter-timber; and forward, at the stemson (73).

78. The length of the ship is too great for the strakes to be obtained in one length, each strake or range is therefore composed of several, and where they meet lengthways is called the butt; the foremost and aftermost plank in each strake is called the fore and after hood (Fig. 18 and 19), and the extreme ends

* Frigates and upwards, are mostly built on temporary keels, made of fir of the most inferior qaulity; as it was found on account of the long standing of these classes of ships, that the permanent keel becomes decayed.

where they abut against the fore part of the rabbet of the stem and after part of the rabbet of the stern post, are called the hooding ends.

79. The several lengths of plank in each strake are not always wrought with fair edges, but sometimes with the plank formed to give strength, or to aid the conversion*. When it is required for particular strength, it is worked what is called anchor-stock, that is, with one edge fair and the other with an angle in the middle of each plank where it is considerably wider, that the butts which are in one strake, placed in the middle of the other, may be reduced, to give strength by a smaller portion of the two strakes being cut off.

80. When it is wanted to aid the conversion of the plank, it is worked what is called top and butt, that is, with the top end of one plank one fourth the length from the butt end of the other; at this distance upon one edge, an angle is formed, where the plank is left as wide as it can be conveniently got to reduce the top end of the plank in conjunction; every other seam, both in anchor-stock and top and butt, produces a fair edge (Fig. 17 and 27).

81. When the edges of the strakes curve up or down, they are said to *hang* or *sny*; if down, to hang; and if up, to sny.

---

* This has the advantage as to conversion, by bringing the top or upper end to the butt or wide end, making the breadth of the two equal to the breadth of the wide and narrow end together; whereas, if they are worked parallel, the breadth of the two could only be equal to the two narrow ends.

82. The strakes are not parallel, but of such a breadth as the form, the places where they are situated, and the circumference of the body, at any given distances upon them, may require; narrowing at some places, and widening, technically called fanning, at others, according as the body gives the form of the edges to hang or sny. The sny in full ships is frequently so great as to require the foremost and aftermost planks in several of the strakes to fall short of the stem and stern-post; these planks are called steelers (Fig. 18 and 19, *a*); and most ships require one, two, or more, to bring a proper edge.

83. The principal strakes, both of the exterior and interior planking, are named either singly or in assemblages.

## Exterior Assemblages.

84. The principal strakes or assemblages of strakes, that compose the exterior planking in three deck ships (Fig. 25), are the channel wale (*z*), middle wale, and main wale (*t*); in two deck ships, the channel wale and main wale; in frigates and all lower class of ships, the main wale only. All ships, except the small class brigs, have an assemblage of strakes called sheer strakes (*k*). The other principal strakes which most ships have, are plank sheers (*h*), the black strake (*w*), diminishing plank (*v*), plank of the bottom (*y*), and garboard strake (*x*). The different strakes that come between the ports are named according as they are situated; if in the range of the gun deck ports, they are called the short plank between the gun deck ports; and so for the ports of every deck.

85. The wales and sheer strakes shew the longitudinal form of that part of the ship which is elevated above the water, by their being placed to the curve that forms what is called the sheer. Upon the degrees of curvature given to the sheer, the beauty of the form will greatly depend, so far as it affects the appearance of that part of the body subject to view.

86. The sheer given to ships of war has been lately considerably reduced, in relation to the ports. It is now made to conform to the curve of the deck or the batteries, except at the foremost extremity, where it is made to rise about eight inches above them, thus preserving the sheer and line of the batteries nearly the same. This gives effect, and produces a degree of symmetry in appearance, which could only be done by painting the form before; and the principal strakes which were before cut off by the ports, are preserved whole, by the sheer of the ship and the decks being the same*.

87. In forming the sheer of ships of war, a proper disposition of the strakes with the ports is the first thing to be attended to. They ought to be placed so as to give the greatest strength, and by their form as much convenience as possible for fighting the guns; care being taken at the same time to produce a good effect as to beauty and symmetry. The sheer of ships of war ought to be as straight as circumstances will admit of, by which means the battery has an uniform and formidable appearance, and the guns can be worked with more ease, and pointed

---

* It was not uncommon before this alteration, for one, two, or more strakes of the main and other wales to be cut off by the ports.

with greater certainty\*. In other vessels, particularly
pleasure vessels, a sheer with a greater degree of
curvature is more suitable, since thus they are rendered apparently lighter, and more lively.

### Interior Assemblages.

68. The principal strakes of the interior planking (Fig. 22 and 25), are the strakes in the hold,
and the assemblages in union with the different
decks: the strakes in the hold are called the footwaling; and those connected with the decks, the
clamps, quick work, and spirketting: these are
named according to the deck to which they are
connected, as upper deck clamps, quickwork, and
spirketting, quarter-deck, forecastle, middle deck,
and gun or lower deck.

### Planksheers, Gunwales, and Drift-pieces
### (Fig. 17 and 22).

89. The planksheers (Fig. 17, a, and 22, h)
are planks lying horizontally upon the heads of the
upper extremity of the timbers, and edges of the
exterior and interior planking; they form the upper
boundary of the longitudinal section, and are covering planks for the top side.

90. The drift-pieces (Fig. 170) are pieces placed
at the fore part of the round-house, and at the
boundary of the waist; those in the waist are commonly called the main and fore drifts, and have
their lower ends mitred into the planksheer, and their
upper ends forming a square abutment under them.

---

\* If the sheer is too quick, it increases the difficulty at every recoil
of bringing the guns, at the extremities, to their proper training.

91. The planksheers have the port, and every third or fourth timber, let up into them, and a rabbet taken out $1\frac{1}{2}$ inches up from the lower edge, and as much on from the outside as the thickness of the exterior planking, and on the inside as the interior; this rabbet will form, in the wake of the quarter-deck and forecastle, the upper stop of the ports.*

92. Between the main and fore drifts, the covering planks are commonly called gunwales (Fig. 17, *n*), and were formerly wrought much thicker. The planksheers on the quarter-deck, forecastle, and round-house, had formerly the timbers that supported a rail, called the fife-rail, let through them. These timbers formed a resistance to their rising, when caulking between them and the upper edges of the interior and exterior planking.

93. The planksheers and gunwales, when not obtained in one length between the drifts, are in general scarphed with a vertical scarph, on the quarter-deck and in the waist, about three feet in length; and on the forecastle, when there is any considerable round, from eighteen inches to two feet; these scarphs are in general bolted with from two to three bolts. On the round-house, where the roughtree timbers† pass through them, they abut square in the wake of one of the timbers.

---

* Port stops are the ends and edges of the planks left round the ports, from one inch and half to two inches and quarter, from the sides of the timbers and upper and lower parts of the sills, to receive the port lids and half ports.

† Roughtree timbers are timbers that run up for supporting a rail, called the roughtree rail (*see Rails*).

94. The planksheers at the quarter-deck, forecastle, and round-house are sometimes fastened with nails, driven into the edges of the exterior and interior planking, about two feet apart in each edge, and with bolts called tie bolts* in each port timber; and at other times they are fastened only with nails in the edges of the planking, from 12 to 14 inches apart: when they let over timbers, there is one horizontal bolt driven through each timber.

95. The gunwales are fastened with short bolts driven into the edges of the planking, from 18 to 24 inches apart, with sometimes one bolt driven through it, and through the upper sill of each upper deck port, and clenched upon the under side of the sill.

## Exterior Planking.

### The Main Wales (Fig. 22 and 25, t).

96. The main wales are an assemblage of planks placed upon the widest part of the body, and extending the whole length of the ship; they are the thickest planking, and form one of the principal longitudinal ties, as much from their situation as their substance. The fastenings of the principal deck pass through them.

97. The main wale is composed of from two to six strakes, wrought anchor-stock (79), or top and butt (80); if only two, they should be worked anchor-stock, to give the greatest strength; if more than two, they may be wrought either way,

---

* The best mode of fastening these rails is with tie bolts, with saucer-heads, let in and fastened to the inside and outside of the timber, since they form a better resistance when caulking the upper edge of the exterior and interior planking.

## The Channel Wale (Fig. 25, z).

98. The channel wale consists of thick strakes placed between the middle and upper deck ports in ships of three decks, and gun and upper in those of two decks; they receive the chain and preventer plate bolts*, and are for giving strength to the top side, or upper works. This assemblage is composed of three or four strakes worked top and butt, and receives the fastenings of the upper deck.

99. The lower edge of the channel wale is placed two inches, or the depth of the port stop, above the upper part of the ports at midships; but, at the extremities, if the sheer of the ship is more than the ports, it will rise the difference, which will now be only the case forward (86).

## The Sheer Wales.

100. The sheer or middle wale is thick strakes, in three deck ships, placed between the gun and middle deck ports, giving additional strength to this class of ships: they are in general wrought anchor stock, or top and butt, and the fastenings of the middle deck pass through them.

101. The disposition of the sheer wale is the same with the gun or lower deck ports, as the channel wale (99) is to the ports it is placed over.

---

* The chain bolts are the bolts that secure the chains of the dead-eyes, and the preventer bolt passes through a plate, called the preventer plate, at some distance down, for aiding the chain bolt, when the strain from the shrouds is brought upon them.

## The Sheer Strakes (Fig. 22 and 25, k).

102. The sheer strakes lie between the upper deck ports and what is called the top-timber line, or the upper boundary of that part of the side that ranges the whole length of the ship : above this line the top side was originally formed by scrolls, worked one above the other, called drifts, to give an elegant appearance, and to prevent an abrupt termination of that part of the top side above it ; but now, to shelter the crew, by presenting a more complete barrier against small shot, in the time of action, the planking and timbers are continued up a sufficient height to form a barricading to the quarter-deck and forecastle. This assemblage was formerly in two strakes, and was the principal longitudinal tie to the upper part of the top side, for which reason the several lengths were scarphed together, between the drifts, with a hook scarph, bolted up and down with two or three bolts; but they are now wrought in as many strakes as the breadth between the ports and under side of the planksheer (92), in midships, may require : if three strakes, the two upper may be worked anchor-stock, or top and butt, the lower one fair edged ; but when appearance is studied, the whole of the edges should be worked fair.

103. The lower edge of the sheer strakes is the same in relation to the upper deck ports, as the middle and channel wales are to the ports to which they are placed over (99 and 101).

104. The sheer strakes, in such classes of flush deck vessels as have them, should always be scarphed, as they form a principal tie to the top side.

### Black Strake (Fig. 22 and 25, w).

105. The black strake is the strake lying upon the upper edge of the main wales, for graduating between the thickness of the plank of the top side, immediately above it, and these strakes; formerly the black colouring of the lower part of the upper works was terminated by its upper edge.

106. This strake is of a parallel breadth, and works up, in two and three deck ships, to the depth of the stop below the lower port sill.

### The Diminishing Plank (Fig. 22 and 25, v).

107. The diminishing plank is the planking immediately below the main wales, for graduating the difference of the thickness between the plank of the bottom and main wale; this planking is in general composed of from two to six strakes, or a sufficient number to prevent, by their diminishing too fast, their forming an angle with the plank of the bottom.

108. The diminishing plank is in general worked anchor-stock or top and butt, but mostly top and butt, to aid the conversion.

### The Plank of the Bottom (Fig. 22 and 25).

109. The plank of the bottom may be considered as the planking from the main wales to the keel, or the whole of the exterior planking, which, by its being water-tight, causes the ship to float; but here it is only reckoned from the lower part of the di-

minishing plank (107) to the keel, or the whole of
the planking below the main wales that is of equal
thickness.

110. The plank of the bottom is wrought top
and butt to some distance beneath the light water
line, or as low as the English oak is worked; below
which, Dantzic plank, or plank of the same quality,
is used, as it is better preserved under water;
and this species of plank being nearer of a parallel
breadth, the strakes are wrought fair edged. Sometimes several strakes, out from the keel, are of elm,
as a suitable place to use this kind of plank, and it is
not so soon injured by rubbing, in the event of the
ship taking the ground; these strakes are likewise
wrought with a fair edge.

*The Garboard Strake* (Fig. 22 and 25, x).

111. The garboard strake is the lowest strake of
the plank of the bottom, with its lower edge formed
in a rabbet taken out of the upper edge of the keel.

112. This strake is in general of elm, and
worked fair edged.

*The Strakes in which Circular Coaks are placed.*

113. To prevent an extension in the way of the
butts of the sheer strakes, channel, middle and main
wales, black strake, and four upper strakes of diminishing plank, they are coaked to the timbers*.

---

* These coaks are placed in general in the strake above and below
the butt, and in the timber next, on each side the butt timber.

# Interior Planking.

### The Footwaling (Fig. 22 and 25, r, q, p, and o).

114. The footwaling, sometimes called cieling, is the interior planking below the orlop clamps, immediately opposite to the plank of the bottom, for given strength to the frame (42) and preventing the ballast, &c. from getting into the openings between the timbers. It is composed of several assemblages of thick strakes, and others of diminished thickness; two, of thick strakes, are wrought over the abutments of the timbers, called the thick strakes upon the floor (p) and first futtock (q) heads; one, near the keelson, called the limber strakes (o), and one under the orlop clamps, called the thick strakes under the orlop clamps. The plank between these principal strakes is of less thickness; and are distinguished into the strakes between the limber and thick strakes upon the floor-head, and those between the thick strakes upon the floor and first futtock heads.

115. The footwaling is of oak planking; in general the refuse of the other planking through its being shaken*, or otherwise defective, but not in a state of decay. It is wrought top and butt with its joints quite close, to prevent the filth, if possible, from getting between the timbers.

116. The whole of the footwaling, except the limber strake, is now left out below the thick strakes under the orlop clamps.

---

* Shaken or shaky, is when the adhesion of the fibre is overcome, or when the timber or plank is full of splits or clefts, the same as wind shocks (*see shaken*).

### The Limber Strake and Limber Boards
### (Fig. 22 and 25, o)

117. The limber strake is a strake placed on each side the keelson, for forming a water course, from the extremities of the ship to the pump well. Formerly there were two strakes of equal thickness, wrought top and butt, and sometimes one of less thickness without them; but these three strakes were in general reduced to one forward and aft.

118. The limber strake is placed, in the full part of the ship, 11 inches from the side of the keelson, and at the termination of the water course, 5 inches. The water course continues as far towards the extremities as the acuteness of the body may require*, and beyond its termination, or where the limber strake is worked against the keelson, limbers are formed by taking off the lower angle of the midship edge of the strake.

119. This strake has its midship edge worked parallel to the side of the keelson to the distance of the water course, and a rabbet taken out to 3 inches down and about 1½ inch on, to receive boards called limber boards (Fig. 22, i), for forming the upper part of the water course or limber passage. The limber boards are made of oak plank from 3 inches to 3½ inches in thickness, and fitted with one edge or end in the rabbet taken out of the limber strake, and the other against the keelson, with their upper surface lying with a descent from the upper part of the

* The water course is formed by the midship edge of the limber strake, as far towards the extremities as the rise of the body will admit, so that the limber boards may be sufficiently above a level.

keelson to the upper part of the limber strake.
They are worked with the grain or range of fibre up
and down under the hatchways, and at the other
parts fore and aft, in lengths of about three feet.

120. The limber strake is now worked without
any other strake in union, and has one circular coak
in each cross chock (48) when the first futtocks
(45) run down; but when the floors are made*,
the circular coaks are placed in the half-floors.

### The Thick Strakes on the Floor-heads
### (Fig. 22 and 25, p).

121. The thick strakes upon the floor-head are
strakes wrought to give support to the abutments,
or what is commonly called the joints of the second
futtocks and floors (45); these strakes are in number
according to the rate of the ship. Ships of the line
have two thick strakes worked over the abutments,
and two above and below, of diminished thickness,
the whole of them wrought top and butt, and diminished to four strakes at the extremities. Large
class frigates frequently have the same, while those
of the middling class have in general but one strake
worked over the abutment, and two above and
below, wrought top and butt, and reduced at the
extremities to three; and the smallest class have but
three strakes in the whole; one over the abutment,
and one above and one below, and reduced to two.
Smaller vessels have but two worked top and butt
over the joint, and reduced to one at the extremities.

122. These strakes are likewise reduced about

* See floors made—*Vocabulary.*

one-third in thickness at the fashion-piece and apron, continuing their whole thickness within from eight to ten feet of these timbers.

### The Thick Strakes on First Futtock-heads
(Fig. 22 and 25, *q*).

**123.** The thick strakes upon the first futtock-heads are for supporting the abutments of the first and third futtocks (45). They are placed immediately over the abutments. Ships of the line and large frigates have two thick strakes over the abutments or joints, worked top and butt, and one above and below of diminished thickness, and reduced to three at the extremities; smaller ships have three, and reduced to two. The whole of these strakes are reduced to two-thirds the thickness of the thickest strakes at the apron (12) and fashion-piece (27), but continue their whole thickness within, from eight to ten feet of these timbers.

### The Clamps (Fig. 22, 25, and 26).

**124.** The clamps are ranges of thick planks extending the whole length on the interior of the frame, for supporting the ends of the beams of the different decks; they are in one or more strakes, according to the deck they are connected with.

**125.** The orlop clamps (*y*) are in two strakes, wrought top and butt: the lower strake was formerly one inch less in thickness than the upper, but is now of the same thickness. The two strakes were reduced to one formerly, at each extremity, but now only forward. The lower one should be worked into the upper with an abutment of about four inches (or what is technically called being worked in with a steeler), if for strength; but for taking out the sny, the upper should be worked into the lower. These strakes are likewise reduced in thickness, at the extremities, to two-thirds the thickness of the thickest strake, or to make the whole of the planking at these places without projection, but maintaining their whole thickness within eight or ten feet of the ends.

(Fig. 26).

126. Below the orlop clamps, in ships of the line, two strakes are wrought top and butt, the upper one from one to two inches less than the clamps, and the lower one to the thickness of the plank of the bottom; these strakes are reduced to one forward, and made to an even surface at each extremity. Smaller class ships have only one strake below the clamps, equal to the thickness of the plank of the bottom.

*Lower Deck Clamps* (Fig. 22, 25, *f*, and 26).

127. The lower deck clamps were formerly in two, three, or four strakes, according to the class of ships; two and three deck ships had three, though sometimes the larger class of two deck ships had four, but more commonly three, and frigates two. When in four and two strakes, they were wrought top and butt, and their edges sometimes tabled into each other with an $1\frac{3}{4}$ tabling*. When in three, two were wrought top and butt, either tabled or

---

* Tabling is the letting of one piece into another, so that they may have an abutment to oppose any strain lengthways.

plain, and the single strake was either placed above or below them; when placed above, it was scarphed with a hook and butt scarph, from 3 feet 6 inches to 4 feet in length. The number of strakes was always reduced to one less at the extremities, and reduced in thickness as described for the orlop clamps.

128. These clamps are now worked in two strakes, wrought top and butt (Fig. 26), with both strakes ranging the whole length.

129. Below the lower deck clamp are worked two thick strakes, wrought top and butt, about three fourths the thickness of the clamps; and upon the end of the orlop beams is one, an inch less than the clamps, with its lower edge scored over the beams, and let down one inch below their upper surface; and frequently upon this, one of the same thickness as the strakes under the clamps, which the distance between the orlop and lower deck beams will determine, as there must always be left for air, an opening of about four inches, either above the upper edge of the thick strake upon the orlop beams, or the strake above it.

130. The lower deck of corvettes and orlop of frigates have no clamps, but the shelves work home to the timbers*.

### Upper and Middle Deck Clamps (Fig. 22, 25, and 25).

131. The upper and middle deck clamps are worked in one strake down to the ports; they were

---

* See shelves.

scarphed formerly with a hook and butt scarph, about four feet six inches in length; but now, instead of a hook, the scarph has two circular coaks placed in it, about one-fourth of its length each way from the lips; the lips are always brought upon the timbers, and have one up and down bolt in each, placed abreast the opening between the timbers nearest the lips.

132. These clamps are always reduced in thickness at their lower edges, called bearded; formerly they were reduced one-fifth, commencing at the middle of their depth down, where they maintain the whole substance; but now one-tenth, commencing from the lower side of the shelf. These clamps used to be left, the whole substance, in the wake of the center of the ports, to receive the muzzle of the guns when housed*, but now they are bearded quite through.

133. The upper deck clamps of frigates, and all single deck ships, are in two strakes, wrought top and butt, and range the whole length of the ship, as explained for the lower deck clamps.

*Quarter-Deck and Forecastle Clamps* (Fig. 22, 25, and 26).

134. The quarter-deck and forecastle clamps are in two strakes; wrought, in general, anchor-stock, sometimes with one edge worked into the other with a hook. The lower edge is worked

---

* The guns are housed when they are run in, the coins takes out, and the muzzle lashed to two eye-bolts, in the side, above the port.

down to the upper deck ports, and bearded half an inch ; formerly from half their depth down, but now from the under side of the shelf.

135. In the waist, or to that part of these strakes which was commonly called the string, additional security used to be given, by placing one bolt in each timber, to pass through them and the sheer strakes, driven from the outside and clenched upon the inside; and in the room of having square butts, they were scarphed with a hook and butt scarph, with the scarphs placed between the ports and the scarphs of the sheer strakes. They used, likewise, here to work up to the gunwale, which was wrought over their edge. To form clamps for the beams that came in the waist, a strake was worked upon them, which extended at least six feet abaft the foremost beam of the quarter-deck, and before the after beam of the forecastle ; this strake was fastened with bolts, about 18 inches apart, driven from the outside and clenched upon the inside ; but now the clamps continue the same through the waist, as the great support which has lately been given to this part renders any additional strength with the clamps unnecessary.

### Round-house Clamps.

136. The round-house clamps are in two strakes, worked down to the quarter-deck ports, with their lower edge bearded ; formerly, one-fourth their thickness and to half their depth, but now to one-eighth, and from the under side of the shelf.

137. Before the shelf and other modes of

security were introduced, these clamps had an additional bolt under each beam, and one or two between,
driven from the outside and clenched upon them.

### Clamps in general.

138. The whole of the clamps are, in general,
worked with their lower edges square to the timbers,
and their upper edge level, and of such a height
that the beams may let into them at least $\frac{3}{4}$ of an
inch; but when the body falls out, they must be
placed high enough for the beams to have a bearing
on the inner part of their upper edge.

139. The clamps are coaked to the timbers;
when more than one strake, a circular coak is placed
in the strake above and below the butt in the timbers, on each side of those upon which the butt is
situated; and when but one strake, if scarphed, a
coak is placed in each timber, next to that upon
which the lip is placed; and if with a square butt,
they are placed next to the butt timber.

140. That the strakes in each assemblage of
clamps may be brought to act in union in resisting extension, they are bolted together with up-and-down
bolts; one is placed opposite the opening between
the timbers, on each side of the timbers upon which
the several butts are situated, and one opposite, to
about every third or fourth opening, according to
the distance between the butts; these bolts are in
general clenched upon the upper or lower edge, according to the way in which they can be most conveniently driven.

F

58

*The Spirketting* (Fig. 22, 23, and 26).

141. The spirketting is composed of thick strakes, lying immediately above the waterways; when there are ports, they fill up the space from the waterway to the port-sill. This assemblage is in general composed of two strakes worked anchor-stock, with the middle of each plank as wide as possible, for giving strength in the wake of the butts; formerly their edges were worked with a hook between each butt.

142. The outer part of the upper edge of these strakes is made in a line with the port-sill, therefore if the timbers fall in from a vertical line, as the upper edge is worked perpendicular to them, and the sills lie horizontal, the inner part of the upper edge must be placed as much above the sill as the timbers incline inwards in the thickness of the plank, when the inner part of the upper edge is taken away level and fair with the sills in the wake of the ports.

143. The spirketting has one bolt passing through it, driven from the outside, and clenched, in each butt, through the timber next to the one upon which the butt is placed; and has likewise two through each port-sill.

*The Quickwork* (Fig. 22, 23, and 26).

144. The quickwork is the planking lying between the clamps and spirketting; formerly, when the planking above the sheer strakes was ornamented with trophies, it was likewise called the quickwork.

145. When this planking comes between the ports, it is worked with fair edges; in other places, as on the lower deck of frigates, it is in general worked top and butt.

### Trusses between the Ports (Fig. 27).

146. To give longitudinal support, there are now between the ports, instead of quickwork, trusses*, forming their abutments against the clamps (124), spirketting (141), and abutment pieces (w), which are firmly fixed to the port timbers for that purpose.

### Abutment Pieces (Fig 27).

147. The abutment pieces (w) have one edge coinciding with the port, and are in breadth, to the gun deck ports, 13 inches, and to the middle and upper deck 12 inches ; they extend from the clamps to the spirketting, with their ends let into them, as far up into the clamp and down into the spirketting as the moulding that is stuck upon the edges of these planks : but before they are let down into the spirketting to the gun or middle decks†, a score is taken out of their lower ends, of $1\frac{1}{4}$ inch on the port side of each abutment piece for the port cants.

148. These pieces are bolted at their upper

---

* Between the trusses the surface of the timber is covered by plank, similar to the quickwork.

† The gun deck to ships of the line is the principal battery or lowest gun deck.

parts with two in-and-out bolts, and abut 3 inches from each end, with one fore-and-aft bolt; the other fastenings consist of the ring and eye bolts to the ports, and the treenails that come through above them. To aid in resisting any action that may be brought upon them by the trusses, they are coaked to the port-timbers with one coak opposite to the end of each truss.

*May 3* *1828*

### Truss Pieces (Fig. 26).

149. The truss pieces ($u$) have their ends that tend towards the extremities elevated to an angle equal to the diagonal of the figure formed by the clamps, spirketting, and abutment pieces*. The lower end forms an equal abutment against the spirketting and one abutment piece, and the end elevated, against the clamp and the other; they are in breadth 11 inches to the gun-deck ports, and 10 inches to the middle and upper deck, and in thickness ½ inch less than the abutment pieces.

150. When the ends of the trusses come opposite to the openings, by the abutment pieces exceeding the breadth of the port timbers, a small sill of about an inch in thickness and of a breadth suffi-

---

* While the angular form of the parts is preserved, and there is an extension above the neutral axis, the trusses, with their present position, will not be brought into action; but when the stiffness is overcome, and the different parts yield to the forces impressed, the extremities will have a tendency to drop, which will then be resisted by the abutment of the trusses; for if the parts at the extremities were only subject to the influence of compression and extension, and not to drop vertically, it would be difficult to account for the angles formed by the edges of the quickwork and port timbers, being altered so much in ships that have broken their sheer to a considerable extent.

cient to take the ends, is let into the timbers across the opening, to form a stop for the oakum when their ends are caulked*.

151. In two spaces between the ports in mid-ships, instead of a single truss there are cross trusses placed. The whole of the trusses are fastened by the treenails that pass through the side.

## The String.

152. The string is strakes, inside, immediately opposite to the sheer strakes (102). In ships with a quarter deck and forecastle, it is only that part of the clamps lying in the waist; but in flush decked ships it extends the whole length, and is in one strake, scarphed with a hook and butt scarph, or as described for the middle and upper deck clamps (131), worked down to the ports and up to the under side of the planksheer.

153. The string, when in more than one strake, is coaked and fastened as the clamps to which it is connected; and in flush deck vessels, when in one strake, one bolt and one circular coak is placed in each port timber, and one or two bolts between the ports: the bolts are driven from the outside through the sheer strakes and clenched upon the string. The circular coaks, to aid the scarphs, are placed the same as described for the clamps of a single strake (131); and the scarphs are from 2 feet 6 inches to

---

* In the smaller class of ships that have trusses, frequently pieces are fastened on to the side of the port timbers to make them sufficiently wide without the sills.

3 feet in length, so as to bring the lips upon timbers; they are placed between the ports as far from the scarphs of the sheer strakes as possible.

*May 10th 1828*

## *Planking Generally.*

### *Placing of the Butts.*

154. The butts are properly placed, or what is technically called properly shifted, when they are suitably disposed in relation to the ports and to each other; and when the butts of the exterior and interior planking are the farthest separated.

155. In placing the butts in relation to the ports, the best disposition is obtained, when the butts are placed in the middle between them, but this can only take place with the two strakes that come next, either above or below the ports, as the butts of the third must come under the port, or the distance of the butts of the other strakes from the ports must be less, which would not give so good a shift, excepting where there are row ports; it may then require to place the butts nearer the ports to obtain a good shift. When the planks overrun two ports to the middle between the other, it is called a two port shift, and it will require planks from 19 to 23 feet; and when three ports, it is called a three port shift, and will require the planks from 29 to 33 feet in length; both these shifts should be introduced, as in general, the more the lengths are varied within certain limits, the greater is the certainty of making the least possible consumption of plank. The first butt is always placed where the pump-dale scupper

will pass through, as this scupper will cut off one strake*.

156. When the butts are properly placed in relation to each other, they are apart, or have a scarph of ¼ the length of the planks under 24 feet; but when above, if the length of the planks, the joint of a timber, or any circumstance occasioned by any of the timbers of the frame require it, the length of the scarph can be reduced to 6 feet. There are always three planks between every two butts, and the butts are placed not to form steps or follow with the length of the scarph in regular succession from each other, but the butts in the second strake are placed in the middle of the planks of the first, the butts of the third the length of the scarph beyond the butts of the second, the fourth double the length of the scarph beyond the butts of the third, and the fifth with the butts under the butts of the first. The fore and after hoods (78) are never less than six feet.

### The Projections left to the Exterior Planking.

157. Formerly there were projections left from one inch to 1½ inches on the upper and lower edges of the sheer strakes, sheer, channel, main wales, and upper part of the black strake; but now projections are only left at the upper part

---

* The pump-dale scupper is that to which the dale lends, that conveys the water from the pumps to the side on the lower deck of large ships.

of the main wale and black strake, and at the
lower edge of the sheer strake, sheer, and channel
wales.

*May 11th 1828*

*Upon the Fastening of the Planking.*

158. The fastening that connects the planking
to the frame (44) of the ship is distinguished by
treenail and metal; treenail when the fastenings
consist chiefly of treenails, and metal when the
planking is fastened wholly with copper or iron
bolts, screws, or nails.

159. When the planking is treenail fastened,
the strakes are either double, double and single, or
single fastened; that is, so as to have in each strake,
when double, two treenails in every timber; when
double and single, to have two in every other timber, and one in the intermediate; and when single,
to have only one in each timber.

160. Formerly, large frigates and all upwards
were double fastened, and smaller ships double and
single from the black strake (105) down. Above,
the large ships were double and single, and the
smaller ships single; though sometimes when the
timbers were of little scantling, the smallest class of
vessels were single fastened only; and the larger
class frequently double fastened throughout. Now,
all ships when they have thick waterways and a
shelf, have the strakes single fastened in their wake,
as the bolts that pass through them become fastening for the planks, and often, with this number of
treenails, more than required, through which the

timbers of the frame and planking become unnecessarily injured.\* When the ceiling is left out, the
strakes of the bottom are single fastened below the
thick strakes under the orlop clamps, as the bolts
in the trussed frame add considerably to the fastenings. And when the ship is built with the small
timber frame (59), the planking throughout is
likewise only single fastened.

**161**. The treenails that fasten the exterior
planking pass likewise through, and form the principal fastening of the interior; but as the exterior
and interior planking cannot be placed on the timbers at the same time, the exterior is brought on
first, and the holes for the treenails bored through
it and the timbers ; but to secure it to the frame till
the treenails can be driven through both, there
was formerly one bolt placed in every fourth timber
in each strake, called hanging or fastening bolts ;
but now the outside planking is held to the frame
by a temporary fastening, consisting of screw eye
bolts ; these bolts are in length, from a shoulder
left just beyond the eye, about the thickness of the
plank, and $6\frac{1}{2}$ inches, and have a worm cut on from
their ends about $6\frac{1}{2}$ inches†. When the planking
is properly placed upon the timbers, or what is technically called set to, or well timbered, the holes are
bored through, to a proper size for the screw bolts,
at the stations of the treenails, and at such places

---

\* The number of bolts that necessarily pass through in the wake of the
decks, cut the timbers considerably in some parts without the treenails, and
it frequently occurs that a bolt and treenail pass close to each other, or
that the treenail is cut partly by the bolt.

† To plank, from 3 to 6 inches in thickness, the diameter of the bolts
are 1 inch, and to all thicknesses above, $1\frac{1}{4}$.

as is necessary to bring or keep the plank to; and
to prevent the shoulder of the bolt making an indent
in the plank, an iron plate is put behind it, to receive the pressure. When the interior planking is
brought on, the holes for the treenails are bored
through it, and the screw bolts are removed as it
becomes necessary to drive the treenails. If after
the treenails are driven, and the whole of the fastenings of the internal works, it is found there is
not sufficient security in the planking, then other
bolts are added; if to the outside planking, the bolts
pass all through from the outside, and are clenched;
and if for the inside planking, in the thick strakes,
short bolts, called dump bolts, are driven $\frac{3}{4}$ through
the timbers; but if the planking is thin, nails are
then used instead of bolts.

162. To fasten the butts, the butts were formerly brought upon the middle of the timber upon
which they were placed, and had one treenail and
one short bolt in the butt of each plank in the butt
timber, and one through bolt, called the butt end
bolt, in the timber next the butt; this bolt had a
ring under the head, or what is technically called,
was driven upon a ring, and was clenched on the
inside; but now the butt is brought, to timbers of
small siding, about two inches from one edge of the
timber, and has one treenail and the butt end bolt
in the butt timber, in the plank that is farthest on it;
and one treenail and the butt end bolt in the timber
next the butt, in the plank that is the least upon the
butt timber. The hooding ends forward (Fig. 18)
have a bolt driven about five inches, and a treenail
about ten inches, from the rabbet of the stem.
Aft (Fig. 20, m), where the planks fan and butt

against the rabbet of the post there is one bolt, and one treenail in each butt; and as high up as the acuteness of the body will allow, the bolts and treenails pass through, and are fastenings to the planks on both sides. Where they come upon the transom and butt against the tuck-rail ($u$), there is sometimes one bolt and one treenail in each, and at other times two bolts in each butt, which is far the best, as treenails are bad fastening near the butt.

163. The treenails have both their ends caulked, to form a resistance to separation in the direction of their length. The large treenails are caulked four ways, as &#x2b22;; the middling, three ways, as **A**; and the small, twice, as &#x2b22;. In the garboard strake (111), and one or two strakes above, according to the form of the body, the treenails do not pass through, but are driven about three times the thickness of the plank into the timber. In the transoms the holes are bored through, but sometimes the treenails are driven short. This should not be the case; for if the hole is left, there is a receptacle for substances that soon create decay.

### Metal Fastening.

164. Metal fastening either consists of copper or iron. Copper is used below water, and to about two feet above its surface, and at the bows all the way up; and iron in the remaining part of the upper works. Formerly ships were fastened with iron throughout; but this species of fastening, after the bottoms of the ships were coppered, was soon destroyed, and though every pains were taken to pre-

vent the communication of the two metals, still oxidation took place very fast, when combined with the salt-water, and the iron was soon destroyed.*

165. Ships seldom have their planking entirely fastened with metal; when it is the case, then only ships built of fir and a small class of vessels; each strake is then fastened either double, or double and single, with dump metal bolt nails, commonly called, or with nails, with one through bolt placed in about every fourth timber, instead of the nail or dump bolt, driven on a ring and clenched. The butts of the planking, in metal fastened ships, are secured the same as those with treenails, excepting that there is a nail or dump bolt in the butt, instead of the treenail.

166. Treenail fastening will better resist any transverse strain than metal, according to the present proportion of the diameter of the bolts with the treenails; but the metal will better resist the direct strain or separation; therefore if the treenails are used in numbers, as the bolts are in treenail fastened ships, and bolts or screws the same as treenails, there is no doubt of increased strength and greater durability; for since the resistance to separation is the same, but the fibres cut off by the fastening less, the

---

* A much greater degree of oxidation goes on when the iron fastening is combined with the salt-water and the acids contained in the oak, than when exposed only to the oxygen of the atmosphere, or in fresh water; but an active galvanic combination is produced, and oxidation goes on still faster when the bottom is coppered and there is iron fastening; because then there are two metals possessing different degrees of oxidability, combined with a fluid (fresh or salt-water) that is capable of oxidating either.

strength must be increased, and the greater the number of joints of wood and wood, not in close contact, the greater the exposure to decay. —

### The Beams.    *May 31 - 1828*

167. The beams are horizontal timbers extending across the ship, for uniting the two sides and for supporting the different batteries, called decks and other platforms. These timbers rest at each end upon the clamps, and in the middle upon pillars; they are disposed on the principal decks in general, one under each port and one between, excepting in the places of the hatchways, masts, and mizen step, where this order is not exactly observed, but deviated from as little as possible, that they may give the best support to the guns.

168. Abaft the mizen mast, the beams of the middle deck in three deck ships, and upper deck in ships of other classes, are placed at equal distances and nearer together; as they cannot have pillars under them on account of the tiller. The beams likewise of the round-house, quarter deck, and in three deck ships, the upper deck, are placed in a similar manner, to preserve uniformity, and to present no obstruction in the accommodation, by having pillars under them in the officers' apartments.

---

* The introduction of half beams generally, which give the flat of the deck a greater degree of firmness against the recoil and percussion o f the gun when firing fast, makes it of less importance that the beams should be under the trucks.

## Fig. 21.

169. The beams are distinguished into single pieces, two (*b*), three (*c*), and sometimes four piece beams (*f* and *g*): the length of the beams and the timbers that can be provided to make them will determine the number of pieces they are to be composed of, which should always be as few as possible; for the quantity of timber required to make them will be increased with the number of pieces, because the number of scarphs is increased*.

170. When a beam is made or composed of more than one piece, the pieces are united together with vertical scarphs. If in two pieces (*b*), the scarph is $\frac{1}{7}$, if in three pieces (*c*) $\frac{1}{4}$, and when in four pieces (*f* and *g*) $\frac{1}{3}$ the length of the beam*.

171. The scarphs are distinguished into right and left hand scarphs, and are named by the hand that is on the side of the angle, or the side from which the wood to form the scarph is taken off; when at the side end, the face is towards the scarph and looking upon the upper surface; they are bolted with from seven to nine bolts; so as to make their distances apart from 16 to 18 inches, placed alternately, about $2\frac{1}{2}$ to $3\frac{1}{2}$ inches from the upper and lower part of the beams. An equal number of them is driven from each lip side and clenched upon the

---

* The quantity will be increased in about the following proportion. If a single piece be 1, a two piece will be 1.16, a three piece 1.25, and a four piece beam 1.3; but the increased expense will not be so great as these proportions, because timber increases in value in a greater proportion than its dimensions.

opposite; in addition to these bolts, one nail is driven into each lip on the opposite edge to the nearest bolt, and one bolt is frequently driven up and down in each lip to prevent its splitting.

172. The lips of the scarphs are in thickness, to beams from 7 to 9 inches sided, 2¼ inches; from 9 to 12, 3 inches; from 12 to 14, 3½ inches; and from 14 inches sided upwards, 4 inches thick. The lips of fir beams are ¼ of an inch thicker. The breast beam of the quarter deck and forecastle, if in two pieces, has the lips of the scarphs let in flush, and the beams are sided the thickness of the lip more than the common siding; but if a three piece beam, the side of the beam that has the lips flush, is placed towards the waist, and if the two end pieces are short of each other, a piece is let in the thickness of the lips between them, so as to make the side of the beam fair.

173. When the beams form the side of the hatchways or ladderways, if a two piece beam, the lip is made to go beyond the hatchway; but if a three piece beam, they are placed so that the fair side of the beam may be to the hatchway.

174. In each scarph there are as many circular coaks, within one, as bolts placed upon alternate edges, about the same distance from the edge as the bolts; formerly they were spaced for the bolts to pass through them, but now between the bolts.

### Uniting the two Sides.

175. The two sides are preserved at their pro-

per distance from each other by the beams (167), which are firmly combined to them by different methods, according to the idea of the ship builder at different periods, or according to the necessity of the times.

176. To make the most effectual combination of the beams to the sides of the ship is of the first consequence, both as it regards the safety of the ship and the comfort of the crew, since upon this security the transverse strength chiefly depends; for it has to sustain the whole force and working of the side, when acted upon by the weight of the guns, stress of the mast under a press of sail, and pressure of the fluid when the ship is inclined by the force of the wind, or when rolling.

177. The stresses that act upon the side of the ship have a tendency principally to separate the side from the beams, and to cause successive variation of the angle formed, transversely, by the side of the ship and the beams, which produces the working.

178. To give the best disposition to the fastenings that form the combination of the side to the beams, so as to oppose the greatest resistance to separation, they must be placed as much in a line with the beams as practicable, for they will be acted upon by a greater force, in degrees proportionate to the distance they are above or below them.

179. To prevent working, such modes of security should be applied, that while they oppose the change of form, they may resist when motion takes place, the alteration bringing a transverse action on

the fastenings, which soon destroys the compactness of the connexion.

180. The methods of security should be such, that the beam ends may be easily replaced, if injured by shot or premature decay.

*To secure the Side by Lodging and Hanging Knees* (Fig. 23 and 24).

181. The mode of securing the beams to the side, in general use formerly, was by lodging and hanging knees*, when one of each was placed to every beam end. The hanging knee (*a*) was secured to the side of the beam, and to the side of the ship, with the plane of its side vertical, or in the same plane with the side of the beam. The lodging knee (*b*) was secured to the opposite side of the beam, lying horizontally, or with its upper surface in the same surface with the upper part of the beams, and lodging upon the clamps (124).

182. The arms of the knees secured to the ship's side were called the side arms, and those to the beams, the beam arms. The side arm of the hanging knee, which was fayed to the inside of the interior planking, was likewise called the hanging arm; and the side arm of the lodging knee, which was fayed to the timbers, the fore-and-aft arm.

183. The athwartship arm of the hanging knee extends out from the side of the ship, from 3 to 5

---

* Knee timbers are formed by the trunk and branch of the tree.

G

feet; and the hanging arm down from the upper part of the beam to about 9 inches below the upper part of the spirketting. The lodging knee is brought against the aft side of the beam in the fore body, and fore side in the after body\*. The athwartship arm extends from the side, so that the toe† may be nearly in the same fore-and-aft line with the toe of the hanging knee. The fore-and-aft arm extends the whole distance between the beams, when practicable; but always a sufficient distance from the beam to receive from three to four bolts.

184. The upper part of the beam arm of the hanging knee is always below, at the outer part, the upper surface of the beam, an inch or $1\frac{1}{2}$ inches, that when the variation of angle, or working takes place, the toe of the knee may not act against the under side of the flat of the deck.

(Fig. 23).

185. When the beams come over a port, so that the plane of the side of the knee cannot be in the same plane with the side of the beam, without lying before it, the knee is brought with the plane of its side diagonally from the beam, when it is called a dagger knee (e), or formed with a curve to clear the port, when it is called a cast knee (d).

---

\* The lodging knees are placed on the aft side of the beam before the middle and fore side abaft, that the knees may be obtuse angles, or without a square, for the ease of getting them, and that they may be of less expense.

† The toes of the knees are the extreme ends; they are in general rounded off.

186. The orlop and platform beams are secured with a lodging and standard knee, the latter of which is similar to a hanging knee inverted. The standard knee extends from the under side of the beam to which it is connected, to about 3 inches below the lower side of the beams of the deck above. When a rider passes up by the side of a beam, the standard knee is omitted.

187. When on account of the direction of the edges of the interior planking, or what is technically called the flight, crossing the direction in which the surface of the deck cuts the side, the beams then, instead of being brought against the timbers of the frame (42), and lying upon the clamps (124), form their abutment against the plank, which is the case at the after and sometimes at the fore port of the orlop, and after port of the lower deck; the lodging knees will then have their side arm against the planking.

## The Fastenings of the Knees.

188. The bolts that fasten the knees are distinguished into in-and-out and fore-and-aft; the in-and-out are those that connect them to the side, and the fore-and-aft to the beam. The in-and-out bolts in the hanging knees are from five to seven in number; the lower one is in general placed in the upper strake of spirketting, the upper one on a level with the under side of the beam, or as high up as practicable, and about one-fourth the breadth of the knee from the edge nearest the beam; this bolt stives upwards as much as possible, so as to come below the upper part of the knee, at the side; the second bolt is 5 inches below the upper one, at an equal distance

from the opposite edge; the third is about 9 inches below the second; and the others are placed at equal distances between the third and lower one, upon alternate edges. The whole of the bolts below the upper one take their shortest distance through the side.

189. The in-and-out bolts in the lodging knees are never less than one in each timber, or less than four in each fore-and-aft arm. One bolt passes into the beam and through the timber behind the beam end, and one bolt about 5 inches from it, which passes through the nearest edge of the timber next the beam. The other bolts are placed as nearly at equal distances as the timbers will allow, and the whole are placed upon alternate edges, at about one-fourth the depth or siding of the knee from the edge. When the lodging knee extends the whole distance between the beams, the upper bolt of the hanging knee passes through it.

190. The in-and-out bolts are driven from the outside, and clenched upon the knees, excepting that frequently one bolt in each knee, to draw it to the side, is driven from the inside and clenched upon the outside.

191. The fore-and-aft fastening consists of from three to five bolts, which unite the knees to the beam, by passing through both and the beam. They are driven from the hanging and lodging knee sides alternately, and the two bolts next the toe are clenched.

192. The in-and-out fastenings are driven before the fore-and-aft, that the knee may be brought firmly against the side.

193. When the riders take the places of the standard knees, two of the fore-and-aft bolts that pass through the lodging knee are then driven through the rider.

194. To aid the fore-and-aft bolts in resisting the separation of the side from the beams, or to take the transverse action off the bolts, two circular coaks are placed in the lodging knee and beam, and two in the hanging knee and beam, in the firmest wood between the bolts.

195. The principle of security, with the lodging and hanging knees, was in general use for a long time, and the first alteration from the former method was owing to necessity, through the great want of knee timber, and not from any proof of the inefficiency; though it was evident the association was not complete, as only part of the fastenings could be of any considerable use in resisting a separation or opening. Nor was there any considerable degree of firmness in the combination, as frequently the bolts near the toe of the hanging knee were broken off, and when the ship was labouring in a sea, the first seam on the flat of the deck would open considerably.

*The New Mode of Uniting the two Sides.*

196. The plans now in general use for uniting the beams to the side are formed by the combination of wood and iron; wood to give the support when motion takes place, and iron to form the tie, this being considered the best disposition for such mate-

rials; for if the iron had entirely to receive the pressure or give support, it would evidently be made weaker at every motion (177), because the elasticity of this metal is so inconsiderable, that it would have little tendency, when bent, to recover its figure; every change would therefore reduce its tenacity; or if the wood had to form the tie, the substance required to give equal strength with the iron would be so great, that its contraction or shrinking would soon render it useless, by the combination losing the firmness required.

### Uniting the Beams to the Side with Chocks and Plate Knees (Fig. 25 and 26).

197. The plan first introduced, of any consideration, as a substitute for the hanging and lodging knees, was the chock and plate knees. This plan had a chock under the beam (Fig, 25, b), bolted through the side, to receive the stress, and a plate knee (Fig. 25, c) fixed on each side of the chock and beam, immediately opposite to each other, to form the union between the chock, beam, and side.

### The Chocks.

198. The chocks are the same breadth as the beams at the upper part and tapered to the lower part, where they are from 2 to 4 inches less; they form an abutment under the beams, and extend down on the head immediately under the beam (Fig. 25, m), where they scarph to the orlop beams, about 4 feet 6 inches; to the gun deck, they extend to about 6 inches below the upper part of the thick

strakes over the orlop beams\*; *to the upper deck* they extend, generally, from 6 to 8 inches below the gun deck spirketting; *and to the quarter deck, forecastle, and round-house beams,* they form their abutments on the spirketting of the decks below. Above the spirketting and thick strakes over the orlop beams, the strakes should be carried back, the breadth of the chock, from an inch to $1\frac{1}{2}$ inches into the plank above, to give a firmer abutment to the lower end of the chock, so as to receive the stress, and take the action off the bolts.

199. Formerly the upper end of the chock had a tenon in the under side of the beam, but now the beams form a hook upon the ends of the chocks, against which wedge-like keys are driven, with a view to bring the beam and side in close contact. The keys are of iron, and in general driven in a copper case, to prevent the wood from yielding too much by the compression.

200. The chocks are of oak, and project from the interior planking at the upper part, sufficiently to receive the plate knee; or to the orlop and gun deck, about two feet two inches; the upper and middle decks, one foot eleven inches; quarter deck and forecastle, one foot five inches; and to the round-house, about one foot two inches; at the lower part they are from three to six inches, and have their ends rounded off.

---

\* Sometimes to this deck they have been nearly of a parallel breadth, and their lower ends have formed an abutment on the orlop beams.

### Bolting the Chocks.

201. The chocks are in general bolted with six bolts; the two upper are placed abreast of each other, from five to seven inches below the under side of the beam, or as high up as is practicable. They are driven in general from the inside, and clenched on the outside, to draw the chock to the interior planking. The next bolt is from eight to ten inches below the upper. The lower bolt, when the side falls home to the middle and upper deck, is frequently in the spirketting to the gun deck; it is placed about four inches above the thick strakes over the orlop beams; and to the other decks, about four inches above the spirketting: the remaining bolts are placed between these at equal distances, and upon alternate edges, about $\frac{1}{4}$ the breadth of the chock from the edge. They are driven from the outside and clenched upon the chock.

### The Circular Coaks in the Chocks.

202. In the chock and interior planking are frequently placed one or more circular coaks, to take the strain off the bolts, when, by the ship's rolling, the pressure is brought upon the head of the chock.

### The Plate Knees.

203. The plate knees are formed with two arms; one extends along the side of the beam, from 3 to 4 feet, and is returned against the side of ship about 14 inches, or so as to receive two bolts; and the other, about $\frac{1}{4}$ out, down the chock, nearly

the same distance. These two arms to the orlop, gun, middle, and upper decks, are supported by a brace connected to each, nearly at the middle.

204. The knee plates are placed one on each side the beam and chock, immediately opposite to each other, so that the fore-and-aft bolts may pass through both; and they are let in for their outer surfaces to be fair with the outside of the chock and beam.

205. To the quarter-deck, forecastle, and round-house, where the knee plates have no brace, the arm connected to the chock has its lower end inclined towards the side, so as to bring it in the direction in which the motion takes place, when there is a tendency for the beam to separate from the chock.

### Bolting the Plate Knees.

206. The plate knees are bolted with from three to four bolts in each arm, and one in the brace; one of the bolts in each arm is placed immediately opposite the brace. The bolts are either collar or saucer headed*, and driven from each side alternately, and clenched upon a ring. The part of the arm that is returned against the side is bolted with two in-and-out bolts, collar headed, driven from the inside, and clenched upon the outside.

### The Fillings between the Beams.

207. Between the beams a filling is placed,

---

* Saucer heads are large flat heads of a circular form (*see Bolts*).

about 1 inch less in thickness than the clamps (124), with its upper edge well with the upper part of the beams, and of a breadth so as to leave an opening above the clamps of about 2 inches; this filling is fastened with the treenails that pass through the side in its wake, and the in-and-out bolts of the plate knees.

208. The method of securing the beam ends to the side, by chocks and plate knees, appears to have been a combination, that the labouring of the ship produced but little effect upon, so far as destroying its compactness; but as the association with the side is only local, it cannot be considered alone as adding any longitudinal strength, or as being complete.

209. The bolts that fastened the plate knees to the beams were formerly placed in the same range of fibre, which order frequently caused the beam end to split; to remedy this disadvantage, the beam arms of the plate knees have been made of a serpentine form, and two up-and-down bolts driven about 10 inches from each end at $\frac{1}{4}$ the breadth from the side of the beam.

210. The plate kness have sometimes been found broken at the part where the brace is welded to the beam arm, which may be caused by the parts not being properly incorporated; but most likely for want of sufficient strength at this place, as the principal action will be produced upon the brace when the ship is labouring.

*Upon the Method of Uniting the Beams to the Side
when the Union is assisted by a thick Waterway
and Shelf.*

*Upon the Shelf* (Fig. 27, a).

211. The shelf is a combination of timbers ranging the whole length of the ship, contiguous to the
clamps (124), and fixed to the underside of the
beams, for forming the whole of the side and beams
in one compact union.

212. The shelf is broad from the clamps, at
the upper part from 10 to 15 inches, and in depth
below the beams against the clamps, from $5\frac{1}{2}$ to 9
inches, according to the rate of the ship and the
deck it is connected with. The several pieces that
compose it are united together with vertical scarphs
(Fig. 28, c), from 5 to 6 feet in length, and have
four circular coaks in each. The scarphs are placed
between the ports, and for the front lip to be nearly
well with the side of a beam, for a bolt to pass
through it to an advantage.

### (Fig. 28.)

213. When the breadth of the shelf is such as
to cause a great consumption of timber, to work it
of a parallel breadth, the top ends of the tree are
brought together and connected by an angular piece
(b); the lips of this piece are brought the same in
relation to the beams as the front lips of the scarphs.
To the orlop and lower deck, instead of the lips being let in their whole thickness, they are sometimes

only let in half. The angular or connecting piece is coaked to the shelf with five circular coaks in each piece.

214. The shelf that is connected to the orlop beams, in all classes of ships having the trussed frame, and to the lower deck of frigates at the extremities, instead of being contiguous to the clamps, is brought upon the timbers of the trussed frame, and the spaces between them from the shelf to the side are filled up by pieces called ekeings, of the same depth with the shelf; their outer parts are worked square, and project beyond the timbers as much as they fall in from a square, that the shelf may not be cut into at the lower part.

215. To the smaller class of ships that have no orlop, the lower deck shelf is brought against the timbers of the frame (42), and scarphed and coaked the same as to the other decks.

216. The front of the shelf, up and down, is worked in the direction of the chocks that are brought under them for receiving an iron knee.

217. The shelf is fastened with bolts, one placed about 12 inches from the middle of each beam, and the others at equal distances of from 18 to 20 inches; and immediately under the middle of the beams there is a bolt in it that passes through an iron knee; when this is not the case, a bolt must be added*.

* The distances given for the bolts which combine various parts of the structure, it will be found cannot frequently be rigidly observed from circumstances that will be found often to occur in practice, as the opening between the timbers, &c. when they must be placed as these circumstances point out.

**218.** To the orlop, lower, middle, and upper decks, of two and three deck ships, and to the upper deck of frigates, there is placed in the shelf two circular coaks in each beam, and one in each beam to all other decks.

*30th August 1828*

*Upon the Waterways.*

**219.** The waterways are pieces brought against the timbers upon the ends of the beam, extending the whole length of the ship; their thickness governs the distance of the lower edge of the spirketting (141) from the beams, which is worked upon the upper part; formerly, they were only formed for keeping the water from lying against the side of the ship, but now they are formed for assisting in uniting the beams to the side.

### The original Thick Waterways.

**220.** The thick waterways formerly were formed according to various methods; but were worked in general, either for the beams to form a dovetail in a score taken out of them, or to have a circular coak in them and the beams. They had their outer edges formed for the flat of the deck to come against them, and caulked up and down the same as the deck.

**221.** These waterways were bolted down to the beams and through the side, according to the idea of the projector, but mostly with two up-and-down bolts through the beams, and bolted through the side, with the bolts placed opposite to the flat of the deck, or above, from 20 inches to 2 feet apart.

## Thick Waterways in the present System of Building (Fig. 26, e).

222. The thick waterways, now in general use, are of the same size each way, with their upper parts a little inclined downwards from the spirketting, to prevent the water lying against the seam, and with their inner or front parts rounded off. They rabbet over the flat of the deck three inches, so as to caulk in, instead of up and down. The rabbet is above the beam the thickness of the flat of the deck at its inner edge, and inclined downwards, so that at its inner part it may be above the beam less than the thickness of the deck by $\frac{4}{8}$ of an inch; and the butts of the flat of the deck are taken off, or what is called bearded away, to correspond, for the convenience of getting them under and caulking.

223. These waterways have a score taken out of them, so as to face $\frac{1}{2}$ an inch upon the sides of each of the main beams, and to let their lower side be below the upper surface, from 2 to 3 inches; and when there are half beams (167) between the main beams, the scores are taken out of them, and not out of the waterway, to allow their being let down.

224. The butts are not, as is usual to other waterways, placed upon the beams, but between them, so that they may be the better fastened, and be the least liable to yield where there is the greatest strain. To receive the butts, carlings to the breadth of the waterways are let down between the beams immediately under them, with their upper sides well with the upper surface of the beams; and the lower part of the waterway, to the depth of the score, is

taken off; and to give firmness and form a connexion, there are two circular coaks in the carling,
in each piece of waterway, on each side of the butt.

225. The waterways to the lower, middle, and
upper decks have two circular coaks in each beam,
and to the other decks one; and when the side falls
home, so that the waterway could not be got into
its place on account of the circular coaks not being
parallel to the timbers, pieces called ekeings are
wrought against the timbers, with their outer parts
perpendicular to the upper surface of the beams, and
of such a thickness at the upper edge as to allow the
waterway to rise what the coak is above the beam,
without coming in contact with the timbers. The
butts of the ekeings are placed clear, or to give shift
to the butts of the waterway, and they score over the
beams the same as the waterway.

226. The waterways are bolted with one up-
and-down bolt in each main and half beam, and one
in each butt, through the carling, unless the bolt
through the half beam answer for the butt; the
butt bolt is then omitted. The whole of the up-and-
down bolts pass through the shelf, and are well
clenched upon the under side; as the center of
motion being on the outer part of the shelf, there is
a great tendency for the beams to rise. The bolts
are therefore placed as far in at the lower side of the
shelf as is practicable; and those through the beams
stive clear of the chock.

227. There is one in-and-out bolt immediately
over the middle of each beam and half beam, about
the middle between the upper part of the deck and

*September 6th*

upper part of the waterway; the bolts stive a little down, and are clenched upon the waterway. *1828*

### Letting-down Strake (Fig. 26).

228. When the flat of the deck is laid diagonally, there is then, in addition to the waterway and shelf, a strake, called the side binding or letting-down strake (o); it is from 5 to 6 inches deep, and 10 inches broad, with its upper part fair with the upper surface of the beams, and its outer edge 3 inches from the inner edge of the waterway.

229. This strake is for forming the flat of the deck and sides of the ship in one continued combination, for which purpose it is firmly united to the beams and side; to the beams, by a score taken out of them the breadth of the strake, and from $2\frac{1}{2}$ to 3 inches deep, and a score out of the strake sufficient to admit of its being let down, so that its upper part may be well with the upper surface of the beam; this score is faced on each side of the beam $\frac{1}{2}$ an inch. The half beams have a score taken out of them half the depth of the binding strake, and the other half is taken out of the strake.

230. To unite the binding strakes to the side, one bolt is driven in the middle between every beam and half beam; these bolts pass through the lower part of the waterway, and are inclined a little upwards, and clenched upon the binding strake.

### The Chocks and Knees under the Shelf
### (Fig. 26 and 27, a).

231. A chock (a) is placed immediately under each beam, forming an abutment under the shelf,

and at the lower deck it extends to the orlop; in a frigate, it extends to the platform beams, and at the other decks to the spirketting (141), where they likewise form an abutment; and as the projection of the spirketting would form but a small abutment for the lower ends, the strake above, to the breadth of the chock, is taken away, from 1 inch to $1\frac{1}{2}$ inch.

232. The chocks are from 6 to 10 inches wide, or sided, according to the class of ships and the deck to which they are connected, and project from the interior planking at the upper part to be the same breadth as the shelf, and with their fronts straight; those at the lower deck project sufficiently at the lower ends to receive a circular plate that connects them to the orlop beams; at the other decks the lower end is fair with the outer part of the spirketting.

(Fig. 27, *m*).

233. The chocks under the orlop shelf are inclined as the timbers in the trussed frame, and extend down about 4 feet below the head of the timber that abuts under the thick strakes below the orlop clamps; this chock is fair with the outside of the shelf at the upper part, and answers for a connecting piece to the two upper timbers in the trussed frame; it is bolted with six bolts, three in each timber; the upper one is about 5 inches below the shelf, and the others from 12 to 14 inches apart; they are clenched upon the chock.

*The Iron Knees, &c. connected with the Chock, Shelf, and Beam* (Fig. 26 and 27).

234. To form a firmer connexion between the

H

side, beam, shelf, and chock, they are united together by *forked, iron knees,* or *plate bolts.* To the
upper deck of frigates, and to the lower, middle, upper and quarter deck, and forecastle, in ships of the
line, are placed *forked knees;* to the lower deck of
frigates are placed *plate bolts;* and to the quarter
deck and forecastle in ships of 50 guns and frigates,
and to the principal decks of the smaller class vessels, are placed *iron knees* under the beams, and to
the round-house of all ships *plate bolts.*

### The Forked Knees (Fig. 26).

235. The forked knees are made to clasp the
beams to form an abutment under them, and to extend down sufficiently low to have one bolt in the
spirketting (141), and at the lower deck, to have
one in the thick strake over the orlop beams (129).
These knees have five in-and-out bolts, one up-and-
down, and at the lower deck three, and at all other
decks, two fore-and-aft bolts. The in-and-out bolts
are placed, one to pass through the shelf (211),
and one through the upper part of the spirketting
or thick strake over the orlop beams; the remaining bolts are placed, so as regularly to increase in
distance from 1 to 2 inches from the upper one;
they are in general driven from the inside and
clenched upon the out. The up-and-down bolt is
driven through the throat or thick part of the knee,
and passes through the beam and flat of the deck,
and is clenched upon the flat. The fore-and-aft
bolts pass through the beam, and are driven from
the sides alternately, and clenched upon the opposite.

### The Iron Knees under the Beams.

236. The iron knees under the beams have one arm extending out from the side immediately under the middle of the beam, and the other down the chock. The arm connected to the beam is from 2 feet 3 inches to 2 feet 9 inches in length, and is bolted with from three to four up-and-down bolts, which pass through the beam, and are clenched upon the upper part of the beam, or upon the flat. The arm that extends down the chock is similar to the up-and-down arm of the forked knee, and is bolted the same.

### The Plate Bolts.

237. The plate bolts are for keeping the beams down; they have a plate that extends down the chock, like the side arm of the forked knee, and bolted to the side, with the in-and-out bolts, the same. Connected with the upper end of the plate is a bolt that passes through the beam, and clenched upon the upper part. For driving the bolt through the beam there is a shoulder formed upon the upper part of the plate, projecting from the outer surface about $\frac{1}{2}$ an inch.

### Side Plates (Fig. 26, n).

238. To ships of the line, the orlop beams are secured at their ends, in addition to the shelf, by a circular side plate, which lets into the sides of the gun deck chock and orlop beam. These plates are placed on one side of the beam only, with their outer surfaces fair with the sides of the chock and beam, and are bolted with four fore-and-aft bolts, two through

the chock, and two through the beam; they are driven from the plate side, and clenched upon the opposite side.

239. The chocks to the lower deck of frigates abut on the orlop or midship platform beams, as far as it extends, but have no side plates connected with them.

240. The beams to the orlop and platform, and the foremost and aftermost beams of the lower deck *in frigates,* and the whole of the lower deck beams in the smaller class of vessels, have two or three bolts in each, driven through their ends from the outside, and clenched upon the beams.

### The Riders.

241. Riders are interior timbers placed upon the inside planking for giving additional strength; those below the lower deck, are in two and three deck ships; and in bombs, under the bomb beds;* they are placed to some extent in the full part of the ship, for giving support to the body when it takes the ground, and against the pressure of the fluid, especially the vertical pressure in the neighbourhood of the keel. The riders above, were in general placed in all classes of ships, and extended nearer to the extremities; they were for supporting the upper works.

### (Fig. 22).

242. The riders below the lower deck are dis-

---

* Bombs have in general six floor riders, extending on each side without the bed, about 3 feet. They are brought on thick strakes.

tinguished into floors (*d*) ; first (*c*), second (*b*), and third (*a*) futtock riders ; and that they may act in conjunction in giving support to the body below water, they were formed into bends. Three deck ships had in general eight, and two deck ships six bends on each side ; five of which in three deck ships, and four in ships of two decks, were connected by floor riders.

243. The floor riders were mostly placed over the first futtocks in the frame (45), and extended from 12 to 16 feet on each side of the middle. The first futtock rider was placed to the side of the floor, when there was one connected with the bend, and had its lower end from 2 to 4 feet from the keelson, and extended from 7 to 9 feet above the head of the floor rider. The second futtock rider scarphed or abutted on the head of the floor rider ; if it abutted, it was connected to the floor by a chock and extended to the orlop beams. The third futtock rider scarphed or abutted upon the first, and extended to the gun deck beams, and if it formed an abutment upon the first, they were connected by a chock ; this rider was in general faced upon the orlop beams and bolted through them with two bolts.

244. The first futtock riders were frequently connected from opposite sides by a cross chock (Fig. 22, *d*), scarphed with a hook and butt scarph upon the heel of each ; the scarph was from 4 to 5 feet in length, and had three small bolts in the upper lip.

245. The floor riders were bolted with from 10 to 12 bolts, the cross chocks with from 6 to 8,

and the second and third futtock riders with from 7 to 9 in-and-out bolts. The bolts, that could be driven from the outside, were clenched upon the riders, the others were clenched upon the plank of the bottom.

246. The riders were likewise bolted to each other, with from 2 to 3 fore-and aft bolts in each over launching part, and the cross chock to the floor rider with from 6 to 8.

*Single Riders in the Hold* (Fig. 25, *n*).

247. Single riders have been partially introduced into ships of the line, instead of the method of forming the riders into bends (242). These riders were in one piece, and placed immediately under the orlop beams, with the chocks (Fig. 25, *m*), that united the orlop beams to the side, scarphed upon their heads, and extending down within 5 or 6 feet of the keelson, or so as to give good shift to the floor heads. These riders were about twelve in number on each side, lying in the full part of the ship, between the fore part of the fore hatchway and the after part of the after hatchway.

248. The bolts in the single riders were from 16 to 18 inches apart, placed upon alternate edges, about one-fourth from them. Where it was practicable, the bolts were driven from the outside, and clenched upon the rider; where it was not, they were driven from the inside, and clenched upon the plank of the bottom.

249. The riders above were for supporting the

topside, and were distinguished into the breadth and top riders, and sometimes in three deck ships, middle riders. The *breadth riders* extended from within 6 inches of the upper side of the orlop beams to the under side of the middle or upper deck beams, according to the class of ship. The *middle riders* had their lower ends sufficiently clear of the lower deck waterway seam, and extended to the under side of the upper deck beams. And the *top riders* were placed with their lower ends clear of the middle or gun deck waterway seam, according to the class of ship, and extended to the under side of the quarter deck and forecastle beams.

250. The breadth riders were in general thirteen on each side in three deck ships, and twelve in two deck ships; they were bolted with from nine to eleven in-and-out bolts. The middle riders, when three deck ships had them, were thirteen on each side, and were bolted as the breadth riders. The top riders were in three deck ships thirteen, in two deck ships twelve, and in frigates from eight to ten on each side, and were bolted with from nine to eleven in-and-out bolts; the whole of these riders were in general placed in a diagonal direction, not that this direction could give any support to the body, but that they might be placed in the best manner in relation to the beams and ports; and it was considered that by their crossing several timbers (45), which this position would effect, additional strength would be obtained; but as the bolt had no support transversely, the riders could resist no other strain than that which was communicated in the direction lengthways of the bolts. These riders were formed with a swell in-and-out, at the decks, and had their

ends rounded; when they were brought against the side of a beam two fore-and-aft bolts were driven through them and the beam. *Oc After 2th = 1728 —*

*The Support formerly given to the Topside by Standards instead of Riders.*

251. When the riders (249) were omitted, the top side used to be supported by knees, similar to inverted hanging knees, placed immediately over the beams, and against the side, called standards; extending out from the side, from 3 feet 6 inches to 4 feet 6 inches; and above the deck from 5 to 6 feet. There were in general from nine to twelve on each side, fixed on pieces upon the deck, called a shole, from 3 to 4 inches in thickness.

The standards were of wood or iron; and in general bolted with nine bolts, four up-and-down, and five in-and-out; the up-and-down bolts were collar headed, and driven from the upper part of the standard, and clenched upon the under'side of the beam. In general, the toe bolt, when the standard was of wood, was driven through a plate that clasped it, as in the working of the topside there was a great tendency for the toe to separate from the deck, and frequently to split. The in-and-out bolts were driven from the outside, and clenched upon the standard. When the standards were of iron, the whole of the bolts were collar headed; and the in-and-out bolts were then driven from the inside.

*The increased Support given to the Structure by the present System of Building.*

252. To increase the resistance which the body

opposes to any alteration of form and to save materials, considerable alteration has been made in the internal structure of the ship. To increase the resistance to extension and to give a firmer support to the sides, timbers called shelf pieces (211) have been placed in combination with each deck. To oppose a greater resistance to compression, and to save materials*, by taking away the foot waling (114), the openings between the timbers at the lower part of the frame (42) have been filled in; and to oppose a resistance to any change of form, by the abutments of its components, and to separate and make the fastenings more general, a truss frame has been introduced in the place of the common riders (241).

253. To increase the resistance to any alteration of form and to give firmness to the fabric, to structures like ships, is of the greatest consequence, since they are bodies that have not only to sustain immense weights, in addition to the weights of the parts of which they are composed, but have to support themselves by their stiffness, in an agitated sea, where the forces produced by the wind and waves are constantly changing. The disposition of the timbers is therefore required to be such, that they should be brought as much as possible into action by extension or compression, since they are not so elastic as to react with forces equal to those impressed, to recover their former figure; nor is their combination such, as to allow, when the compactness is destroyed, by the fastenings being improperly acted on, and in part overcome, of the same degree of firmness that existed in the original state of the structure; but as

---

* See *Philosophical Transactions*, 1814, part II. page 301.

a deformation takes place and the resistance of the
body is overcome, there will be a movement amongst
the parts, and working will take place, and as the
different forces operate will be continually increasing
and producing effects, more and more disasterous to
the system.

## The Shelf.

254. The shelf (211), in common with the interior and exterior planking, and the other parts of
the structure, that form longitudinal ties, oppose a
resistance to extension; but the shelves in a greater
degree, on account of their substance, and the firmness with which they are combined to those parts
of the ship to which they are contiguous.

## To fill in the Openings between the Timbers.

255. The openings between the timbers were
filled in formerly no higher than the floor heads, but
now they extend up, in all ships having orlops,
within 4 inches of the strakes under the orlop
clamps (126); and to smaller vessels, within 4
inches of the strake under the lower deck shelf, if
there is one; if not, within 4 or 6 inches of the under side of the shelf; their upper ends are formed to
an inclination downwards, from the outer part, below
an horizontal line, that the water which passes between the timbers may run into the hold.

256. The fillings between the timbers were formerly the same breadth in and out as the timbers
themselves, and when the openings were more than

3 inches, the range of fibre was placed in the same direction as the timber.. These fillings were formed wedge-like, so that one of them might be driven from the inside or out to give firmness. When the openings were less than 3 inches, they were likewise formed wedge-like and driven from the inside and out opposite to each other, with the range of fibre perpendicular to the timber. In both cases the fillings were caulked upon the same edge, inside and out, for the oakum to meet ; upon the other edge, and at the butts of the timbers, and fillings, they were only chinced*.

257. The fillings are now, from frigates upwards, put in from the outside and in, with the range of the fibre the same as the timbers, of about 3 inches in depth, and of such lengths as can be provided out of offal timber. The butts of the different lengths rabbet over each other to form a stop for the oakum. When the outer fillings are caulked, which it is upon both edges, those in the interior of the ship are taken out, and the space between the fillings filled in with a composition†. The interior filling is replaced and caulked as the outer fillings.

258. The smaller class of vessels have now the openings between the timbers filled in, with the fillings, having the range of fibre the same as the timbers, and of the same breadth with them ; they are of any lengths, that can be got out of offal timber, so as to give shift to the heads and heels of the timbers. These fillings are well caulked inside and out.

---

* To chince or chinse, is a slight mode of caulking any seams or butts.

† Parker's Roman cement ⅔, drift sand ⅓.

259. Before the keelson (69) is got into its place, in all classes of ships, the fillings are put in so as to extend to some distance on each side, and are well caulked.

260. The openings are filled in to render more secure the bottom of the ship, in the event of any disaster, to prevent decay by the exclusion of the impure air from the sides of the timbers*, to prevent the accumulation of filth in the openings, which may endanger the health of the crew, by the noisome vapour arising from it, and to prevent hogging.

261. Before the body can deflect, or what is technically called break the sheer, an extension must take place above a certain point within the body, called the neutral-axis, and a compression below it; this extension and compression are quite evident in all ships that have broken their sheer to any extent. The body will therefore deflect in corresponding degrees as the parts above are extensible and the parts below compressible; and the neutral axis or point of revolution will be lowered or raised according as the resistance to compression or extension exceeds in influence upon the structure. Now as in the former mode of building, the resistance to compression existed principally on the planking, the timbers having but little else to prevent their mutual approach but the fastenings; whereas now, by the timbers being made a solid mass, the body is rendered as incompressible as the nature of the sub-

---

* See *Philosophical Transactions*, 1814, Part II.

stance of which it is composed will admit; consequently the resistance which the same surface opposes to compression is greatly increased, therefore the neutral axis must be lowered, in order to equalize the moment of extension and compression round that line ; and consequently, since the resistance to deflection varies as twice the moment of the resistance to extension in each case*, the resistance to arching will be increased.

### The Truss Frame (Fig. 26 and 27).

262. The trussed frame is a combination of timbers brought in contact with the frame of the ship (42), below the thick strakes under the orlop clamps (126), and above upon the interior planking ; it is for supporting the ship principally against bending in the direction of its length (252), which all ships, according to their strength, form, or stowage, are subject to, more or less, and as a substitute for the foot-waling (114) and the former riders (241). This frame is composed of timbers, or riders, fore and aft, or longitudinal pieces, and trusses. The timbers or riders may be considered as braces or principals in this frame ; they are laid at an angle of about 45° vertically, with a longitudinal line, inclined forward in the after body, and aft in the fore body. The longitudinal pieces are placed between the riders, immediately over the heads and heels of the timbers in the frame, forming an abutment

---

* This may be inferred from natural principles, for after the ship has assumed a curved form, there is an equilibrium round the neutral line ; therefore the effect to prevent extension, is equal to the effect to prevent compression, and the sum of these two, or twice the effect to prevent extension, since they are both equal, is the resistance to arching.

against their sides, to prevent their mutual approach; these therefore, with the aforesaid riders, from rhomboidal spaces. The trusses are inclined in a contrary direction to the riders, forming an abutment against their sides, and dividing the rhomboids into triangles.

### The Timbers or Braces (Fig. 26 and 27).

263. The timbers ($x$) in ships of the line are in three lengths, with the two lower timbers scarphed side by side; the lower timber extending from the limber strake to about 2 feet 6 inches above the floor head*, on the aft side of the middle timber in the fore body, and fore side in the after body; the middle timber extends from about 2 feet 6 inches below the floor head to about a foot below the lower edge of the thick strake under the orlop clamps; and the upper timber abuts on the middle, and extends up within about 6 inches of the gun deck shelf and snapes against the gun deck chock (Fig. 27, $d$); and that they may not snape too much, and have the proper inclination, the aft side of the orlop beams in the fore body, and fore side in the after body, have 6 inches if required, taken off their lower angle. The two upper timbers are made to correspond at their abutments, and as a connecting piece to the two, a chock ($m$) is brought under the orlop shelf and to give a proper scarph, it extends down about 4 feet 6 inches below the upper part of the middle timber; this chock, at the upper part, is fair

---

* These timbers on each side, forward and aft, meet at their lower ends, and are united by a circular plate of iron (Fig. 99, $b$), so as to answer for the hooks and crutches.

with the outside of the shelf, and the lower end is rounded off.

264. The upper timber has one circular coak in one of the thick strakes under the orlop clamps, and one in the lower strake of the lower deck clamps; the middle and lower timbers have them placed in the timbers of the frames (42), one about a foot above and one a foot below the joint, or heads and heels; the lower timber has likewise two others, one of them about a foot from the lower end, and the other near the middle.

265. In frigates, when they had a trussed frame, the timbers were in two lengths; the upper one extending from about 6 inches below the lower deck shelf, to the longitudinal piece at the floor head. Three of these timbers, at each extremity, extend from the same distance below the upper deck shelf; the lower timbers extend from the limber strake, except forward and aft, where they meet at the middle line and are made to form hooks or crutches, by their being united by a circular iron plate, as Fig. 29, *b*; to form an abutment against the truss, as the lower timber in the fore body is placed on the aft side of the upper, and in the after body on the fore side.

*Upon Bolting the Timbers.*

266. The upper timber has an iron plate about 12 inches from the upper end, with two bolts passing through it; the next bolt is placed about 14 inches down from these two, one passes through the middle of the shelf, and one about 5 inches above; the intermediate bolts between this and the

one under the plate, are about 18 inches apart; the middle timber has one about 6 inches from the lower end, the next 12, and the remaining bolts from this to the lower bolt in the chock are about 18 inches apart. The lower timber has one bolt about 6 inches from each end, and one about 18 inches; the other bolts are spaced, between these, to be about 18 inches apart. The chock under the shelf, or connecting piece to the two upper timbers, is bolted with two bolts opposite to each other, about 5 inches below the shelf, and two about 8 inches from the lower end; between these, two bolts are placed in each timber nearly at equal distances apart. The whole of the bolts are placed upon alternate edges; those at the ends and one between, in each timber, are driven from the inside and clenched upon the outside plank; the remaining bolts are driven from the outside and clenched upon the riders. In frigates the timbers or riders are bolted the same as in ships of the line, unless there is no chock. The scarphing or over launching of the diagonal timber, or where they come side by side, is bolted with two fore-and-aft bolts.

### The Longitudinal Pieces (Fig. 27, n).

267. The longitudinal pieces are brought immediately over the joints of the floor and first futtock heads, with their abutments fitting closely between the diagonal timbers, and are of the same depth in and out. These pieces have one circular coak in each end in the diagonal timbers, and are bolted with two bolts, about 8 inches from each end, abreast of each other; and between them, as many bolts as the space will admit of, at equal distances of about 20

inches. The end bolts and one in the middle are driven from the inside, and clenched upon the outside; the remaining bolts are driven from the outside, and clenched upon the longitudinal pieces. In frigates, such of the treenails as compose the security of the outside planking and will make good fastenings, by passing through these pieces at a proper distance from the edge, are made to answer for part of their fastenings, and only as many bolts driven through them, as to make up the deficiency in addition to the end bolts.

## The Trusses (Fig. 27, y).

268. The trusses are placed in the diagonal of the rhomboid, formed by the timbers and longitudinal pieces, and abut as firmly as possible against both. They are of the same depth as the other parts of the trussed frame, and are bolted, with one bolt about 8 inches, and another about 20 from each end, on opposite edges. The other bolts, between these, are at equal distances apart of about 20 inches; but in frigates, when the treenails will form a proper fastening, only such bolts, in addition to those at the ends, are added as may be necessary.

## The Resistance the Truss Frame opposes to any Longitudinal Bending.

269. It is difficult to give to the body of ships sufficient stiffness to overcome the tendency they have to arching, or sinking at the extremities. It is therefore of consequence, in the distribution of the materials, that such a combination should be made, with the different assemblages, as to give a general

I

support; and such a disposition as not to cause a separation, opening, or working of the several parts of the structure, when the body is bent. To obtain this object, the components of the trussed frame are uniformly distributed throughout that part of the body, which has to receive the stress when arching takes place.

270. When the body arches upwards, or is hogged, the deflection commences at a certain distance afore and abaft the middle; within this limit the body is stationary, or if any alteration takes place, it is a bending downwards, or sagging, rather than arching upwards. From the neutral or stationary points, any parts that before formed right lines will now become by the arching curvilinear. And supposing the union of all the parts to be complete and unchanged, the parts above will be thus extended, and those below compressed; but if this union and combined support be overcome, the different parts will drop, and the angles formed before by the timbers and planking, &c. will be altered.

271. With a trussed frame this arching is so inconsiderable as to remove all its disadvantages, for the body can arch no more than to bring its parts into an uniform action, except what the flexibility of the materials of which the whole frame is composed will allow; for through the inclination of the riders, the ends towards the extremities must be depressed more than the others, because their distances from the neutral points are greater; therefore if the upper ends of the riders were inclined towards the extremities, they would resist arching by compression; but if inclined in the contrary direction, or as they

are at present placed, by extension. It is therefore
evident, that arching cannot take place, without destroying the strength of the fibre in one case and the
fastenings in the other. And since if the timbers
were applied as in the first case, and brought into action by compression, they would tend to produce
extension on that part of the fabric, which by its
position, becomes extended by any bending; one
support would be thereby endangered, in order to
obtain another. But supposing, as in the second
case, the riders to be inclined from the extremities,
they act solely as braces, and put the whole frame in
action to resist any alteration of form, without
acting partially themselves, or producing any derangement, as the stress is then communicated more
generally.

272. The riders have been considered as right
lines; whereas in practice they are curved to the
form of the body, but it is shewn, that the chords
must be elongated or shortened according to the
manner in which they are inclined; the curve also
must be lengthened or shortened, which will be
prevented by the fastenings.

273. Again, to allow the body to arch, the
riders must approach each other; but they are prevented from approaching by the longitudinal pieces.
The body therefore cannot arch till acted upon by a
force sufficient to destroy the strength of fibre of
these pieces. In the same manner, no change can
take place without altering the angular positions of
the rhomboids that are formed throughout the
frame; and as their perimeters will remain the same
under every change that takes place in their angles,

the diagonals of the rhomboids must be lengthened or shortened; and since the riders must approach each other under any alteration, and the trusses form the diagonal that would be shortened, they also must suffer by compressions; and in order for the body to assume a new position, they must yield, which cannot take place, because the pressure produced by their abutments is uniformly resisted throughout the frame; consequently the body cannot bend (more than the imperfection of the materials and workmanship will admit) while the strength of the longitudinal pieces and trusses is able to resist any forces that may act upon the body.

274. The strain produced upon the trusses and longitudinal pieces by compression, has a tendency to force the body out; but, as the riders will sustain the whole pressure, they will resist it, by being brought into a state of extension; whereas if they were placed in the contrary direction to what they are at present, they would act with the trusses; and the result would be, that when the body was powerfully acted upon, racking motion or working would take place in the materials.

#### The Iron Riders or Trusses.

275. The iron riders are placed in the larger class of frigates instead of the trussed frame; they are composed of iron plates, of about 6 inches broad, and $1\frac{1}{4}$ in thickness, and are in two lengths. The upper length extends from about 4 inches below the lower deck shelf to about 3 feet below the first futtock head; the lower one, from 3 feet above the first head to such a distance down, as to receive two bolts

below the floor head; though sometimes, in frigates
of 46 guns, they extend no lower than to receive a
bolt through the thick strakes upon the floor heads;
especially when it is not the small timber frame (59),
as then the floors do not extend out so far.

276. These riders or trusses are placed to about
the same inclination as the timbers in the trussed
frame, but inclined with their upper parts forward in
the fore body, and aft in the after body; and as low
down as the thick strake upon the ends of the orlop
or platform beams, they are brought upon the
plank, and below, in contact with the timbers (42).
The bolts in these trusses are from 18 to 20 inches
apart, with one always placed about 4 inches from
each end.

### The Thick Strakes worked over the Joints of the Timbers.

277. To all ships without the trussed frame
there are thick strakes worked over the heads and
heels of the timbers. To give firmness to these
joints, in brigs, there are in general two worked over
the floor heads; in all other classes of ships, there
are two worked anchor stock (79) over the floor
and first futtock heads; and to the smaller class of
ships without the midship platform, that have neither
the trussed frame nor iron riders, there is, in general, a thick strake worked below the lower deck
shelf. The thick strakes are always brought over
the iron riders, in those ships that have them, and
the bolts that come in their wake are driven through,
and clenched upon them.

*Nov.* for 29 1806

## The Framing of the Decks.

278. The framing of the deck consists of half-beams, carlings, and ledges, or all that may be placed for supporting the flat, in addition to the main beams. It is for giving firmness, both for supporting the artillery, and when caulking the seams of the flat.

279. The framing consisted, formerly, chiefly of carlings and ledges. In ships of three decks, there were, in general, from three to four tiers of carlings, and in other ships from two to three, ranging fore-and-aft, between the beams; one tier with their midship sides ranging with the inside of the hatch and ladderways, and one tier about 6 inches within the toes of the knees; the other tiers, if more, were placed equally between. These carlings varied in size according to the deck and rate of the ship, from 6 inches to $11\frac{1}{2}$ in breadth, and from $4\frac{1}{2}$ to $16\frac{1}{2}$ inches in depth. Extending from carling to carling, and from the carling without the toe of the knees to the throat of the lodging knees, or to a filling let down on purpose, were ledges, lying parallel to the beams, with the common distance between them, about 12 inches; though they varied according to the space between the beams, from 10 to 16 inches. These ledges were in breadth from 3 to 6 inches, and in depth from $2\frac{1}{2}$ to 5 inches, according to the deck or class of ship.

280. The carlings were scored upon the beams, at the upper part, from $1\frac{1}{2}$ to $1\frac{1}{4}$ inches, with the

score less at the lower part about $\frac{1}{4}$ of an inch; and the ledges were scored into the carlings, with a score about $\frac{1}{4}$ of an inch less than those for the carlings.

*November 29th 1828 — Knbotte*

281. Instead of ledges to the upper and middle decks, abaft the mizen mast, there were, in general, placed half-beams; they varied in breadth from 7 to 11 inches, and in depth from 5 to 10 inches. The carlings that received the midship ends of the half-beams, and those to receive the comings, were from $\frac{3}{4}$ to $1\frac{1}{2}$ inch broader than the other carlings. *December 8th 1828 — X.*

282. In the present mode of framing the deck, one or more half-beams are introduced between each main beam, in place of the ledges; they are of more substance, and are combined with the carlings and ship's side, so that a greater degree of firmness is not only given to the flat, but the side and flat are united more as one combined mass; instead of being an unconnected assemblage of materials, as they were with the ledges*.

283. To receive the midship ends of the half-beams, carlings are let down between the main beams. When the deck is laid fore and aft, one tier on each side is placed with their midship sides ranging with the inside of the hatchways; excepting where the masts, pumps, capstan partners, and standard to the riding bitts require the carlings to be

---

* The ledges, after being some time in the ship, shrink from the scores; they therefore could give but little firmness to the flat, and the manner in which they were fixed could form no tie to the different parts of the structure to which they are in conjunction, no more than their connexion with several strakes.

placed differently to conform to them. With the diagonal deck, one tier, ranging the whole length on each side, is placed with its midship edge, at such a distance from the comings, that the side edge of the two binding strakes may lie about 2 inches upon them; and, to receive the comings, capstan partners, standard to the riding bitts, pumps, &c. others are let down at their proper distances from the middle line.

284. The half-beams are placed one between each main beam, except in the spaces between the beams that form the hatchways and mast rooms, where there are in general two; they have their side ends abutting against the timbers of the frame, and resting upon the shelf, to which they are connected with one circular coak. Their midship ends are scored into the carlings, and are secured to them with a plate or dog bolt; the bolt passing through the carling, and clenching upon it, and the plate bolted with one or two fore-and-aft bolts through the half-beams, and clenched upon the opposite side of them. The half beams are of fir, excepting under the cable tier, where they are of oak, and are of the same depth as the carlings, only that their side ends as far out as the shelf to the fore-and-aft decks; and from 14 to 20 inches without the letting down strake (228) to the diagonol deck, they are left the same depth as the main beams, to rest upon, and coak to the shelf.

285. When the flat is laid diagonally, from two to three tier of ledges are let down between the half-beams, and half and main beams; they are from nine to ten inches broad, and from four to five

inches deep, and are laid at right angles to the
direction of the strakes of the flat; the side tier have
their side ends about 12 inches from the side binding
or letting-down strake (228); and the midship tier,
with their midship ends, about two feet from the
carlings that receive the side edges of the midship
binding strakes, and midship ends of the diagonal
deck. These ledges, as well as all the carlings, are
of oak.

386. Between the carlings in midships, and
between the carlings for the midship binding strakes,
and those for the comings, ledges are let down, to
give firmness to the flat in these parts; and in general, on the aft side of the riding bitts, a ledge is let
down, as broad as the bitts; and frequently these
bitts, as well as all others, are framed on each side
of them, to form a stop for the oakum, in case of
their working. And in all cases where scuttles are
placed in the flat, and for the wing gratings, carlings
or ledges are first let down to form them.

*Thin Waterways* (Fig. 22 and 26, *k*).

387. The thin waterways are in general worked
from one to two inches thicker than the flat of the
deck; but hollowed out, or what is called chined
down, to the thickness of the flat from the outer
part of the spirketting. The inner edge is close to
the timbers (42), and always of a breadth, or sufficiently out, to caulk the outer edge, or first seam on
the flat: when the side tumbles home considerably,
their outer edges are frequently inclined in the direction of the side, but no more than is necessary, as
the caulking will have a tendency to bring it from
the beams.

**288.** These waterways are always made as tight as possible between the beams and spirketting, that when the joint, or what is called the waterway seam, is caulked, they may be brought as firm as possible upon the beams; for it has always been found, that with all the force that can be used, this seam will still open when the ship is labouring in a sea.

**289.** The thin waterway is in general fastened as the flat of the deck, altogether with nails, or with nails in the beams and treenails in the ledges, and sometimes with an additional bolt placed in each beam.

### The Flat of the Deck.

**290.** The flat of the deck is the flooring or covering over of the beams and framing with planks or deal, from 2 to 4 inches in thickness. To the lower or gun deck of ships of the line, the flat was formerly laid with four-inch Dantzic plank, extending in strakes, curved as they approach the side, the whole length, with the second and third strake from the comings on each side, forming binding strakes, for which purpose they were one inch thicker, and scored over the beams and ledges the additional thickness; this flat was fastened with two three-quarter inch short bolts in each beam, and one deck treenail in each ledge, in every strake. The flat of all other decks were mostly of Prussian or Dantzic deal, with the strakes extending fore and aft, excepting two strakes next the comings, which were oak for binding strakes, one inch thicker than the common flat, and scored over the beams and ledges as before described; and frequently, between these strakes in midships was oak, especially to the upper and middle deck, with the strake at the middle line one inch thicker, to place the pillars upon; and sometimes from three to five strakes out from the side they were likewise of oak, to train the guns upon; the flats laid in this manner were fastened with deck nails in general, two in each beam, and one in each ledge, in every strake.

291 The butts of the binding strakes were always placed at the greatest distance possible from the hatchways, mast partners, and riding bitts, and they scored over the beams always as tight as possible, and they were mostly faced upon the beams.

292. The fore-and-aft decks are now laid with fir, except the two strakes next the comings, which are oak, and one inch thicker; but instead of being scored over the beams as the other binding strakes, they project above the flat, and have one circular coak and two bolts in each beam; these flats are fastened with two nails in each beam, and one in each half-beam, in every strake. The weather decks are fastened with nails made of mixed metal; the other decks with iron.

293 When the flat is laid diagonally, which is the case now, to the lower, middle, and upper decks of ships of the line, to bring the strakes to act as braces in combining the beams and sides of the ship in one compact association (229), the strakes are laid to an angle of about 45°, with a fore-and-aft line; these strakes have their midship ends abutting against two binding strakes, that range the whole length, and their side ends abutting against the waterways, which rabbet over them (222). Each

strake is fastened at the side butt with two treenails
through the side binding or letting down strakes
(228), excepting when the up-and-down bolt in the
forked knee (235) passes through their ends, or
when their ends come over a half-beam (in which
case, a bolt is driven in their ends, letting down
strake, half-beam, and shelf, and clenched on the
under side of the shelf), when only one treenail is
driven in each end. The treenails pass quite
through the letting down strakes, but those in their
ends, that pass into the main beams, are to be no
more than from 9 to 10 inches in length; only one
is to pass through the half-beam. The midship
butts are fastened to the main beams or carlings
(283), with two bolts in each butt; between the
butts each strake is fastened to every main beam
with two bolts of 5-8ths of an inch diameter, and to
every half-beam with two, and every ledge with one
treenail. The bolts in the beams are from 8 to 11
inches in length; but the holes for them are bored
quite through the beams.

294. The binding strakes, which are two on
each side, for receiving the abutments of the diagonal decks, are 1 inch thicker than the flat, and each
strake has one circular coak of 3½ inches in diameter, and two up-and-down bolts in every beam,
and are treenailed, with one deck treenail in each
ledge.

NOTE.—In the alphabetical index at the end,
will be found a description of the more minute parts
of the structure, as the head, stern, capstan, bitts,
blocks, comings, &c.

# INDEX AND VOCABULARY.

ABAFT (Swedish, *akter, akterlik*; Danish, *agter, agterlig*; Dutch, *agter, agterlig*; German, *agter, agter-lich*; French, *arrière*; Italian, *in poppa*; Spanish, *in popa*; Portuguese, *em popa*) behind, nearer to the stern. Ex. As the fore or main sheet bitts are before the mast, and the jeer bitts abaft, that is, the sheet bitts are nearer the head, and the jeer nearer the stern than the main mast.

ABOARD (Swedish, *om bord*; Danish, *om bord*; Dutch, *aan boord*; German, *an bord*; French, *abord*; Italian, *abordo*; Spanish, *abordo*; Portuguese, *abordo*), the inside; to be on board, that is, to be within the ship or upon the ship.

ADVICE BOATS (Swedish, *adisbat*; Danish, *advis-baad*; Dutch, *adviesboot*; German, *advisboot*; French, *bateau d'avis*; Italian, *barca d'avviso*; Spanish, *embarca-cion de aviso, de correo*; Portuguese, *embarcaçaom de aviso*), small vessels intended to carry dispatches : vessels built for swift sailing.

AFLOAT (Swedish, *flyta*; Danish, *være paa flot*; Dutch, *vlot zyn*; German, *flot seyn*; French, *flotter*; Italian, *galeggiare, essere a gala*; Spanish, *flotar, estar a flote*; Portuguese, *estar a nado*), to float upon the water; the ship is said to be afloat when she is clear of the ground and borne entirely by the fluid.

AFORE, or right a-head (Swedish, *observrea just rätt sörut*; Danish, *observere just lüge forud*; Dutch, *regt van vooren observeeren*; German, *recht von vorne, etwas beobachten*; French, *droit avant*; Italian, *dritto per la prua*; Spanish, *observar algo derecho por la proa*; Portuguese, *observar direito pela proa*). See ABAFT.

AMIDSHIPS (Swedish, *mittskepps* ; Danish, *midt-skibs* ; Dutch, *midschips;* German, *mittchiffs* ; French, *au milieu d'un vaisseau* ; Italian, *nel mezzo della nave* ; Spanish, *medinania* ; Portuguese, *mediania*), signifies the middle of the ship, both as it regards the length and the breadth.

ANCHOR (Swedish, *ankar, ankars* ; Danish, *anker* ; Dutch, *anker* ; German, *anker* ; French, *ancre* ; Italian, *ancora* ; Spanish, *ancora* ; Portuguese, *ancora, ferro*), a strong and heavy instrument by which the ship is held, by means of a cable, in any place. It is formed of three principal parts,—the *shank* (Swedish, *läggen;* Danish, *læggen* ; Dutch, *ankerroede;* German, *die ankerruthe* ; French, *la verge;* Italian, *la verga* ; Spanish, *la canna* ; Portuguese, *a astea*) : the *flukes* (Swedish, *flyna, flyet* ; Danish, *sandbørerne, sands paane, floyene* ; Dutch, *an-kertanden of handen, klouwen* ; German, *die ankerflügal oder flünke* ; French, *les pattes* ; Italian, *le patte, le marre, le zampe* ; Spanish, *las unnas* ; Portuguese, *as unhas, as patas*) : and the *stock* (Swedish, *ankerstocken* ; Danish, *ankerstok* ; Dutch, *ankerstok* ; German, *der ankerstock* ; French, *le jas* ; Italian, *il cepo* ; Spanish, *el cepo* ; Por-tuguese, *o cepo*). The flukes or arms are welded to one extremity of the shank, and the stock is fixed afterwards, at right angles to them at the other. The part where the flukes or arms of the anchor connect to the shank is called the *crown* (Swedish, *ankarkors* ; Danish, *ankerkrydset* ; Dutch, *ankerkruis* ; German, *das ankerkreutz* ; French, *la croisée, la crosse, le diamant ;* Italian, *la croce, il diamente;* Spanish, *la cruz* ; Portuguese, *a cruz*) : the wide parts connected to the flukes are called the *palms* (see FLUKES) and the extreme point of the fluke, the *bill* (Swedish, *ankarnäbben* ; Danish, *næbbet* ; Dutch, *de punt* ; German, *die ankerspitzen* ; French, *le bec* ; Italian, *la punta, il becco* ; Spanish, *el pico* ; Portuguese, *o bico de papapayo*) : the part between the flukes and shank is called the *throat* or *clutch* (Swedish, *ankarhalsen* ; Danish, *det stærkeste of læggen hvortel armene ere smedede* ; Dutch, *ankerhals* ; German, *ankerhals* ; French, *le collet, le fort de l'ancre* ; Italian, *il collare, la parte la pin' forte del usto* ; Spanish, *el cuello* ; Portuguese, *Cœllo*) ; and a *ring*

(Swedish, *ankarringen*; Danish, *ankerringen*; Dutch, *ankerring*; German, *der ankerring*; French, *l'arganeau*; Italian, *la cigalla*, *l'anello*; Spanish, *el arganeo*; Portuguese, *o anele*) passes through the end upon which the stock is connected for securing the cable; and upon the square of the shank, which lets into the stock, a projecting part called the *nut* (Swedish, *nötter*; Danish, *nöddern*; Dutch, *de neuten van het vierkant*; German, *die nüsso des ankerschafts*; French, *les tenons*, *les tourillons*; Italian, *le prese*, *le orecchia*; Spanish, *las orejas*; Portuguese, *as orelhas*) is left for confining it. The large part of the shank, which is from the throat equal to the length of the arms from the throat to the bill, is called the trend or trent.

The anchors supplied to ships are distinguished into the *Sheet* (Swedish, *pligtankaret*; Danish, *pligtankeret*; Dutch, *pligtanker*, *stopanker*; German, *der pflichtadker*, *hanptanker*; French, *la grande ancre*; Italian, *l'ancora d'esperanza*; Spanish, *el ancla de forma*, *de esperanza*; Portuguese, *ancora de forma*, *ou de esperanza*): *Best Bower* (Swedish, *dageliga ankaret*; Danish, *daglig ankeret*; Dutch, *het dagelyks anker*; German, *der tägliche anker*; French, *la seconde ancre*, *ou ancre de veille*; Italian, *la seconda ancora*; Spanish, *el ancla de uso*; Portuguese, *segunda ancora*): *Small Bower* (Swedish, *tög ankaret*; Danish, *tög anketret eller fortöynings anker*; Dutch, *tuyanker*, *vertuyanker*; German, *der ley-oder tauanker*; French, *l'ance d'affourche*; Italian, *la terzar ancora*; Spanish, *el ancla de leva*; Portuguese, *terceira ancora*): *Spare Anchor* (Swedish, *reserve ankar*; Danish, *reserve anker*; Dutch, *ruimanker*; German, *der raumanker*; French, *ancre del la cale*; Italian, *ancora di riserva*; Spanish, *ancla de respeto*; Portuguese, *ancora de respeito*): *Stream* (Swedish, *varp ankaret*; Danish, *varp ankeret*; Dutch, *werpanker*; German, *der wursanker*; French, *l'ancre à jet ou de touèe*; Italian, *l'ancoretta*, *l'ancorotto*; Spanish, *el anclote*; Portuguese, *ancorote*, *ou ancora de reboque*, *ancoreta*): and *Kedge*. The sheet anchor is the heaviest and strongest, though varying but little in weight from the bowers and spare anchors; it is used when the other anchors come home or drag, or in extreme cases. The bower anchors are the working anchors of the ship. The stream anchor is to ride in rivers, or to bring up for a short time, &c. The kedge is a light anchor, used for different purposes, as to prevent the ship from yawing from side to side, or to keep her steady when riding at single anchor, or in working up rivers.

The anchor-stocks are either of wood or iron, for keeping the anchor in its proper position when it takes the ground. Iron stocks are seldom placed to anchors above 28 cwt.; they are in length the length of the shank and half the diameter of the ring, and are in size to the forelock hole equal to the small of the shank. The wood stocks are in length the length of the shank and half the diameter of the ring, and in size, at the middle, 1 inch in a foot, and at the the ends, half an inch in a foot of their length. The stock is made straight, in the direction of the shank, on the part towards the ring; but the other way it is tapered equally on each side, commencing the tapering, both ways, at once, its largest size from the middle.

The stock is in two pieces, which are united together by four bolts, placed at half the largest size on each side of the middle, and a quarter from the edge; three or four treenails are placed at equal distances, and two hoops on each side, under 40 cwt.; and three to all anchors above. The two pieces have an opening left between them, at the shank, of about half an inch to an inch and a quarter: a chock about three inches wide is placed between them.

ANCHOR LININGS (Swedish, *anker fodringen*; Danish, *ankerfoeringen*; Dutch, *ankervoedering*; German, *die, ankerfütterung*; French, *un coussin d'ancre, un renfort*; Italian, *un parabordo per l'ancora*; Spanish, *una concha*; Portuguese, *huma repoza*), are planks fastened to the side of the ship to prevent the bill injuring it, or to prevent the bill from catching under any projection. The anchor lining is placed with its middle at a distance from the stopper cleat on the cat head, equal to the distance from the centre of the ring to the bill, and made to a curve for the bill to sweep up parallel to the fore part. When the anchor is stowed with the bill on the fore end of the channel, a bolster is then bolted to the side, of a height for the lining which is well with the outside of the channel rail at the upper part, to be in the direction of the chains, with from three to four bolts, extending from about 10 to 15 inches before the lining; and upon it two or three stanchions are fixed, with their upper part rather less than the thickness of the lining within the outer part of the channel rail, and the lower end snaping so as to form an equal abutment against the side, and on the bolster; to these stanchions the lining, above the bolster, is fastened; below the bolster, one or two breadths of lining is fastened to the side, with their lower parts rounded into the side. When the anchor is stowed with the bill before the fore end of the channel, the bolster is placed at the height of the channel, and the lining is placed close to the side, from the first projection of the wale to the under part of the bolster. When the anchor stows on the channel, a bill-board is placed with its outer part resting upon the outer part of the channel, and the inner end against the side of the ship, to the height of the forecastle sills, or to such an inclination that the anchor will slide off when the shank painter is let go. The bill-board should be placed for the bill to rest upon it when the anchor is hung by the stopper, and when it is stowed with its end abaft the aft side of the cathead. Its fore side should be therefore about six or eight inches less than the length of the anchor from the bill to the ring abaft the fore side of the cathead in a vertical line with the stopper cleat, and its aft side, about six or eight inches more than the length of the anchor from the extreme end to the bill, from the aft side of the cat head, at a distance out that the anchor would stow (for length see tables). Upon this board as high up as the bill of the anchor comes, or home to the side, and down the bill anchor lining about 9 inches, is fixed a plate of iron, called the bill-plate, to prevent the bill from rubbing the wood. Bill-plates are likewise placed upon the bolster when it is at the height of the channel for the same purpose.

## *Weight and Length of Anchors supplied to the different Classes of Ships.*

| CLASS OF SHIPS. | Weight of Anchors supplied. | | | Whole Length. | | | | Length from the Ring to the Bill. | | | | Length from extreme End to the Bill. | | | | Weight of small Anchors. | | | | | |
|---|---|---|---|---|---|---|---|---|---|---|---|---|---|---|---|---|---|---|---|---|---|
| | | | | Pering. | | Common | | Pering. | | Common | | Pering. | | Common | | Of Stream. | | | Of Kedge. | | |
| | No. | Cwt. | qr. | ft. | in. | ft. | in. | ft. | in. | ft. | in. | ft. | in. | ft. | in. | No. | Cwt. | qr. | No. | Cwt. | qr. |
| Guns | | | | | | | | | | | | | | | | | | | | | |
| Three-deck Ships..120 | 4 | 95 | 0 | 18 | 7½ | 19 | 2½ | 14 | 10 | 15 | 5 | 15 | 5 | 16 | 0 | 1 | 21 | 0 | 1<br>1 | 5<br>10 | 0<br>2 |
| 110 | 4 | 90 | 0 | 18 | 4½ | 19 | 0½ | 14 | 7 | 15 | 2 | 15 | 2 | 15 | 9 | 1 | 21 | 0 | 1<br>1 | 5<br>10 | 0<br>2 |
| 104 | 4 | 84 | 0 | 18 | 1½ | 18 | 8½ | 14 | 4 | 14 | 11 | 14 | 11 | 15 | 6 | 1 | 21 | 0 | 1<br>1 | 5<br>10 | 0<br>2 |
| 98 | 4 | 76 | 0 | 17 | 7½ | 18 | 2 | 13 | 11 | 14 | 6 | 13 | 5 | 15 | 1 | 1 | 18 | 0 | 1<br>1 | 4<br>9 | 2 |
| Two-deck Ships ...86 | 4 | 81 | 0 | 17 | 11½ | 18 | 6½ | 14 | 2 | 14 | 10 | 14 | 8 | 15 | 4 | 1 | 18 | 0 | 1<br>1 | 4<br>9 | 2<br>0 |
| 81 | 4 | 81 | 0 | 17 | 11½ | 18 | 6½ | 14 | 2 | 14 | 10 | 14 | 8 | 15 | 4 | 1 | 18 | 0 | 1<br>1 | 4<br>9 | 2<br>0 |
| 82 | 4 | 70 | 0 | 17 | 7½ | 18 | 2 | 13 | 11 | 14 | 6 | 14 | 5 | 15 | 1 | 1 | 18 | 0 | 1<br>1 | 4<br>9 | 2<br>0 |
| 80 | 4 | 76 | 0 | 17 | 7½ | 18 | 2 | 13 | 11 | 14 | 6 | 14 | 5 | 15 | 1 | 1 | 18 | 0 | 1<br>1 | 4<br>9 | 2<br>0 |
| 78 | 4 | 76 | 0 | 17 | 7½ | 18 | 2 | 13 | 11 | 14 | 6 | 14 | 5 | 15 | 1 | 1 | 17 | 0 | 1<br>1 | 4<br>8 | 2<br>2 |
| 76 | 4 | 76 | 0 | 17 | 7½ | 18 | 2 | 13 | 11 | 14 | 6 | 14 | 5 | 15 | 1 | 1 | 17 | 0 | 1<br>1 | 4<br>8 | 2<br>2 |
| 74 | 4 | 76 | 0 | 17 | 7½ | 18 | 2 | 13 | 11 | 14 | 6 | 14 | 5 | 15 | 1 | 1 | 17 | 0 | 1<br>1 | 4<br>8 | 2<br>2 |
| 58 | 4 | 49 | 0 | 15 | 6½ | 16 | 0 | 12 | 4 | 12 | 9 | 12 | 10 | 13 | 3 | 1 | 11 | 0 | 1 | 5 | 2 |
| Built as Frigates...60 | 4 | 57 | 0 | 16 | 1 | 16 | 7 | 12 | 9 | 13 | 3 | 13 | 3 | 13 | 8 | 1 | 15 | 0 | 1 | 7 | 2 |
| 50 | 4 | 48 | 0 | 15 | 5½ | 15 | 11 | 12 | 3 | 12 | 8 | 12 | 8 | 13 | 2 | 1 | 12 | 0 | 1 | 5 | 0 |
| 48 | 4 | 48 | 0 | 15 | 5½ | 15 | 11 | 12 | 3 | 12 | 8 | 12 | 8 | 13 | 2 | 1 | 12 | 0 | 1 | 5 | 0 |
| 46 | 4 | 46 | 0 | 15 | 3½ | 15 | 9 | 12 | 1 | 12 | 7 | 12 | 6 | 13 | 0 | 1 | 10 | 0 | 1 | 5 | 0 |
| 44 | 4 | 42 | 0 | 14 | 11½ | 15 | 5 | 11 | 10 | 12 | 4 | 12 | 5 | 12 | 9 | 1 | 10 | 0 | 1 | 5 | 0 |
| 42 | 4 | 42 | 0 | 14 | 11½ | 15 | 5 | 11 | 10 | 12 | 4 | 12 | 5 | 12 | 9 | 1 | 10 | 0 | 1 | 5 | 0 |
| 34 | 3 | 29 | 2 | 13 | 11 | 14 | 4 | 11 | 4 | 11 | 5 | 11 | 6 | 11 | 10 | 1 | 8 | 0 | 1 | 3 | 2 |
| 32 | 3 | 29 | 2 | 13 | 11 | 14 | 4 | 11 | 4 | 11 | 5 | 11 | 8 | 11 | 10 | 1 | 8 | 0 | 1 | 3 | 2 |
| 28 | 3 | 25 | 0 | 13 | 2½ | 13 | 7 | 10 | 5 | 10 | 10 | 10 | 9 | 11 | 3 | 1 | 7 | 0 | 1 | 3 | 2 |
| 26 | 3 | 25 | 0 | 12 | 10½ | 13 | 3 | 10 | 2 | 10 | 7 | 10 | 6 | 11 | 11 | 1 | 7 | 0 | 1 | 3 | 2 |
| Flush-deck Vessels, Tons. 455..20 | 3 | 25 | 0 | 13 | 2½ | 13 | 7 | 10 | 5 | 10 | 10 | 10 | 9 | 11 | 3 | 1 | 7 | 0 | 1 | 3 | 2 |
| 460..18 | 2 | 22 | 0 | 12 | 8½ | 13 | 1 | 10 | 1 | 10 | 6 | 10 | 3 | 10 | 10 | 1 | 7 | 0 | 1 | 3 | 2 |
| | 1 | 25 | 0 | 13 | 2½ | 13 | 7 | 10 | 5 | 10 | 10 | 10 | 9 | 11 | 3 | | | | | | |
| 400..18 | 2 | 20 | 0 | 12 | 6 | 12 | 10 | 9 | 10 | 10 | 3 | 10 | 2 | 10 | 7 | 1 | 7 | 0 | 1 | 3 | 2 |
| | 1 | 21 | 0 | 12 | 6½ | 12 | 11 | 9 | 11 | 10 | 4 | 10 | 3 | 10 | 8 | 1 | | | | | |
| 382..18 | 3 | 20 | 0 | 12 | 6 | 12 | 10 | 9 | 10 | 10 | 3 | 10 | 2 | 10 | 7 | 1 | 7 | 0 | 1 | 3 | 2 |
| 255..16 | 3 | 20 | 0 | 12 | 6 | 12 | 10 | 9 | 10 | 10 | 3 | 10 | 2 | 10 | 7 | 1 | 7 | 0 | 1 | 3 | 2 |
| 235..10 | 3 | 17 | 0 | 11 | 10 | 12 | 2 | 9 | 4 | 9 | 9 | 10 | 7 | 10 | 0 | 1 | 6 | 0 | 1 | 3 | 0 |
| Cutters ....160..10 | 3 | 10 | 2 | 9 | 8½ | 9 | 11½ | 7 | 8 | 7 | 11 | 7 | 11 | 8 | 2 | | | | | | |

**Note.** These lengths are taken from the establishments; but it will be found that anchors frequently vary considerably from them, it would therefore be most correct, when circumstances will allow in determining the place of the cathead, to stow the anchors properly in relation to the dead-eyes, and fixing the bill board and anchor linings, to take the dimensions from the anchors that are appropriated to the ship.

*Anchor Chock*, a chock bolted upon the gunwale abaft the fore drift, for the flukes of the sheet and spare anchors to rest upon, when these anchors are stowed; it is of a height for the palm to be above the deck, and sufficiently aft for the stock to stow between the ports. If the bill is not abaft the channel when stowed, a bill-board is placed upon the channel to carry the anchors clear; if it comes abaft, a bolster is frequently bolted to the side, and a bill-board upon it. To prevent the stock, when the anchor is stowed, from rubbing the channel rail, a plank is bolted to the under side of the channel, extending from the side of the ship to about 2 inches, without the rail, and a stanchion or shore is placed under it, in general extending down to one of the projections of the strakes; this plank is bolted with saucer-headed bolts, driven down and fore-locked on its under side.

APRON (Swedish, *följare innan på forstäefven*; Danish, *indenstevnen paa forstevnen*; Dutch, *binnensteven*; German, *binnensteven vorne*, *oder binnenvorsteven*; French, *contre-étrave*; Italian, *contraruota diproa*; Spanish, *contrabranque*; Portuguese, *contraroda*), (12).

ASH, *Fraximus excelsior* (Swedish, *ask*; Danish, *ask*, *aske*; Dutch, *esche*, *esch*; German, *eschen-holz*; French, *frêne*; Italian, *frassino*; Spanish, *fresno*; Portuguese, *freixco*). This timber is used but for few purposes in a ship, principally for capstan bars, handspecks, and oars. See TIMBER.

ATHWART (Swedish, *tvärt*; Danish, *tvœrs eller tverts*; Dutch, *dwars*; German, *dwars*; French, *à travers*; Italian, *al traverso*; Spanish, *al traver*; Portuguese, *ao travez*), transversely, lying or reaching across the ship, perpendicular to the longitudinal axis horizontally.

BADGE (Swedish, *galleriets undre delen med fönster och trummor för äfträde*; Danish, *side galleriets undre delen*; Dutch, *germakken onder de zydegalleryen*; German, *seiten gallerie*; French, *bouteilles*; Italian, *camere fotto i giardini*; Spanish, *pié del jardin*; Portuguese, *pé do alforge*), in ships, an ornamental port, in small vessels and yachts, fixed near the stern, or where the quarter galleries in larger ships are placed, excepting that it is unconnected with the quarter pieces; it mostly has a sash for giving light, or for the convenience of the after cabin, which is in general of an oval form, sometimes richly ornamented with a canopy, marine figures, and the different genii, or with trophies; at other times it is a simple carved moulding encircling the sash.

BALCONY (Swedish, *altan*; Danish, *agter gallerie*; Dutch, *agter gallery*; German, *hinter gallerie*; French, *galerie de poupe*; Italian, *galeria*; Spanish, *corredor, galeria*; Portuguese, *jardim*), a gallery, sometimes called sternwalk, formed formerly in the stern of large ships. Two-deck ships had one, and three-deck ships two; the lower one in three-deck ships connected with the admiral's, and the upper one with the captain's cabins.

BALLAST (Swedish, *barlast eller ballast*; Danish, *baglast*; Dutch, *ballast*; German, *ballast*; French, *lest*; Italian, *savorra*; Spanish, *lastre*; Portuguese, *lastro*), heavy substances placed in the hold of a ship to regulate the trim, and to bring the centre of gravity of the system in its proper place. It is distinguished into metal and shingle. Metal is composed of lead or iron, but mostly of iron pigs, some 6 inches square and 2 feet 11½ inches long, seven of them making about a ton weight; others 1 foot 5½ inches long, and 5 by 4½ inches, eighteen making a ton; 1 foot 4½ inches long, 5½ inches by 4½ inches, twenty making a ton; and 1 foot long and 4 inches square, forty making a ton. Shingle consists of gravel, but now is very seldom used.

BARS OF THE CAPSTAN (Swedish, *bräckbommar*; Danish, *vindebommer*; Dutch, *windboomen*; German, *wind bäume, spill bäume*; French, *barres du cabestan*; Italian, *manovelle dell' argano*; Spanish, *barras del cabrestante*; Portuguese, *barras do cabrestante*), are levers used to turn the capstan, when a great power is required; they are in number, to the capstans of sloops, nine; frigates and two-deck ships, twelve; and to ships of three decks, fourteen; and in length, to sloops 10 feet, frigates 12 feet, and to ships of the line 14 feet.

*Bars to the Hatches or Scuttles* (Swedish, *járn böglar til luckor*; Danish, *böyler til lugen*; Dutch, *beugels over*

*de luiken* ; German, *eiserne bügel über den luken*; French,
*barres d'écoutilles*; Italian, *barre dei boccaporti*; Spanish,
*barras de las escotillas* ; Portuguese, *barras ou barroues
das escotilhas*), plates of iron made to secure them down,
to prevent embezzlement, &c.

*Bars of the Ports,* generally called port cants, are
used for securing in the port-lids. They fix into a score
taken out of the quick work or abutment pieces (147) for
their outside to come against the timbers, and have two
hooks that pass through a mortice ; these hooks fix to the
shaokle in the port-lid, which are drawn in tight by means
of iron wedges or keys.

BARGE (Swedish, *capitains slup* ; Danish, *chess
sluppe* ; Dutch, *kapiteins sloep* ; German, *kapitains
schlupe* ; French, *canot du capitaine ou grand canot* ; Italian, *lancietta del capitano*; Spanish, *bote del capitano* ;
Portuguese, *bote do capitaom*), a boat sometimes supplied
to ships, but mostly boats of state, in general richly decorated (see BOATS).

BARK (Swedish, *bark* ; Danish, *bark* ; Dutch, *barks-
chip*; German, *barke order barkschiff*; French, *petit
bâtiment destiné au service d'un port. Vaisseau marchand
a trois mâts qui n'a ni poulaine ni bouteilles* ; Italian,
*fregatta mercantile, seuza polena* ; Spanish, *fragatta mercantil sin alas de proa*; Portuguese, *fragata mercantil
sem beque*). A ship with three masts without a mizen
topsail, or a general name given to small ships, especially
those with broad sterns without a knee of the head and
rails.

BARCA-LONGA, boats used in the Mediterranean,
principally by the Spaniards, for fishing boats ; they are
worked with two or three lug sails.

BARRICADING (102).

BARREL OF THE CAPSTAN (Swedish, *axel trumma* ;
Danish, *spillets tap* ; Dutch, *wel van't spil*; German,
*welle eines gangspill* ; French, *mèche de cabestan*; Italian, *campana dell' argano* ; Spanish, *mecha del cabrestante, molinete del cabrestante* ; Portuguese, *madre do
cabrestante*), the principal piece in the capstan (see CAP-
STAN).

*Barrel of the Steering Wheel* (Swedish, *trumma* ;

Danish, *trumle*; Dutch, *wel vau't stuur-rud*; German, *welle des steuerrades*; French, *cilindre ou marbre de la roue de gouvernail*; Italian, *massa della ruota del timone*; Spanish, *masa*; Portuguese, *cylindro daroda do leme*), that part into which the spokes are fixed, and round which the wheel ropes pass (see WHEEL).

BATTEN (Swedish, *lackter, ribbor*; Danish, *legter*; Dutch, *latten*; German, *latten*; French, *latte*; Italian, *latte*; Spanish, *latas, barrotines*; Portuguese, *latas*), thin and narrow strips of wood (see TIMBER). Grating battens are those strips which unite the ledges that form the covering for the hatchways (see GRATING). Battens to the hatchways are battens used for securing the tarpaulings over the hatchways in a storm, to prevent the sea finding a passage between decks.

BEAKHEAD, a platform at the foremost extremity of the ship, generally at the height of the port-sill; its fore part is formed with the bow, and its aft part terminated with the barricading which encloses the fore part of the ship, and from the forecastle to that platform, terminates the fore part of the forecastle, called the beakhead bulk-head. Ports were formed in this barricading which answered for doors to the head of the ship. The beakhead was formerly common to all two-deck ships and upwards, but now is discontinued (Fig. 15), and the round bow is continued quite up (Fig. 18).

BEAMS (Swedish, *balkar*; Danish, *bielkerne*; Dutch, *balken, deksbalken*; German, *balken, deckbalken*; French, *baux*; Italian, *latte, bai*; Spanish, *baos*; Portuguese, *vaos*), (167).

BED OF THE BOWSPRIT, is a solid bearing, formed out of the head of the stem and apron, to support the bowsprit; it is in general lined over with lead or copper to prevent the water getting below, should the different joints become slack by shrinking.

BEECH (*fagus sylvatica*) (Swedish, *bok eller bök*; Danish, *bög*; Dutch, *beuken-of boeken-hout*; German, *buchen, holz*; French, *hêtre*; Italian, *faggio*; Spanish, *haya*; Portuguese, *faiu*). The common beech is used but for few purposes in ship building; principally shot-racks, chocks, as boom chocks, &c. and sometimes for some of the lower strakes of the plank of the bottom, as a substitute for elm (see TIMBER).

BENDS (46) (see FRAMES).

BENDS, the main-wales (84 and 96) are frequently called by seamen the bends of the ship, or the widest part of the ship transversely.

BETWEEN DECK (Swedish, *mallandäck*; Danish, *imellem-dœk*; Dutch, *tusschen deck*; German, *das zwischen-deck*; French, *entrepont*; Italian, *corridore*; Spanish, *entrepuente*; Portuguese, *entre cubertas*), the space between any two decks.

BEVELLING (Swedish, *skefning*; Danish, *skevning*; Dutch, *het in den haak schaaven van een stuk houts*; German, *das schmiegen, die schmiegung*; French, *équerrage*; Italian, *lo squadrare ad angoli acuti o ottusi*; Spanish, *accion, de cuadrar con la salta regla*; Portuguese, *a xeura*), the angles formed between one surface and another, as between the side of the timber and the outer surface, on the side and end, &c. When it is without a square, or an obtuse angle, it is called a standing bevelling, when within, or an acute angle, an under bevelling.

BILANDER, a name given in different parts of Europe to different kinds of vessels; but more particularly to those with a fore-and-aft mainsail, bent on a yard which has its peak considerably higher than the common fore-and-aft mainsail; and with the tack brought considerably before the main mast, and the sheet to the taffrail.

BILL (Swedish, *intappa*; Danish, *indpinde*; Dutch, *pennen, inpennen*; German, *pinnen, einpinnin*; French, *enter*; Italian, *indentare*; Spanish, *endentar*; Portuguese, *enxertar*), a part that projects to fit into a mouth or aperture, for giving strength or uniting two pieces so as to preserve them in one relative position.

BILL (see ANCHOR).

BILL-PLATE (see ANCHOR LINING).

BILL-BOARD (see ANCHOR LINING).

BINDING STRAKES (309) (Swedish, *skarstockar*; Danish, *skierstocker*; Dutch, *schaarstokken*; German, *scheerstocken, oder scheerstroken des decks*; French, *hiloires*; Italian, *corde*; Spanish, *cuerdas*; Portuguese, *sicordas*), strakes that unite several parts in one continued mass, as the *binding strakes of the deck*, &c.

BIRTHING (see PLANKING).

BINNACLE or BITTACLE, a case for fixing the compasses, &c. in.

BITTS are square timbers fixed to the beams vertically and enclosed by the flat of the deck; they are for securing the cables to, and for leading principal ropes connected with the rigging, &c.

*The Riding Bitts* (Swedish, *beting*; Danish, *beting, eller beding*; Dutch, *beeting*; German, *beting dil grosse*; French, *les bittes*; Italian, *le bitte*; Spanish, *las bitas, o' abitas*; Portuguese, *as abitas*), are for securing the ship to when riding at anchor, and are placed upon the gun or lower deck of all two-deck ships and upwards, and upon the upper deck of ships of smaller classes. Ships of 28 guns and upwards in general have two pair, below which they seldom have more than one pair, fixed to the aftside of the beam abaft the foremast; they extend from about 4 feet to 5 feet 3 inches above the deck to which they are placed, to about 4 inches below the under side of the beam of the deck below, except in flush deck vessels, when they extend down to the foot-waling, or timbers; they are of a parallel breadth to the lower side of the beam of the working deck, below which they are tapered on the aft side, and side and side, so as to be at the lower end one-sixth less, and are scored and faced upon the beams about one inch and a half. These bitts are bolted to each beam with two bolts, and when they extend down to the foot-waling or timbers, they have one short bolt in each heel.

Upon the aft side of the bitts is fixed a timber called the *cross-piece* (Swedish, *betings-kalf*; Danish *tœbeting eller bedings-puden*; Dutch, *beeting-balk*; German, *betingbalken*; French, *traversin des bittes*; Italian, *stramazzo delle bitte, traversa del bitte*; Spanish, *cruceta de la bita*; Portuguese, *traversaom da abita*) lying horizontally, with its lower side, in three-deck ships, one foot nine inches; in two-deck ships, one foot eight inches; in frigates, one foot seven inches; and in sloops, one foot six inches above the deck. These timbers score and face upon the bitts from $1\frac{1}{2}$ to $2\frac{1}{4}$ inches, and extend to a certain distance without them on each side. They are confined to the bitts with a hook and eye; the hook is fastened to the bitts with a collar-headed bolt, and the eye passes through the cross-piece, and is clenched on the aft side.

The cross-piece is sustained by a shot locker, which is in general fixed under them; if not, by a bracket that is fastened to the side of the bitts, and projects aft sufficiently to support it.

To take the rub of the cable from the cross-piece, a face-piece from five to six inches thick is brought on the aft side of it, of elm, and fastened with treenails about 16 inches apart on alternate edges.

The face-piece is rounded off on the aft side, on the upper and lower edges, to a circle, the radius being equal to its thickness.

To give support to the bitts, where the ship is riding heavy, a knee called the *standard against the riding bitts* (Swedish, *betingsknän*; Danish, *betingknœer*; Dutch, *beetingsknien*; German, *betingsknien oder stockknien der beting*; French, *courbes des bittes*; Italian, *bracciuoli delle bitte*; Spanish, *curvas de las bitas*; Portuguese, *curvas das abitas*), is placed against them. They are fayed in general upon a carling, which was formerly about an inch below the upper surface of the beams, for the standard to score over them to act against the pressure forward; but now the carling is mostly fair with the upper surface, and the standard has two or three circular coaks in it and the carling.

The standard to the after bitts extends and forms an abutment against the foremost; and to the foremost bitts, a piece sometimes is worked to the height, and forms the mast partners, abutting against the foreside of the bitts, and extending to the fore part of the bowsprit partners. When this is the case, the standard is brought upon it, and has its fore end let into this piece about four inches, with an abutment to resist against the bitts. The standard has likewise two or three circular coaks in the piece upon which it is fayed, and has two bolts and one circular coak in each mast beam, and two circular coaks in each carling, abaft the mast beams. The arm of the standard connected to the bitts extends as high as the upper part of

L

the cross-piece. In the lower part of it a hole is cut through for a stopper.

The standards are bolted with two bolts that pass through the bitts above the deck, one that stives below the deck, and one through each beam; others are likewise driven through the carlings, so that those before the one which passes through the beam, to which the bitts are connected, may be about 18 inches apart. The bolts are driven from above and clenched below.

Fixed to the fore side of the bitts, extending from the under side of the beam of the working deck, to the upper side of the beam below, is a cleat for preventing the bitts from working, two-thirds the breadth of the bitts, from 7 to 9 inches thick at the upper, and tapered to two-thirds the thickness at the lower part. This cleat is in general bolted with five bolts, one placed four and one eight inches from the upper end, and three at equal distances below. The bolts pass through the bitts, and the two upper are clenched upon the aft side.

*Carrick Bitts* (Swedish, *bradspelbeting*; Danish, *bradspilbeding*; Dutch, *braadspitbeting*; German, *bratspill-beting*; French, *les bittes latérales du vindas*; Italian, *le bitte del mulinello*; Spanish, *las abitas del molinete*; Portuguese, *columnas das abitas do molinete*). These bitts are for fixing the windlass, and are therefore only to such ships as have them, where they answer every purpose of riding bitts. They are brought with their aft side to the center of the windlass, and extend from a sufficient height above the working deck, sometimes down to the footwaling, where their foreside is scored and faced upon the beam, and bolted through it with two bolts; at other times they are fixed to a carling, that is attached to the beams of the working deck. When this is the case, the carling takes two beams abaft the bitts, and two or three before, and is scored over and faced on each side of the beam about ¼ at the upper part, ⅛ of an inch at the lower, or as much as the moulding at the lower part of the beam, if there is one, so as to be well with the lower part; and of a depth sufficient, so as to be 1½ inches or 2 inches above the upper surface of the deck; and of a breadth, so as to be at least 3 inches on each side wider than the bitts, to support the caulking.

The bitts have two tenons, each one-fourth the size of the bitts fore and aft, and four-fifths the size of them athwart-ships; the after tenon is brought to the after part of the bitt, and has its upper part taken off to form a dovetail; the foremost tenon is placed with its fore part about one-fourth the breadth of the bitts from the fore side; they let quite through the carling, and are both formed so as to dovetail on the aft side of the tenon, and are forced upon the dovetail by a key driven up from the under side on the fore side of each. The bitts let down their whole size into the carling, about 2 inches, so as to caulk round them. On the fore side of the carrick bitt is placed a knee, or standard to support them. If they run down, there are carlings placed to receive them, the same as to the standards against the riding bitts; but when the bitts are fixed in carlings, the standards are brought upon them. The standards are bolted up and down with one bolt through each beam, and two between. The two bolts that pass through the gudgeon (see WINDLASS) answer for two of the fore-and-aft bolts, which are in general four in number.

To the aft side of the carrick bitts is fixed a circular chock, with its lower end let into the deck about ¼ an inch, and confined to the bitts, in general, by a strap, and the upper end by a nut and screw; sometimes both ends are secured to the bitts by nuts and screws. It is fastened in this or a similar manner, that it may be easily removed to take down the windlass.

*Paul Bitts* (Swedish, *palbeting*; Danish, *palbeding*; Dutch, *palbeeting*; German, *pal beting des bratspills*; French, *cadre de charpente et potence établie vers le milieu du vindas, où lon établit les élinguets ou éliquets*; Italian, *le bitte delle castagne del mulinello*; Spanish, *bitas del pal del molinete*; Portuguese, *abitas dos linguetes (ou do pal) do mölinete*). The paul bitts are for fixing the main pauls of the windlass, and have therefore a great stress communicated to them; and they form one of the principal supports of the windlass when the ship is riding heavy.

These bitts run down, or let into a deep carling, the same as the carrick bitts.

*Topsail Sheet and Jeer Bitts* (Swedish, *twärbetingar*; Danish, *tvärbetinger*; Dutch, *kruisbeetingen*; German, *kleine-betingen, kreuz-betingen*; French, *bittons*; Italian, *bittoni*; Spansh, *abitones, escoteras*; Portuguese, *esco-teiras*). These bitts are placed to the fore and main masts. for bringing the topsail sheets and jeers to. The jeer bitts are placed on the aft side, and the sheet bitts on the fore side of the mast. The fore sheet and jeer bitts are placed on the forecastle. The sheet bitts are brought on the aft side of the beam before the mast, and extend down, and tenon into the mast partners on the upper deck; formerly these bitts, below the forecastle, were curved to meet at the middle, when they were called Y bitts. The fore jeer bitts are brought on the fore side of the beam, abaft the mast, and extend down, and bolt with two bolts to the upper deck beams: they have sufficient cast at the lower part for their midship side to clear the mast partners. Both the sheet and jeer bitts are scored and faced 1 inch upon the forecastle beams, and are bolted with two bolts in each.

In flush-deck vessels, the sheet bitts are in general brought on the foreside of the beam, and bolted to the side of the bowsprit partners; and the jeer bitts are formed by knees, which extend from the beams abaft to the beam before the mast.

These bitts have a cross-piece on their aft sides, scored and faced 1 inch upon them, and bolted with two bolts in each bitt, punched up, and plugs driven upon them. The main jeer and sheet bitts, in most ships, are placed on the upper deck; the sheet bitts in general to the aft side of the after beam of the main hatch; and the jeer bitts to the fore side of the foremost beam of the after hatch. These bitts formerly tenoned into the quarter-deck beams, and were secured to them by a T plate, but now they are only sufficiently high to receive the rhodens of the pumps and the head above, and extend down 3 inches below the under side of the beam of the deck below; they score and face 1 inch upon each beam, and are bolted with two bolts.

The sheet bitts have a cross-piece on the fore and jeer bitts on the aft side. The cross-piece scores and faces 1 inch upon the bitts, and is bolted with two bolts in each. The bolts are punched considerably within the wood, and a plug driven upon them.

Sometimes bitts formed with knees are fixed on the

fore and aft sides of the mizen masts; those before, extend from the beam before the mast to the next abaft; and those abaft, from the beam abaft the mast to the next abaft; these knees are bolted with two bolts in each beam, and have a cross-piece on their aft sides scored and faced on the bitts, and bolted with two bolts.

*Gallows Bitts* (Swedish, *galge*; Danish, *galge*; Dutch, *galg*; German, *galgen*; French, *potence*; Italian, *potenzie*; Spanish, *guindaste*; Portuguese, *bonecas*). These bitts are fixed in flush-decked vessels for stowing the booms upon; there are two pair; the after pair in brigs is placed on the fore side of the after beam of the fore hatch, and in corvettes on the aft side; which answers likewise for the main sheet bitts, and has a cross-piece fixed to them the same as the main sheet bitts to other ships. The foremost pair is on the fore side of the foremost beam of the fore hatch; these bitts extend down to the lower side of the lower deck beams, and have a cross-piece upon their heads, which they tenon into. The upper part of the cross-pieces is in general 5 feet above the deck. These bitts are scored and faced upon the beams, and bolted the same as the jeer and sheet bitts.

*Fore-Brace Bitts.* These bitts are on the aft side of the main mast, upon the quarter-deck, for bringing the fore, fore topsail, and fore top-gallant braces to, and other ropes. They are placed on the fore side of the beam abaft the mast; and, as they do not extend to the deck below, a chock equal to the depth of the beam, and of the same breadth, is bolted to the lower side of the quarter-deck beam with five or six bolts, to give greater support to them. These bitts are made to incline aft, sufficient to lead the ropes fair when they lead aft, and are considerably wider athwartships than other bitts, for fixing shivers for fair leaders. They score upon the beam at the upper part, sufficient to incline them aft, and are bolted to the beam with three, and to the chock with two bolts. These bitts have a cross-piece on the aft side scored, faced, and bolted the same as the cross-piece to the other bitts.

BLACK STRAKE (105) (see STRAKE).

BLOCKS (Swedish, *stapel-block*; Danish, *stapel-blok*; Dutch, *stapel-blok*; German, *stapel-block*; French, *tins*;

Italian, *tacchj*; Spanish, *'picaderos*; Portuguese, *pica-deiras*), short pieces of timber upon which the structure is erected (1). There are several tiers, one above the other; the upper tier is of a thickness equal to the excess of thickness of the permanent keel over the temporary keel (76); the next down is equal to the thickness of the false keels; and the next, which is called the splitting-out cap, should not be less than seven or eight inches, and free from knots, that it may be easily split out when the ship is launched.

*Block*, the piece from which the figure-head is carved.

*Fixed Blocks*, are blocks fixed to the sides of the ship for leading principal ropes connected with the yards and sails, and for removing or transporting the ship. The principal blocks are the fore and main sheet, main tack and brace, transporting block, and blocks for catfalls. The fore tack is in general led on board through the fore transporting block. Other blocks are sometimes, with kevel heads, fixed against the side, abreast the main and fore mast, inside, for the main and fore lifts; and for the top-sail hallyards, sufficiently abaft the masts to clear the tops; and outside in relation to the mizen mast for the derrick and mizen jeers.

The fore sheet block is in general fixed when the ship is worked below, so as to be in an opening before the gangway. It is fair inside and out with the outer surface of the planking, and the outside laps upon the timber to the thickness of the planking two-thirds of its breadth; and if a port timber, it laps as far as the stops; two bolts are driven through each lap and clenched upon the inside planking. When worked above, a block is fixed horizontally upon the gunwale, and extends as far out as the outer part of the hammock stantions, just before the gangway. The fore sheet block has in general two shives, one for the sheet and one for the studding sail guy.

The main sheet block in two-deck ships was formerly brought to an outrigger, commonly called a spider, at the most convenient part abaft the main channel, and led into the port, and to prevent its rubbing against the stops a roller was fixed against the side; but now in all ships it is in general fixed in the quarter-deck barricading.

The main tack was formerly brought to the chesstree, and led through the side by a block similar to the fore sheet, but now it is in general fixed to the most convenient place inside, to be worked above.

The main brace is sometimes brought to a spider fixed in the quarter piece, and led through a fixed block, placed as far aft as possible; at other times it is led directly through them. When there is only a rough-tree-rail, it is fixed in the space between the side counter and one of the rough-tree-timbers faying upon the plank sheer; but when there is regular birthing, it is let through it, and its upper part is well with the lower side of the plank sheer.

It is of importance to the trimming of the main and fore courses that the blocks for the tacks and sheets should be properly placed, so that when the tacks are down and sheets home, the canvass may present as flat a surface as possible to the wind; and as it is known that for the impulse of the wind upon the sails to produce the greatest effect in impelling the ship, when sailing by the wind, the yards should be braced to an angle of about 25° with the keel*; but this will be found considerably sharper than they can possibly be braced, on account of the shrouds and stays, which will not allow of their being brought nearer than about 30°, and that only with the trusses eased off considerably. Therefore to place the blocks in the best position for the tacks and sheets, produce a line from about a foot from the diameter of the mast, placed at an angle of 30° (or less if the yards can possible be braced to it), with a fore and aft line, till it cuts the side of the ship; or if a spider is to be fixed in the side, to the outside of the spider; this will give the places for fixing the blocks, &c. which should be abided by as near as circumstances will admit of; bringing the tacks as near to the middle line as possible, as by this means they will be brought more directly down, according to the present breadth of the ship

---

* See Chapman on Finding the Proper Area of Sails, English Translation, p. 18; Euler's Theory of the Construction of Ships, English Translation, p. 247; Gower on the Theory and Practice of Seamanship, p. 20; and Encyclopædia Britannica, Vol. X, p. 74—article, Seamanship.

and length of the yards. The position of the fore end and length of boomkins will likewise be determined from this angle and the length of the fore yard, produced from the fore mast.

The block for bringing in the cat fall is placed immediately over the cat head on the under side of the plank-sheer, betwen the timbers that are brought up on each side of it.

In the transporting blocks there are in general two shives placed opposite to each other in each block, for the warp to communicate with both, that it may be brought to act in any direction.

BOARD (Swedish, *bräde* : Danish, *dœle* ; Dutch, *deel* ; German, *diehle* ; French, *bordage mince* ; Italian, *tavola di poca grassezza* ; Spanish, *tabla poca gruessa* ; Portuguese, *taboina*), distinguished from plank, from its being less than $1\frac{1}{2}$ inches in thickness.

*Feather-edged Board,* an inch or an inch and $\frac{1}{4}$ deal, sawed in two lengthways, in the direction of its diagonal, so as to make two boards as near as possible their whole thickness on one edge, and as thin as possible on the other.

BOATS (Swedish, *bat* ; Danish, *baad* ; Dutch, *boot* ; German, *boot* ; French, *bateau* ; Italian, *batello* ; Spanish, *barea* ; Portuguese, *batel*), are small open vessels named and designed according to the purpose for which they are intended : they are impelled by oars or sails.

The principal boats for attending upon ships are launches, long boats, barges, pinnaces, cutters, yawls, jolly boats, life boats, and gigs or galleys.

The launches, long boats, barges, pinnaces, and yawls, are carvel-built ; and cutters, jolly boats, galleys, gigs, and life boats, are clincher-built.

The *Launches* are in general from 34 to 39 feet in length. They are for *watering* and carrying stores to the ship, and are sometimes armed and equipped for cruising at short distances ; they are mostly fitted to carry one twelve-pounder carronnade, and sometimes fitted with swivel stocks.

*Long Boats* (Swedish, *barkas* ; Danish, *barkass* ; Dutch, *barkass* ; German, *barkasse* ; French, *chaloupe* ; Italian, *lancia* ; Spanish, *lanchia* ; Portuguese, *lancha*) are seldom or never employed for the use of British ships of war; they are sharper and wider than launches.

*Barges* are generally 32 and 35 feet in length. These boats are for accommodation, principally for carrying flag-officers and captains; and are lined and panelled above the thwarts, all fore and aft, that they may be richly decorated, if required.

*Pinnaces* are 28 and 32 feet in length. These boats are for similar purposes as the barges, but to carry officers of less rank; they are not therefore fitted up in quite so neat a style, as they are lined and panelled no farther forward than the stern sheets.

*Yawls* are in length 26, 25, 18, and 16 feet. These boats are for carrying light stores, provisions, and passengers, to and from the ship. To the smaller class of ships, they answer all the purposes of a launch.

*Cutters, Jolly Boats, Galleys, Gigs*, and *Life Boats*, are clincher-built, that they may be made as light as possible. *Cutters* are in length from 32 to 16 feet; they are used for various purposes that are common to ship's duty, though sometimes 32-feet cutters are supplied to ships instead of a barge, and used for the same purposes; and sometimes the shorter boats are called and used as jolly boats. *Galleys* are from 28 to 36 feet in length; they are used in enterprises and expeditions against the enemy, and against illegal trade. *Gigs* are in length from 16 to 27 feet; they are for swift rowing, and are supplied to ships when light boats are required. *Life Boats* are from 16 to 22 feet in length; they are for landing in surfs, performing enterprises and boarding ships, and for saving men that fall overboard, in bad or such weather as would endanger the lives of the crew, to use common boats; they are constructed as light as possible and fitted with air tubes of sufficient buoyancy to support the crew, &c.; and in the event of the sea filling them, they have valves in the bottom to allow the water to escape till it is on a level inside and out. The air tubes are made to fix and unfix, that the boats may be used as jolly boats.

Boat-Building. Boat-building consists in forming, erecting, and combining the various parts of different boats; in the performance of which the operation is different

M

according as the boat is carvel, or clincher-built. In the carvel-build it assimilates to that of ship-building, by first laying off the form of the boat on the mould-loft floor, making moulds for and taking the bevellings of the timbers*, and forming them accordingly. The timbers are then erected, and secured in a temporary manner in their position, and the planking afterwards brought upon them. While in the clincher-build, the planking is brought on first to the stem, stern-port, and transom; and to two. or three moulds placed between, to give the form, and the timbers afterwards brought upon the planking.

In erecting boats, a plank is placed edgeways and level, for receiving the keel, on blocks sufficiently high up to work upon the bottom, and to this plank the keel is fixed by several pieces fastened on each side.

The keel is trimmed to its siding from the dimensions and moulding, according to the depth and rising forward and aft, as given in the draught; and a rabbet is taken out, to the thickness of the plank of the bottom, and from its upper edge, from $\frac{1}{4}$ of an inch to $1\frac{1}{2}$ inch down.

The stem is formed to the mould given, with a rabbet taken out of its sides for the planks, and made of a parallel siding according to the dimensions of the boat, but bearded from the rabbet to the fore part, taking less off in bearding, from the head to the lower part of the landstrake. The stem is scarphed to the keel with a side scarph, that goes quite through the keel, leaving the lips about $\frac{1}{4}$ of an inch more than the thickness of the plank of the bottom. The scarphs are fastened to launches and long boats, with four small bolts clenched and a few nails; to other boats, entirely with nails, which are driven half from each lip side, and turned or rivetted on the opposite side.

The stern post is fore and aft as given in the draught, and sided according to the dimensions; out of the side is taken a rabbet for the plank, in general at the upper part,

---

* Boats of the same dimensions and classes are in general of the same form; the moulds therefore when made for one class of boats answer for all the boats that are built for this class, and are preserved for the purpose.

it is brought with $\frac{1}{2}$ an inch or an inch from the aft side of the transom, and at the lower part to $1\frac{1}{2}$ inch from the fore edge of the post. The stern post is tenoned into the keel with a tenon, in length two-thirds the depth of the keel; and in width, the breadth of the post, within from $1\frac{1}{2}$ to 2 inches from the after part, and is fastened with two pegs, in general driven through the tenon and keel. In launches and clincher-built boats, the stern post is on the fore side of the transom, and extends up within an inch of its upper side; but in barges, pinnaces, and yawls, it is on the aft side, and extends up to about the height of the lower edge of the sheer or upper strake; corresponding with which, in pinnaces and barges, is in general a moulding, which it abuts under. The post is in general bearded from the rabbet to the after part.

The transom in launches and clincher-built boats has its aft side on one surface, and well with the rake of the after part of the post; but in barges and pinnaces it is in general in two parts, the upper part lapping over the aft side of the lower and projecting abaft it, to form a moulding on its lower part, well with the lower part of the land strake; and in addition to this moulding, formed by the projection of its lower edge, one is likewise worked above by another projection, worked out of the upper piece, well with the lower part of the sheer or upper strake.

The transom in launches and clincher-built boats are therefore always let in their thickness from the after part; and in barges, pinnaces, and yawls, from the fore part, it is in general fastened to the post with nails, in addition to the ring bolt and gudgeon.

When the stem and stern post are fastened to the keel, and fixed in their proper position, by temporary spars at their heads, a piece of deadwood is then fixed at each extremity (except in launches, where it is only placed forward) for giving additional support, and for fixing the heels of the timbers to, afore and abaft the floors. To launches, the foremost deadwood is in general fastened with three bolts, before the scarph of the stem, which go through and are clenched, and three abaft the scarph, which are driven short. To other boats, the foremost deadwood is in general fastened with short bolts or nails, and the after deadwood has one bolt driven through the post and clenched, and three or four short bolts into the keel. In launches, the after deadwood is formed in the keel, and has one bolt through the stern post.

The timbers in carvel-built boats are formed into frames: as far as the floors extend, three timbers in general compose one frame, consisting of a floor and a futtock on each side, the futtock brought by the side and extending down below the floor-head to give sufficient scarph. Before and abaft the floors, a single timber extends from the deadwood to the gunwale.

Formerly the whole of the timbers were cut to their form from pieces cut out of the tops of trees, or crooks that were near to their growth, called flitches; now only the timbers that abut against the deadwood; the rest are bent to their form, from straight pieces, in brakes made for the purpose.

The floors score over the keel, down to the rabbet; and in launches are fastened with one short bolt into the keel; and to other boats with one nail in each. The timbers that come against the deadwood have their lower ends let in, and are nailed. The futtocks are brought by the side of the floors, and the scarph or overlaunching part, fastened with from three to four nails; one driven from the head of the floor into the futtock, and one from the heel of the futtock into the floor, and one or two between. The futtocks and floors are regularly sided and trimmed from a mould and bevellings given from the mould-loft; and when up in their place, ribbands and harpins are placed, one at the floor sirmark, and one at the main breadth; they have likewise cross-spalls attached to each frame, to keep them to their proper breadth; and the pieces that were nailed upon the timbers to keep them to their forms at the brakes, are kept on till the going on with the works makes it necessary to remove them.

In planking these boats the first strakes brought on are the binding and the garboard strakes, which are permanently fastened; while the strakes between these, when the boat is intended for seasoning, are only hutch-hocked till the boats are wanted, when they are taken down and refayed and fastened.

The garboard strake is fayed into the rabbet of the keel, and is fastened as other strakes, with two nails in each timber, except when it widens aft, when it has sometimes three.

The binding strake is placed to be a parallel distance up from the lower edge of the landing strake, and has its upper edge reduced in thickness, for this strake to fay upon it. The landing strake is then brought on, and the sheer or upper strake, when the gunwale is on, the upper edge of which corresponds with the upper part of the gunwale, to lap on the landing, according to the breadths, as in general shewn on the draught. The space between these strakes and the timbers, which is left by their lapping on each other, is in general filled up by small fillings; and the strakes are fastened with two nails in each timber; and the upper edge of the upper or sheer strake is nailed to the gunwale.

The gunwale, which is the upper boundary of the permanent part of the boat, is in general composed of two or more pieces, scarphed together with a vertical scarph, from about 9 to 12 inches in length; and has its upper side well with the sheer or upper strake. The heads of the timbers are snaped on the inside, from the lower side of the gunwale to about one-eighth of an inch at the upper part, and the gunwale is scored over them.

Above the gunwale is fixed wash strakes, sometimes permanently, and at other times to fix and unfix. When permanently, chocks are let through the gunwale, to extend down to the upper part of the landing strake, inside, and up to the upper part of the wash strake, for fastening them to the chock, and are spaced so as to form the rowlocks, with additional ones on the bow and quarter, according to the space. The wash strakes lap on the outside of the sheer or upper strake, and are fastened to it, in addition to the fastenings in the chocks. They have likewise to support them, sometimes, a narrow strip, called a feather band, nailed to their upper edge, inside; but most commonly they are lined quite through.

On the outside, close under the wash strake, is fixed a piece, rounded to form a fender; and likewise a similar piece, only smaller, is fastened on the land strake, close to the lower edge of the sheer strake, called a land rail. I.... a ..... height, and for supporting the thwarts, ..... .....  strake, called the risings; this strake is in general nailed to the timbers, and the thwarts are let in a small distance.

The thwarts of boats are loose and fixed; in general three are fixed, and are called the fore, main, and after thwarts; those fixed are commonly kneed at each end: to carvel-built boats, in general, the main with two iron knees, and the fore and after with one, which have two nuts and screws or forelock bolts through the side, one of them through the gunwale, and two up-and-down bolts through the thwarts. When the knees are wood, which most commonly is the case in clincher-built boats, they are fastened with nails, which are in general rivetted on roues.

To strengthen the fore part, and unite the bows, two coaks are in general placed across the bow, one on the gunwale, and one at the upper part of the wash strake; they are fastened, in large boats, when attached to the gunwale, in general, with two bolts on each side; and in others, commonly with nails: if wood hooks, the nails are driven from the outside, and rivetted on roues. And aft, to strengthen the quarters, knees are likewise brought against the transom, one on each side, commonly at the gunwale and wash strake.

The internal fittings of boats are different according to their class and service. In launches, the footwaling extends generally from the keelson to the rising; to some boats, to about the height of the floor-head; while others have only bottom boards, to fix and unfix. The bow and stern sheets are likewise not only fitted differently, according to the class of boats, but frequently according to the idea of the captain, officer, or person for whom they are intended; sometimes with regular platforms, and frequently with gratings only. The internal fittings of boats generally are of too trifling a nature to describe; and to explain their detail would be more extensive than important,

since the slightest observation on them, would furnish us
with every particular, especially for the student.

Clincher-built boats have their keels, sterns, stern posts,
and transoms trimmed and fixed as to boats carvel-built;
and to bring the planking on to the form, two, three, or more
moulds, of the form intended to be given, are fixed firmly
at their proper stations on the keel, when the planking is
brought on ; while, sometimes the breadths of the strakes
are set off on the midship timber and the rising taken of
each strake, without the application of moulds, when they
are set fair by the eye, as they are brought on. The first
strake worked is the garboard ; when this is fixed, the
next strake is brought to land upon it, working one strake
on the other in this manner to the upper. The strakes are
in two or more lengths, scarphed with a flat scarph, the
foremost always lapping on the aftermost shift ; and the
scarphs have tarred paper placed in the joints, and are
nailed with flats from the thin end. Forward and aft, the
planks are chased into each other, that is, a rabbet is taken
the depth of the land, and of the plank below, to a sharp
at the rabbet of the stem and stern post, and coming to
nothing from 9 to 12 inches along, for their outer surfaces,
to be fair at the rabbets of the stem and stern post.

To fasten the strakes the stations of the timbers are
set off, sometimes for the floors to be in the middle between the futtocks, and in some boats for the floors and futtocks to be close together. When spaced between, the
fastenings are placed one in the middle between the floor
and futtock, and above the floor-head, in a line with it;
but when the floor and futtocks come together, there are
two nails between each. The nails are all driven from the
outside and rivetted on roues. When the planking is on,
and lands fastened, the timbers are bent round ; in general,
the futtocks abut at the middle line, and the floors extend
across the boat ; formerly they were fayed into the lands,
but now only brought upon them, through each timber ;
at each land is driven one nail, from the outside, and
rivetted on roues.

BOLSTERS OF HAWSE are bolsters to take the rub of
the cable from the cheek, and to prevent the angle of the

hawse-hole from being formed too suddenly. They are sometimes above the upper cheek, and sometimes between the cheeks; they extend up about two-thirds of the hawse-hole, and when between the cheeks, they have a *filling* on them to fill up. They say to the bow, and extend from the stem the whole length of the cheek, and their fore part projects beyond it from two to three inches; their fore end is cut to an angle from a thwartship line, so as to allow the hooding ends (78) to be caulked, and their after end is rounded off in the same manner as the cheeks.

They are bolted with six or eight bolts, driven through the bow and clenched; and to prevent them from injuring the cables, they are punched two or three inches within the wood, and short plugs put over them. There is an eye-bolt, with the eye up and down, driven between the two holes, nearly on a level with their upper parts, for clearing hawse, and sometimes it is used for a boom-kin brace.

*Bolsters for Tacks and Sheets* are pieces formed to a semicircle, and placed on different parts, to prevent the tacks and sheets from chafing.

BOLTS (Swedish, *bultar*; Danish, *bolte*; Dutch, *bouten*; German, *bolzen*; French, *chevilles*; Italian, *perni*; Spanish, *pernos*; Portuguese, *cavilhas*) are cylindrical — or sometimes square (Swedish, *fyrkantige bult*; Danish, *fürkantige bolt*; Dutch, *vierkantige bolt*; German, *viereckantige bout*; French, *boulon, cheville quarrée*; Italian, *perno quadrato*; Spanish, *perno caudrado*; Portuguese, *cavilha quadrada*); of metal, varying in diameter from ½ an inch to 2¼ inches, which are adapted according to the object they are intended to secure. They are for uniting in one mass the different parts of the structure, and are of various lengths according to the places where they are employed; the longest bolts through the dead-wood may be about 17 feet, and the upper bolts through the knee of the head 19 feet.

These bolts are generally made of copper, iron, and what is termed a *mixed metal*, which is a composition of copper and zinc, with a certain proportion of grain tin, to give it a suitable degree of rigidity.

The copper is used below water (164), and the iron above; the mixed metal is used for minor purposes, as a substitute for copper.

Bolts are formed with different heads, according to the purposes for which they are used; they are distinguished into the common, saucer, collar, tee, and caulking-iron headed bolts; they have also sometimes conical heads. The *common head* is used for common purposes in uniting wood and wood; it is but a small swell beyond the iron. *Saucer-head* is a thin head, formed to about twice the diameter of the bolt: these heads are used in bolts that are intended for fastening iron plates to wood, and sometimes for driving into fir or any soft wood. The *collar-head* is similar to the saucer, excepting that it has greater substance in it as to thickness; bolts with these heads are used principally for bolting iron knees, they were likewise used formerly for bolting the standards of wood. The *tee-head* has rather more substance in it than the collar-head; it is nearly formed, with a segment of the circle of the head, taken off on each side, so as to make it one way half the size it is the other; the bolts having these heads are for securing the chain plates, and are called chain bolts; they are formed in this manner for taking down the chain plates without driving them out. The *caulking-iron head* has rather more substance in it than the saucer, but less than the collar, and for a certain distance from the head the bolt has a somewhat conical form: these heads are formed in bolts that are intended principally to be driven in fir planking, and sometimes the knee of the head bolts are formed so. *Conical heads* have but little projection, but the bolt to a certain distance from the head is conical; they are as a substitute for collar heads in iron knees, where the holes are formed to correspond, that the bolts may fit close in them. The length of the conical part is sufficient to extend some distance into the wood, to compress it and resist working.

When the bolts have to resist any strain in the direction of their length, the points of them are secured either by being rivetted, clenched, or forelocked. The former is called a *clenched bolt* (Swedish, *klinkbultar*; Danish, *klinkbolte*; Dutch, *klinkbouten*; German, *klink bolzen*; French, *chevilles clavetés sur virole*; Italian, *perni ribattuti*; Spanish, *pernos rebatidos*; Portuguese, *cavilhas de aninar*); and the latter a *forelocked bolt* (Swedish, *slutningsbultar, splintbultar*; Danish, *slutningsbolte, splitbolte*; Dutch, *oogbouten met spylen*; German, *splintbolzen*; French, *chevilles à goupille*; Italian, *perni à chiavetta*; Spanish, *pernos a chaveta*; Portuguese, *cavilhas de escatelar, ou de escatel, ou cavilhas catelares*). Short bolts are in general forelocked, when they have a mortice made through the point, at right angles to the bolt; and when the bolt is driven, an iron wedge-like key is driven through it; behind the wood and key an iron ring is placed. Sometimes, when the bolts are not clenched or forelocked, but driven short, the points are barbed or jagged, that they may hold the more firmly in the wood; they are then called *rag-pointed bolts* (Swedish, *tagbultar eller hackbultar*; Danish, *hakkebolte*; Dutch, *bouten met takken*; German, *tack bolzen*; French, *fiches, chevilles à grille ou à barbe*; Italian, *perni arponati*; Spanish, *pernos harponados, o niziembrados*; Portuguese, *cavilhas farpadas*): they are more commonly used in putting together the masts than the hull. The French and most other nations use them more than the English. Bolts are sometimes pointed when they have to pass through holes that are not straight, or through openings, and when they are to fasten any iron work, as knees, &c. as the hole in the iron is frequently not in the same direction as that in the wood. The long bolts, through the knee of the head and deadwood, are *pointed bolts* (Swedish, *skarpbultar*; Danish, *skarpbolte*; Dutch, *scherpe of spitse bouten*; German, *scharf-bolzen*; French, *chevilles à pointe aigue*; Italian, *perni con punta acuta*; Spanish, *pernos de punta aguda*; Portuguese, *cavilhas de ponta aguda*).

*Eye Bolts* (Swedish, *ögnebultar*; Danish, *öjebolte*; Dutch, *oogbouten*; German, *aug bolzen*; French, *chevilles à œillet*; Italian, *perni a occhio*; Spanish, *pernas de ojo*; Portuguese, *cavilhas de olhal*), are bolts that have an eye formed upon one end, to project out for hooking tackles, lashing the guns, &c. When over the ports for lashing the guns, they are called *muzzle lashing bolts*; when between the ports through the side, *intermediate*;

and at the ports, *gun tackle eye bolts.* The top tackle eye bolts are those for the top tackles. When the eyes have to resist particular strains not in the direction of their length, they are formed with shoulders that rest upon a plate, to prevent their being forced into the wood, as the fish tackle eye bolts, &c.

*Hook Bolts* (Swedish, *hakebultar*; Danish, *hagebolte*; Dutch, *haakbouten*; German, *haken bolzen*; French, *chevilles à croc*; Italian, *perni a gancio*; Spanish, *pernos de cancamo*; Portuguese, *cavilhas de gato*), are in general for the same purpose as the eye bolts, but mostly used by the French and other nations.

*Ring Bolts* (Swedish, *ringbultar*; Danish, *ringbolte*; Dutch, *ringbouten*; German, *ring-bolzen*; French, *chevilles à boucle*; Italian, *perni a anello*; Spanish, *pernos de argolla*; Portuguese, *cavilhas de arganeo*), have a ring turned into the eye. These bolts are for different purposes; as for the stopper for the cable, called stopper bolts; for the breeching of the guns, called breeching and preventer breeching bolts; for training the guns, &c. called train tackle bolts. When the rings are intended for lashing, they are of a triangular form, that the lashing may lie easy.

*Fixed Bolts* are the ring and eye bolts that are fixed for different purposes, as the eye bolts for the standing parts of sheets and tacks, &c.

*Starting Bolts* or *Drift Bolts* (Swedish, *jagbult*; Danish, *drivbolte at drive bolter ud med*; Dutch, *stempelbout*; German, *stempel bolzen*; French, *rebousse*; Italian, *sportadore*; Spanish, *botador*; Portuguese, *botador*), are used for driving out others.

*Wrain Bolts*, ring bolts that forelock. They are in general placed through the treenail holes and forelocked, and have cylindrical pieces of wood, called wrain staves, placed through the ring, for the purpose of setting to (called bringing to), by means of wedges, the different planks to the frame of the ship, &c.

Bomb Vessel (Swedish, *bomkits*; Danish, *bombarder-galiot*; Dutch, *bombardeer galjoot*; German, *bombardier galiote*; French, *galiotte à bombes*; Italian, *galeotta da bombe*; Spanish, *bombarda*; Portuguese, *galiota de bombas*), a small vessel of war designed to throw shells from mortars into a fortress. These vessels, which are intended for vigorous bombardments, and have to sustain the shock produced by the discharge of the mortars, have an extra degree of strength given them, especially immediately under the mortar beds.

Boomkin, or Bumkin (Swedish, *bottlof*; Danish, *butteluur eller boutteluer*; Dutch, *botloef*; German, *butluf*; French, *minois, portelof, boutelof*; Italian, *minotto, mijotto, o grua per amurare il trinchetto*; Spanish, *servioletta*; Portuguese, *pao da amura do traquete*), is a boom that is fixed to the bow of the ship for hauling down the fore tack; it is secured either by a tenon or a cleat against the bow, and rests upon the false rail, or on a cleat for the purpose, with a strap over it. There is in general a collar-headed bolt that passes through the strap, boomkin, and rail, and forelocked on the under side of the rail, and one bolt driven into the bow. The boomkin should be placed so that the fore end and the fore mast should form a suitable angle (about 25°) with a fore and aft line, at a proper distance before the mast (rather more than half the length of the yard) and sufficiently down, that when the fore tack is aboard, the fore sail may be well down (see Fixed Blocks).

Booms (Swedish, *svängbommer*; Danish, *svängbommer*; Dutch, *loefboomen*; German, *luv-bäume*; French, *boute-hors*; Italian, *pescanti*; Spanish, *pescantes*; Portuguese, *bimbarras*), poles or outriggers for extending or hauling out different sails, &c. as *Main Boom* or *Driver Boom* (Swedish, *bommen af et bomsegel*; Danish, *bommen til et brigseil*; Dutch, *geip boom*; German, *giek baum*; French, *gui au baume*; Italian, *boma*; Spanish, *fotebarra*; Portuguese, *bome*): *Jib Boom* (Swedish, *klysvarebom*; Danish, *klyverbom*; Dutch, *kluiverboom*; German, *klüver-baum*; French, *bâton de foc au boute-hors de beaupré*; Italian, *bastone di focco*; Spanish, *botalon del beaupres, batalon de foc*; Portuguese, *pao da boyarrona*): *Studding-sail Boom* (Swedish, *läsegels bommar*; Danish, *læesejls-spirer*; Dutch, *ly-zeils-spieren*; German, *leesegal-spieren*; French, *boute-hors de vergue, boute-hors de bonnettes*; Italian, *bastoni o lancialuoli dei cor-*

*tellazzi e scopamare*; Spanish, *botalones*; Portuguese, *botalos*) : and booms for booming off, called *Fire Booms* (Swedish, *brandhaker*; Danish, *brandhage*; Dutch, *brandhaken*; German, *brandhaken*; French, *boute-hors pour defendre l'approche des brûlots*; Italian, *bastoni per impedire l'abbordaggio d'un brulotto*; Spanish, *perchas para defender el abordaje de un brulote*; Portuguese, *paos para defender a abordagem de hum brulote.*

The *main boom* is for extending the fore and aft main-sail; the *jib boom* for the jib : a boom is likewise connected with this, called the *flying jib boom*, for the flying jib. The *studding sail booms* are the fore and main lower, top and top-gallant studding sails, and sometimes swing booms for bearing out the lower studding sails (see MAST MAKING).

Bow (Swedish, *bog*; Danish, *bov eller boug*; Dutch, *boeg*; German, *bug des schiffs*; French, *l'avant du vaisseau relativement à sa construction*; Italian, *la pruna*; Spanish, *la proa*; Portuguese, *proa avante*), the curved part of the body forward, from the stem to the loof, or where the curve more suddenly approaches a fore and aft line.

*Full* or *Bluff Bow* (Swedish, *fyllig bog, tvär bog*; Danish, *rund bov*; Dutch, *volle boeg*; German, *voller bug*; French, *avant renflé, avant joufflu*; Italian, *prua piena*; Spanish, *navio muy lleno de proa*; Portuguese, *navio muito cheio de proa*). In proportion as the horizontal tangent to the curve of the bow approaches a perpendicular to the longitudinal axis, the bow is said to be full, or very full.

*Lean* or *Sharp Bow* (Swedish, *skarp bog*; Danish, *skarp bov*: Dutch, *scherpe boeg*; German, *scharfer bug o der schmaler bug*; French, *avant maigre*; Italian, *prua magra o acuta*; Spanish, *chupado de proa*; Portuguese, *proa aguçada*). In proportion as the horizontal tangent to the curve of the bow approaches a fore and aft line, or forms more acute angles with the longitudinal axis, the bow is said to be sharp, or very sharp, or lean.

*Flairing Bow* (Swedish, *springande bog*; Danish, *bogen af et skib som skyder forud*; Dutch, *een vooruits-chietende boeg*; German, *ein springender, oder vorübers-*

*häugender bug*; French, *avant fort élancé*; Italian, *proa che a molto lanciamento*; Spanish, *proa que tiene mucho lanzamento*; Portuguese, *proa que tem muito lancamento*). The bow flairs more or less as it falls out, or increases in breadth at the upper part, and it rakes in degrees, as it is without a perpendicular vertically to the longitudinal axis; when it is perpendicular, the bow or stem is said to be upright.

Bowsprit (Swedish, *bogsprõt*; Danish, *bougspryt eller bovspryt*; Dutch, *boegspriet*; German, *bugspriet*; French, *beaupré*; Italian, *copresso, buonpresso*; Spanish, *baupres*; Portuguese, *gurupes*). The bowsprit is for securing the fore-mast, and for extending the head sails.

Bowsprit Chock (Swedish, *sluthult*; Danish, *slutholt*; Dutch, *slothout van de boegspriet*; German, *schlosholz oder schlotholz des bugspriet*; French, *petite pièce de bois placé entre les apôtres au-dessus du beaupré*; Italian, *chiave sul copresso*; Spanish, *entre miche sobre el baupres*; Portuguese, *chasso sobre o gurupes*), a chock placed between the knight-heads (15), fitting close upon the upper part of the bowsprit, when the planking above is not carried round, but abuts against the boxing of the knight-head. This chock in general laps upon the fore part, and is bolted through the knight-heads.

Boxing. The boxing is any projecting wood, as the boxing for the gripe to abut against, boxing of the knight-heads, post timbers, &c

Boxing Scarphs (11) (see Scarph of the Stem).

Brackets, pieces resembling knees, with their outer parts formed in general with an inflective curve; they are either for support or ornament.

*Hair Bracket*, a piece which is a continuation of the upper cheek, and terminates with a scroll at the back of the figure of the head.

*Console Bracket*, frequently called a canting-livre, is a carved ornament placed at the fore part of the quarter gallery.

*Stern Brackets* are carved ornaments placed upon the munions where the cove springs from.

Brakes (Swedish, *pumpvipp*; Danish, *pompvippe*;

Dutch, *gekstok*; German, *geckstock oder geck der pumpe*; French, *bringuehale*; Italian, *manovella della tromba*; Spanish, *guimbalete*; Portuguese, *embalete*), the handles or levers for working the hand pumps.

BREADTH, EXTREME, (Swedish, *skeppets bredden*; Danish, *skibets breden*; Dutch, *bredle vont schip* : German, *breite eines schiffs*; French, *largeur d'un vaisseau*; Italian, *bocca della mare*; Spanish, *mauga*; Portuguese, *boca*), is one of the principal dimensions of the ship; it is the widest part to the outside of the plank of the bottom without the timbers, whereas the breadth moulded is only to the outside of the timbers.

BREAK, when the quarter-deck or forecastle has a rise to give height between the decks; the parts where the rise terminates towards the waist is called the break of the quater-deck or forecastle.

BREAD ROOM (Swedish, *brödskafferi*; Danish, *brödrommet, brödkammer*; Dutch, *broodkamer*; German, *brodkammer oder brodschafferel*; French, *saute à pain ou à biscuit*; Italian, *pagliott, o paglinolo a biscotto*; Spanish, *panol del pan*; Portuguese, *paiol do biscouto*), a place parted off for receiving the bread, at the after extremity of the ship. It is from the keelson to the upper deck in flush-deck vessels, in all others to the lower deck. The bread rooms are always lined over. A dunnage batten about ½ an inch in thickness is first placed up and down upon the footwaling or timbers, and a feather-edged board with the thick edge upwards fastened longitudinally upon it. The upper part of the crutches, &c. are lined over in the same manner, but their sides are mostly lined with slit or plain deal.

BREAM (Swedish, *brimma et skepp, sväda och bränna et skepp med halm eller rö uti kölhalnning*; Danish, *svide og brænde et skib med halm eller rör udi.kiölhaling*; Dutch, *een schip branden sengen*; German, *ein schiff brennen*; French, *chauffer un vaisseau, donner le feu;* Italian, *dar il fuoco allu nave*; Spanish, *dar fuego al costado del navio*; Portuguese, *queimar hum navio*). The operation of breaming is to clean from the bottom, the seaweed, ooze, or any filth that may have accumulated upon by means of furze, reeds, faggots, or similar materials, kindled and held to the bottom. The flame communicates with the pitch or other combustible substance with which the bottom is payed over, and loosens whatever has adhered to it, so that it may be cleaned off.

This operation is in general done on floating stages, as the water leaves the ship. Previously to its being done, fire engines are placed alongside, in case of any part taking fire, and to wet the upper works. The ports, scuttles, scuppers, &c. are stopped up, and the joints covered with clay, or some substance impervious to fire, to prevent its communicating with the internal part.

Breaming now seldom takes place, as it is not necessary when the bottom is coppered.

BREAST-WORK (Swedish, *skott*; Danish, *skod*; Dutch, *schot*; German, *schott, schot oder schotting*; French, *cloison, fronteau*; Italian, *parapetto*; Spanish, *mamparo*; Portuguese, *antepara*), is formed of rails and newels; the rails (called the breast rails) are formed of different curves, and their edges worked with different mouldings; and the newels are frequently worked with different members, as with a cap, frieze, and necking, and shaft socket and plinth; the whole was formerly decorated, and is now in yachts, with different emblems. The breast-work used to form, in ships of war, a balustrade at the termination of the *Quarter-Deck* (Swedish, *shott för skansen*; Danish, *skod for skandsen*; Dutch, *schot van de stuurplegt*; German, *schott der schanze, schott der steuer pflicht*; French, *fronteau du gaillard d'arrière*; Italian, *parapetto del cassaro*; Spanish, *mamparo del alcazar*; Portuguese, *parapeito-da tolda*): *Forecastle* (Swedish, *backens ackterskott*; Danish, *bakkens agter-skod*; Dutch, *henne-schot*; German, *henne schott oder hintere schott der back*; French, *fronteau arrière du gaillard d'avant*; Italian, *parapetto del castello dietro*; Spanish, *mamparo á la subida del castello*; Portuguese, *parapeito do castello de proa arré*): and *Round-house* or *Poop* (Swedish, *skott til hyttan*; Danish, *hytte-skod*; Dutch, *schot voor de hut*; German, *schotte der hutte*; French, *fronteau de la dunette*; Italian, *parapetto del cafferetto*; Spanish, *mamparo de la toldilla*; Portuguese, *parapeito do tombadilho*).

BREAST RAIL (see RAILS).

BREACH, where the outside of two arms of any pieces formed of knee timber meet, or the angular part, as the breach of the transoms where they coincide with the post or inner post, or floors where they coincide with dead-wood, &c.

BRIDGES or BEARERS, pieces placed across in binns and lockers for supporting the lids ; they are in general dovetailed in the front to prevent their being forced out.

BRIG (Swedish, *brigg*, *bergantin* ; Danish, *brig* ; Dutch, *brig of brigantyn* ; German, *brig oder brigantine* ; French, *brigantinc* ; Italian, *brigantina* ; Spanish, *bergantin* ; Portuguese, *bargantim*), vessels having two masts, rigged similarly to the fore and main masts of ships, and a fore and aft main sail. This term is often applied by seamen of different nations to vessels peculiar to their own marine, and not confined to the manner in which they are masted and rigged in the British service.

*Brig Cutter* (Swedish, *brigkutter* ; Danish, *brigkutter* ; Dutch, *brigkutter* ; German, *brigkutter* ; French, *un cutter gréé en brigantine* ; Italian, *una balandra con guarnimento d'una brigantina* ; Spanish, *balandra con aparejo de un bergantin* ; Portuguesc, *chalupa com apar elho de hum bargantim*), cutter-built vessels rigged as brigs.

BUCKLERS, are lids or shutters for closing the hawse holes, to prevent the encroachment of the sea through them, when the ship is pitching. They are in general of elm, with grooves in them, fitting close over the laps of the hawse pipes. When in one, they are called blind buck-lers, and are used when the cables are unbent ; and when in two, riding bucklers, in which case they rabbet in the middle, at half the hole up, and have a hole in them to fit close round the cable, and are used when riding at anchor, or when the cables are bent. They are fixed between cants that circumscribe about 3 inches clear of the holes, called buckler cants. These cants are fastened to the bow of the ship in general with nails, and the edges of the buck-lers fix close between them. The bucklers when in use, are fixed in their place sometimes by two bars to each hole, that tenon into the hook above and chase into the one below ; between these bars and the bucklers, wedges are in general driven to press them firm to the bow. At

o

other times, especially when there is an iron hook below the hole, there is an iron plate fixed to the upper part of the buckler, which when they are fixed goes about 3 inches into the hook above, and two plates with eyes in their lower end below, which are placed over eyes fixed in the cant through which an iron bolt passes.

BUILGE or BILGE, the full part of the ship's body on each side the keel at the floors, or that part which would be in contact with the supporting surface, if aground.

*Builge trees*, frequently called builge pieces or builge keels. Pieces sometimes brought longitudinally on the builge of small vessels or boats, to prevent their falling to leeward, and to keep them upright when they take the ground.

*Builgeways* (Swedish, *sladarne*; Danish, *slädebalker*, *aflöblings-puder*; Dutch, *sledebalken*; German, *schlittenbalken*; French, *coites*, *anguilles*; Italian, *vasi*; Spanish, *anguilas de cuna*; Portuguese, *cachorras*), a timber placed on each side of the ship to form the cradle upon, for supporting the body when descending the inclined plane in launching. The builgeways are in general about from 0.8 to 0.85 of the length on the deck, and are in breadth about 1 inch in 6 feet of their length; if they have plank brought upon each side, they are less in depth by the thickness of the plank on one side. They are formed with the main piece of fir, scarphed together with scarphs about 10 feet in length, with the lips about 3 inches in thickness, and let in flush. The scarphs have four circular coaks in them, and are bolted with eight bolts; one bolt in each lip is driven from the lip side and clenched on the main piece; the remaining bolts, when the side pieces are brought on, are driven through, from each side alternately, and clenched upon the side pieces. These pieces are of oak plank from 3 to 4 inches in thickness, with the different lengths, where they abut, billed into each other; they are treenailed and nailed to the main piece. At the lower part, a plank of 3 or 4 inches in thickness is brought on, called the sole; this plank is fastened with nails, with their heads driven considerably within the wood. The different lengths of the sole where they abut, have their abutments cut to an angle of 45° or mitre, and placed with the butt of the after plank lying over the foremost one, to prevent the possibility of their catching as they descend. The upper and lower end of the builgeways are rounded at the lower part, and holes athwartships are cut through their ends for making the builge-rope fast, for getting the ways out after the ship is launched. Upon the outside of the fore end of the builgeways is fixed a cleat, called the dog-cleat, for placing a shore against, called the dog-shore, to prevent the ship from descending before it is intended. This cleat is kept up from the lower part of the builgeways at its after end, at least an inch and half more than the depth of the ribband at the deepest part from the lower side of the builgeways, and the fore end up so as to place it as near as possible in the direction of the dog-shore; it has two circular coaks in the side of the builgeways, and is bolted with four to six collar-headed bolts, forelocked. The after end is cut off up and down, so as for the dog-shore, sweeping down, to forsake at the lower end at least a quarter of an inch (see LAUNCH).

BULKHEADS (Swedish, *gäflingar*; Danish, *gevelinger*; Dutch, *gevelingen*; German, *gemelingen*; French, *cloisons*; Italian, *casse sotto la coperta*; Spanish, *arcadas*; Portuguese, *anteparas*), are partitions that separate one part of the ship from the other, and form the several cabins for the accommodation of the officers, and the store rooms for keeping distinct the different stores. The *bulkheads that lie across the ship* (Swedish, *tvärskotten*; Danish, *tvæskaaderne i rummet*; Dutch, *dwars schotten*; German, *dwars-scotten im raum*; French, *cloisons qui traversent le vaisseau*; Italian, *parapetti*; Spanish, *mamparos*; Portuguese, *parapeitos no poraom*), in the hold, are in general from 2 to 3 inches in thickness; those that form the magazine, and spirit and bread rooms, to keep the powder, spirits, &c. more securely from the other stowage, have the edges of several breadths of plank in general rabbetted; and those that form the coal hole, well, shot locker, &c. are in general cypher-edged, to prevent, in the coal hole, the coals from working through the edges, and at the other places to keep the dirt from getting in; therefore in the coal hole the upper planks should have their upper edges over the lower, outside, and the other bulkheads inside.

The store-rooms of the carpenter, gunner, boatswain, captain, and ward-room, with the marine store-rooms, slop-room, &c. are in general built up with 1¼ rabbetted deals; and sometimes bulkheads that separate the wings are formed of lattice-work; they are then called *Lattice Bulkheads* (Swedish, *trall-skott*; Danish, *skōd af rostværker*; Dutch, *traalie-schot*; German, *tralje schott*, *schott von roster-werk*; French, *cloison à jour*; Italian, *parapetto da quartieri*; Spanish, *mamparo da jareta*; Portuguese, *parapeito de xadrezes*), and are formed of battens, nailed across each other so as to form squares or diamonds. The bulkheads upon the deck, that separate the officers' cabins, are in general formed by panels or pieces of framing; the panels are of inch, or what is commonly called whole deal, with three breadths jointed and glued together; they are for bulkheads where the appearance is not so much studied. Framing may be bead and flush, flat or raised-panel, according to the place where it is fixed; each piece of framing is composed of stiles, rails, panels, and sometimes munions; the stiles are those pieces that form the boundary two ways, or the up and down pieces, which extend the whole length from the top to the bottom; the rails lie across, and are tenoned into the stiles; these are the upper, lower, and middle; if four, the next to the top is called the frieze rail. The pieces that fill in between the rails and stiles are called panels, the upper one, between the frieze and top rail, is called the frieze panel. When the panels would be too large, or out of proportion to fill in wholly between the stiles, pieces are placed between them in the same direction, and tenoned into the rails, called munions. Sometimes each piece of framing is fixed between thick pieces that tenon into the beam and deck, with rabbets out of their edges to receive the framing called thick stiles; these stiles are always placed on each side of the doors, and sometimes have on each side or face of them a pilaster with a cap and base for ornament. The pieces of framing should have as small a bearing as possible where they come in contact with the cant or deck below, and cant and beam above, and should be formed to a curve, which is called rockering, that when the ship works they may make as little noise as possible.

BURTHEN (see TONNAGE).

BUTT, the root or largest end of any timber or plank.

*Butt,* the joint where the different planks meet end-ways; likewise the space left between two butts for driving the oakum in. This space is left, because if the butts were close, it would be impossible to drive in sufficient oakum to produce a proper degree of compression.

BUTTOCKS (Swedish, *läring*; Danish, *gattet af et skib eller laaringen*; Dutch, *billen*; German, *billen des schiffs*; French, *les fesses*; Italian, *il rotondo della poppa*; Spanish, *cojenadas*; Portuguese, *alhetas*), the after part of the ship on each side below the margin of the wing transom, or to a certain distance above or below the superior flotation; above, till the longitudinal vertical sections begin to approach a vertical line, and below an horizontal. As these parts are more or less prominent, or have greater or less degrees of convexity, the ship is said to have lean or full buttocks.

CABINS (Swedish, *kajata*; Danish, *kahyt*; Dutch, *kajuit*; German, *kajüte*; French, *chambre*; Italian, *camera*; Spanish, *camara*; Portuguese, *camera*), apartments or *Cabins* (Swedish, *hyttor*; Danish, *kammerne*; Dutch, *kaamers*; German, *kammern eines schiffs*; French, *chambres, cabanes*; Italian, *camerini, camerotti*; Spanish, *camarotes*; Portuguese, *camarotes*) separated from the ship's company, for the accommodation of the officers.

CAMBERING, an hollow or arching upwards, contrary to sheer or hanging.

CANT (Swedish, *kantra, wältra öfverända*; Danish, *kantre*; Dutch, *kantern*; German, *kantern*; French, *tourner ou renverser*; Italian, *rovesciare, tornare, vollare*; Spanish, *voltar, tornar*; Portuguese, *voltar*), any thing that lies oblique; as the plane of the sides of the *Cant Timbers* (Swedish, *kantrings-timmer*; Danish, *spanter*; *som ikke stace ret paa kiölen*; Dutch, *hoek-spanten*; German, *huk-spannen*; French, *couples dévoyés*; Italian, *quaderni che non stanno dritto ful primo*; Spanish, *cuadernas que no estan perpendicularmente sobre la quilla*;

Portuguese, *balizas que naom estan perpendicularmente sobre a quilha*), which though perpendicular to the keel vertically, are horizontally oblique to the plane of elevation. The timbers are canted at each extremity, to bring the plane of their sides more nearly perpendicular to the body. As far as these timbers extend forward is called the fore cant ; and aft, the after cant body ; and the part between these bodies, where the plane of the sides of the timbers is athwartships, is called the square body. This division of the diffcrent bodies can only take place as far as it respects the frame of the ship.

CANT SPARS (see SPARS).

CAPS (see BLOCKS upon which the ship is built).

*Caps for the Mast-head* (Swedish, *eselhufvud* ; Danish, *œsels-hoved* ; Dutch, *eezels-hoofd* ; German, *eselshaupt* ; French, *chouquet ton, tête de more* ; Italian, *testa di moro* ; Spanish, *tamborete* ; Portuguese, *pega*), pieces fixed upon the different masts and top-masts, and bowsprit, for the top-masts, top-gallant-masts, and jib boom to pass through. They are distinguished into the *Main Cap* (Swedish, *stora eselhuvud* ; Danish, *store œsels-hoved* ; Dutch, *groot ezelshoofd* ; German, *grosse eselshaupt* ; French, *choquet du grand mât* ; Italian, *testa di moro di maestra* ; Spanish, *tamborete mayor* ; Portuguese, *pega do mastro grande*), which is placed on the head of the main-mast : *Fore Cap* (Swedish, *fock-eselhuvud* ; Danish, *fokke œsels-hoved* ; Dutch, *fokke ezelshoofd* ; German, *fock-eselshaup* ; French, *choquet de misaine* ; Italian, *testa di moro di trinchetto* ; Spanish, *tamborete de trinquete* ; Portuguese, *pega de traquete*) on the fore mast : *Mizen Cap* (Swedish, *besan eselhuvud* ; Danish, *besan œsels-hoved* ; Dutch, *bezaans-ezelshoofd* ; German, *besahns-eselshaupt* ; French, *choquet d'artimon* ; Italian, *testa di moro di mezzana* ; Spanish, *tamborete de mesana* ; Portuguese, *pega da mezana*) on the mizen-mast : and *Bowsprit Cap* (Swedish, *bogspröts eselhuvud* ; Danish, *bougspryts œsels-hoved* ; Dutch, *ezelshoofd op de boegspriet* ; German, *das eselshaupt des bugspriets* ; French, *chouquet de beauprés* ; Italian, *testa di moro del copresso* ; Spanish, *tamborete de baupres* ; Portuguese, *pega do gorupes*) on the bowsprit. For the top-gallant mast to pass through, there are the *Main Top-mast Cap* (Swedish, *store stäng-eselhuvud* ; Danish, *store stænge æsels-hoved* ; Dutch, *ezelshoofd op de groote steug* ; German, *das grosse steugen-eselshaupt* ; French, *chouquet du grand mât de hune* ; Italian, *testa di moro di gabbia* ; Spanish, *tamborete del mastelero de gabia* ; Portuguese, *pega do mastareo grande*), *Fore Top-mast Cap* (Swedish, *för stänge eselhuvud* ; Danish, *fore stænge æsels-hoved* ; Dutch, *ezelshoofd op de voor-steng* ; German, *das vorstengen-eselshaupt* ; French, *chouquet du mât de hune d'avant* ; Italian, *testa di moro di parochetto* ; Spanish, *tamboreto del mastelero de velacho* ; Portuguese, *pega do mastareo de velacho*), and *Mizen Top-mast Cap* (Swedish, *kryss-stäng eselhuvud* ; Danish, *kryds-stænge æsels-hoved* ; Dutch, *ezelshoofd op de kruis-steng* ; German, *das kreuzstengen-eselshaupt* ; French, *chouquet du perroquet de fogue* ; Italian, *testa di moro di contramezzana* ; Spanish, *tamborete de sobre mesana* ; Portuguese, *pega do mastareo de gata*). (See MAST MAKING).

CAPSTAN (Swedish, *spel gängspel* ; Danish, *spil* ; Dutch, *spil, gang-spil* ; German, *spill, gang-spill* ; French, *cabestan* ; Italian, *argano* ; Spanish, *cabrestante* ; Portuguese, *cabrestante*), a machine used for extraordinary effort, as weighing the anchor, &c. It is of the same mechanical advantage as the wheel and axle. Capstans are either single or double ; single capstans are fixed on board all flush-deck vessels, and are either fixed upon an iron spindle, which is the case to the smaller class of these vessels, or have their barrels (which will be explained hereafter) extending to the deck below that upon which the capstan is fixed, where a step is placed to receive it ; and the barrel, which is then conical below the deck, works on a pivot, in an iron cup or socket.

The double capstans are fixed in all ships with a quarter-deck and forecastle ; but ships of the line have two, called the main and fore *Jeer Capstans* (Swedish, *för spelet* ; Danish, *for-spillet* ; Dutch, *voor-spil* ; German, *kleine gang-spill, vor spill* ; French, *petit cabestan* ; Italian, *argano piccolo, argano di prua* ; Spanish, *cabrestante sencillo* ; Portuguese, *cabrestante avante da esotilha grande*) : these capstans are composed of several pieces united strongly into one body; the principal piece that extends through both capstans, is called the *Barrel*, and has the pivot formed of an *Iron Spindle* (Swedish, *gångs-pellets-tapp*; Danish, *spillets-tap*; Dutch, *pen van de spil*; German, *pinne des gangspills*; French, *pivot du cabestan*; Italian, *anima dell'argano*; Spanish, *peon del cabrestante*; Portuguese, *piaom do cabrestante*). The piece that fixes upon the upper part of the barrel to the upper capstan, to fix the bars in, is called the *Drum-head* (Swedish, *gångs-pels-hufvud*; Danish, *spil-hoved*; Dutch, *kop van de spil*; German, *kopf oder köppels des gangspills*; French, *la tête du cabestan*; Italian, *testa dell'argano*; Spanish, *cabeza del cabrestante*; Portuguese, *cabeca do cabrestante*): to the lower capstan, the *Trundle-head*; and that to which the pauls are fixed, which is only to the *Main Capstan* (Swedish, *stora gäng-spelet*; Danish, *agter-spillet, dob-belt spil*; Dutch, *dubbelde spil, spil boven en onder*; German, *doppelte gang-spill, hintere gang-spill, grosse gang-spill*; French, *cabestan double*; Italian, *argano doppio*; Spanish, *cabrestante doble*; Portuguese, *cabrestante aré do mastro grande*), is called the *Paul-head*. The pieces that lie in the direction of the barrel, and round which the turns of the rope pass, are called the *Welps* (Swedish, *spel-klampar, spel-hvalpar*; Danish, *spil-klamper*; *spil-hvalper*; Dutch, *klampen van de spil*; German, *spill-klampen oder gang spill-klampen*; French, *taquets de cabestan au flasques*; Italian, *fantinetti dell'argano*; Spanish, *guarda-infantes*; Portuguese, *cunkas do cabres-tante*). Between the welps, at the upper and lower parts, are short pieces called chocks. The pieces at the deck, between the capstans, which circumscribe the barrel, and keep the capstan in an erect position, are called the *Part-ners* (Swedish, *gangspels fifker*; Danish, *gang-spillets fifker*; Dutch, *fiffer van de gangspills*; German, *fischen des gangspills*; French, *étambrais du cabestan*; Italian, *fogonature dell'argano*; Spanish, *fogonaduras del cabres-tante*; Portuguese, *eunoras do cabrestante*): and the piece at the lower part, into which a cup is fixed, for receiving the iron spindle that is fixed in the lower end of the barrel for forming a pivot, is called the *Step* (Swedish, *spelspar*; Danish, *spil-spor*; Dutch, *spil-spoor*; German, *spillspukr*;

French, *carlingue de cabestan* ; Italian, *mortaletto* ; Spanish, *castanneta del cabestante* ; Portuguese, *carlinga au
chapa do cabrestante*).  The barrel, which is of oak, is the
main piece of the capstan, and is the piece to which all
the other parts are fixed.  To double capstans, it extends
from 5¼ inches into the drum-head to the lower part nearly
of the paul-head ; and from the lower part of the tenon, at
the upper end, to 2 inches above the upper part of the
partners ; it is formed with ten or twelve squares, according to the number of welps ; from two inches above the
partners to about its diameter down, cylindrical, and from
thence to the lower tenon, it is formed with ten squares.
The tenon at the upper end of the barrel is square, to fix
into the drum-head, and is inscribed within the decagon
or dodecagon, according as the barrel is formed, in length
from 3½ to 5 inches ; and with an iron hoop driven upon
it, in breadth equal to its length.  Below the tenon there
is another hoop, about 2½ inches wide, of the form of the
barrel, with its upper edge well with the lower part of
the tenon, and its outer part flush with the outer part of the
barrel.  The lower tenon is likewise formed square, which
is inscribed within the decagon or form of the lower part
of the barrel ; upon the lower end of this tenon is brought
an iron plate, of about 1⅛ inch to 1¼ inch in thickness,
that lets over the square necking of an iron spindle, which
is driven into the lower end of the barrel, to form the pivot
for the capstan to turn upon ; this plate is bolted with four
bolts, countersunk in the plate, and driven into the end of
the barrel.  Upon the tenon, with its lower edge well with
the lower part of the plate, is driven a hoop, from 5 to 5¼
inches broad, and from 1¼ to 1⅜ inches in thickness.  The
iron spindle extends about two feet into the barrel, and below it from 5 to 7¼ inches ; the part that fixes in the barrel
is from 4¼ to 5¼ inches in diameter, and has a bolt that
passes through it and the barrel about 3 inches from the
end.  The square necking left upon the spindle is from 1¼
to 2 inches in thickness ; and the lower part of the spindle
that forms the pivot is from 5 to 6½ inches in diameter.

Formerly, upon the barrel in the wake of the partners, were let in and fixed iron ribs, to reduce the friction
when the capstan was revolving ; but now an iron hoop,

P

in two parts about 4 to 5 inches wide, that tongue into each other, is bolted to the barrel with three bolts in each part.

Barrels to single capstans extend to two decks, or are short, and work upon an iron spindle. When they extend to two decks, the upper part is formed to the lower part of the welps, or to ¼ of an inch above the partners to ten squares: from an inch above the upper side of the partners, to ¼ of the diameter down, they are formed cylindrical; from thence to the lower end conical, with the lower end about ¼ the diameter of the barrel at the partners: a hoop five inches broad is driven upon the barrel in the wake of the partners: the upper end has a tenon for the drumhead, and is hooped the same as double capstans, and the lower end has a hoop driven on 4 inches wide, and a collar-headed bolt driven into the end upon a plate which is bolted with four short bolts to form the pivot. Short barrels with iron spindles are formed their whole length to ten squares. They have a hoop on the lower end about three inches wide, and the upper end has a tenon formed about four inches long, and hooped the same as to double capstans. The spindles upon which these capstans revolve have their lower ends formed square, which is fixed in a step, from 12 to 14 inches deep, and from about 16 to 20 inches wide, and passing quite through it, with an iron plate let in fair on the upper and lower side of the step and closely circumscribing the square part of the spindle, the upper one fitting close upon a necking or shoulder formed upon the square part, and both of them bolted with four saucer-headed bolts; there is a bolt likewise that passes athwartships through the step and spindle.

These spindles are seldom made less in diameter than from 3¼ to 4 inches; 4 inches to 150 tons, and increasing 1 inch for every 100 tons: their upper end, which forms the pivot, is in diameter about three-fifths of the lower end, which works on an iron plate let into the under side of the drum-head, and has a mortise through it for a forelock to pass over the upper end of the barrel, to prevent the capstan rising. The hole through the barrel for the spindle is about one-eighth of an inch longer than the spindle; and to prevent the friction, an iron plate is let into

the upper and lower ends of the barrel, closely circumscribing the spindle, about ¼ of an inch thick; but they
have a ring welded on them about ¼ of an inch deep, to
make a larger bearing, and are bolted with four saucer-
headed bolts.

The welps or whelps are of oak, and are brought upon
every other square of the barrel, or every other angle is
taken off to form a seating for them; they extend from
1 inch and one-eighth to 1 inch and ⅛, or what they let
into the drum-head, to about ¼ or 1 inch of the partners, or
the smallest distance, that when the capstan is revolving,
their ends may clear the partners; but when there is a paul-
head, they extend no lower than to let into it, from 1¼
inch to 1¼ inch. That part of the welp upon which the
rope passes up and down to the greatest limit, is called the
surge, and the angle this part of the welp makes with a
vertical line is called the surging power; this power ought
to vary inversely with the number of welps, because the
friction decreases with the number; as that part of them,
where the turns are taken, approaches nearer to the form
of a truncated cone, will cause the angles in the rope by
passing round the welps to be small; but on the contrary,
when the number of welps is decreased, the rope will be
brought into greater angles, and the friction will be increased. The common angle given to the outline of the
welp, from a vertical line, is about 9° 30' to 10°; this
surging power, will be found to answer very well with five
welps, but will be too much for six, when 9° will be sufficient. The friction is not only increased by lessening the
number of welps, but it is increased with the strain; and
it is frequently found that the messenger or other ropes with
three turns and half, with a great strain, is obliged to be
slacked, to allow it to rise up the welps, or what is called
surge, while with a smaller strain it will require considerable strength to hold on; therefore to regulate the surging
power under these circumstances, the outline of the welp
up and down is formed to an arc of a circle, and the inclination before given is made the cord of this arc, so that as
the messenger or the ropes descend, they will be brought
upon an increased ascending or surging power.

The length of the surge is in general from 20 to 21

inches, and the lower part is placed, to the welps of the lower capstan, about 6¼ inches, and to the upper, and all single capstans, or those without a paul-head, about 4½ inches above the lower end ; at the upper part of the surge a stop of 1½ inch is formed, and above it the welp is inclined the same as the surge. The outer part of the stop is from 1¼ to 1½ inches above the surge, so as to incline upwards. The upper end of the welp is in general from 9 to 10 inches above the outer part of the stop, or to let into the drum-head and trundle-head 1½ inch.

The welps are in breadth, at the inner part, the same as the square, and are broader at the outer part, so as to increase in breadth about 3¼ inches in a foot ; and in and out, at the upper part of the surge, from 3½ to 7 inches.

The welps when brought upon the squares, are let into the barrel half an inch, and placed with their middle line, in and out, tending to the center of the barrel, or square to the seating. They are fastened with two bolts in each, one above and one below the surge, and one treenail generally at the middle of the surge ; when six welps, the bolts will pass through one and its opposite, and are clenched upon the welps ; but when only four, they are clenched upon the barrel.

The chocks are pieces placed between the welps for aiding them, and forming the whole in one mass ; there are two in each compartment. The upper one both to the lower and upper capstan is from 3 to 3¼ inches deep, and placed with its lower part about one inch and ½ above the upper part of the surge ; the lower one, to the upper capstan, is from 3½ to 4½ inches deep, and has its lower part from one inch to one inch and ½ below the lower part of the surge ; and to the lower capstan it is from 6 to 7¾ inches deep, and its under side fays on the paul-head. The lower chocks have their outer parts formed to an arc of a circle, with radii equal to the distance of their upper and lower edges from the center of the barrel.

The chocks are faced or tailed into the welps about half an inch, and have one short bolt driven through the middle of them, into the barrel.

The drum and trundle heads are pieces formed to circles for fixing the bars in. The drum-head is fixed upon the upper end of the barrel, and is the head of the upper capstan, or the head to all single capstans. They are of elm, and formed of four semi-circular pieces, of a radius equal to half the diameter of the drum-head, so that two of them joined together form the circle; the two upper pieces are in general one inch thicker than the lower, as the upper part is bearded down one inch from half the diameter. The four pieces are united together, so that their joints may be at right angles to each other, with eight bolts, two about three inches without each side of the mortise, and two inches on each side of the joint, and mostly one between each hole: about three inches in from the circumference, sometimes an iron hoop, three inches wide, is let in flush at the under side, about an inch and a half in, with one bolt passing through it, between the holes; at other times, the outer parts are fastened by square staples let in between the holes. The holes are in number according to the rate of the ship (see Bars); they are square at the outer part, from $3\frac{1}{2}$ to $4\frac{1}{4}$ inches, and deep from $10\frac{1}{4}$ to 17 inches, and taper about 1 inch in a foot; the lower part is taken in horizontal.

The drum-head lets on the barrel (see Barrel and Welps), and is fastened down with three saucer-headed bolts, which are driven through the upper chock, and forelocked on the under side. The lower side is in general from 3 feet 3 inches to 3 feet 4 inches above the deck.

The trundle-head is in general about 4 inches less in diameter than the drum-head, but is put together, bolted, let down upon the welps, and fastened down in the same manner; it has two less bar holes, and the barrel passes through it.

The paul-head is a circle, and is for fixing the pauls to: it is of elm, and in general formed of two pieces; its lower part is kept well with the lower end of the barrel, and about one inch above the step, and faces upon the welps (see Welps). Upon the lower and upper sides, 2 inches from the circumference, there is a hoop about 3 inches wide let in flush, and bolted with countersunk bolts, to pass through both, about 14 inches apart, except where the hoop crosses the joint of the two pieces that compose the head, where they are placed 3 inches on each side the joint.

This head is united to the capstan by bolts that pass through it and the lower chock.

The paul-rim is a cast iron rim, into which the pauls catch, to resist the return, or what is called to paul the capstan. This rim is from 4 to 5 inches broad, and from $3\frac{1}{4}$ to $4\frac{1}{4}$ inches deep, and is bolted to the deck with twelve countersunk bolts, or one through every stop. The step is taken away, so as to be well with the inner circumference of the ring, and its upper part on a level with the upper part of the rim. The spaces left between the sides of the step and rim on each side are filled up with two pieces of oak plank, with their upper surfaces on a level with the upper surface of the rim and step.

The paul-head and rim are seldom fixed to the foremost capstan, when there is one.

With a paul-head their are four drop-pauls, placed at equal distances, and fastened to the head with bolts, upon which they revolve, from 12 to 20 inches in length, and from $1\frac{1}{4}$ to $2\frac{1}{4}$ inches in diameter. Sometimes a hoop is placed upon the head to receive them, but most commonly a plate is let in flush, from 6 to 12 inches in length, and from $4\frac{1}{2}$ to 6 inches wide, for each. To hold the pauls up when not in use, ketch or slip bolts are fixed in a plate, which is fastened to the head, to slide in and out; the inner ends of these bolts are in general $\frac{1}{4}$ of an inch larger than the outer, that they may be tight in the iron plate when out.

The step is fixed, lying fore and aft, on the lower deck of ships of the line, and upper deck of frigates; it is a solid piece of oak, from 20 to 24 inches broad, and from 19 to 22 inches deep, kept above the deck the depth of the paul-rim. It is let down between two beams into a score of about $1\frac{1}{4}$ inch taken out of them half-way down, and a face from them to the lower part of the step of about $\frac{1}{4}$ of an inch on; it laps upon the beams to the head-ledge, if the beam forms a hatchway; if not, half-way on.

The steps to single capstans, that revolve on an iron spindle, have the scores in the beams taken down, the after one parallel to the side of the beam and the foremost one to strengthen down, that the step may act against the spindle, the strain being in general forward. The steps are bolted with from two to three bolts at each end, which pass through the beam.

The partners lie athwartships, and enclose the barrel between the two capstans ; they are composed of several breadths, that fill up the space between the two beams, sometimes called the capstan-room, which is always sufficiently large for the capstan to pass up and down. This space or room is framed round with comings and head-ledges, the same breadth and heighth above the deck as those to the hatchways. The comings have a rabbet taken out to receive the ends of the partners. The rabbet is not taken directly down, but inclined, as the partners lap over them part of their thickness.

The several breadths of partners are rabetted together, and the two middle pieces that circumscribe the barrel are left as wide as possible, with their joint at the center of the barrel. Each breadth is bolted with two bolts in each end, that pass through the comings and carling under it.

An iron hoop is placed in the partners round the hole for the barrel, about $4\frac{1}{2}$ inches in breadth, and projecting above the upper part of the partners, about $1\frac{1}{2}$ inch.

*Capstan, patent* ; a capstan with machinery attached to it, for increasing the power when heavy purchases are required, as four to one. In double-barrelled capstans the upper and lower barrels revolve separately, to obtain the power ; and in single-barelled capstans the barrel revolves on an iron spindle, attached to the drum-head, so that when the increased power is applied the drum-head and barrel revolves separately.

For obtaining the machinery for patent capstans, or double-barrels, the height from the upper side of the upper or gun-deck beams to the under side of the partners, with the thickness of the partners, is given ; and for single-barrelled capstans, the height from the upper side of the step to the under side of the partners, with likewise the thickness of the partners, and also the height of the partners above the level of the deck, to regulate the length of spindle.

Carling (see Timber).

*Carling* (Swedish, *karflar*; Danish, *kraveller*; Dutch, *grieten, karvielen*; German, *balkfüllings*; French, *traver-*

*sins des boux, ou barrolins*; Italian, *traversi dei bai*; Spanish, *atraversannor de los baos*; Portuguese, *chassos dos vaos, chassos das cubertas*), between the beams.

*Fore-and-aft Carlings.* These are carlings brought under the beams for particular support. They are placed, one below the mizen step, under the gun-deck beams, extending from the beams before the step to the sternson, or to the fore side of the transom, and are secured to it by a chock (*q*, fig. 11) and a plate (*r*) ; one beneath the galley, under the upper or middle deck beams, extending from the fore beam of the fore hatch to the beam abaft the fore-mast, and one under the orlop beams between the fore and main hatchways. These carlings score and face 1½ inch on the under side of the beams, and are bolted through them.

CARACK (Swedish, *karake*; Danish, *karake*; Dutch, *kraak, karak*; German, *karake*; French, *caraque*; Italian, *caraca*; Spanish, *caraca*; Portuguese, *caraca*), a Portuguese Indiaman.

CARRICK BITTS (see BITTS).

CARVED WORK (Swedish, *bildhuggeri*; Danish, *billedhuggerie*; Dutch, *beeldwerk*; German, *bildwerk*; French, *sculpture*; Italian, *scultura*; Spanish, *escultura*; Portuguese, *escultura*), is the ornamental part of the head, stern, and quarters; and when properly applied, gives a lightness and elegance to the structure.

CARVEL WORK (Swedish, *cravel, bygd på cravel*; Danish, *kravel, bygt paa kravel*; Dutch, *karvielwerk, met karvielwerk opboejen*; German, *karvielwerk, mit karvielwerk aufbugen*; French, *border en carvel à joints quarrés*; Italian, *mettere le tavole delle bande di maniera che i canti si toccano perpendicularmente, ó che fauno un incomento*; Spanish, *tablas unidas con los cantos de manera que hazen una costura or dinaria*; Portuguese, *fiades de taboas unidas de topo e canto*), when the planks of the bottom are brought edge to edge, and the seams are caulked in and out, as the other planking. It is a term applied principally to cutters or small vessels and boats, to shew that they are not clincher built.

CASK (see PROVISIONS).

CAST, any timber that has a turn or bend to clear any

part is said to have a cast ; as the cast knees (*da*, fig. 23), which are made to cast, in order to clear the ports (185).

CAT BEAM, a beam formerly placed with its fore part to receive the stanchions of the beakhead bulkhead, and the after part for securing the inner part of the cathead ; it was mostly in two breadths, tabled and bolted together.

CAT BLOCK (see BLOCKS, *fixed*).

CATHEADS (Swedish, *kranbalk* ; Danish, *kranbielke* ; Dutch, *kraanbalk* ; German, *krahn-balken* ; French, *bois-soir* ; Italian, *grua* ; Spanish, *serviola* ; Portuguese, *turco*) are timbers projecting from the bow of the ship (nearly perpendicular to it horizontally) for hoisting the anchor, after the cable has brought it clear of the water ; they have two or three vertical shives at the outer end, and are of sufficient length for the flukes of the anchor to clear the bow when hoisted, and have considerable flight or rise.

The cathead to large ships has the inner end, or what is sometimes called the cat's tail, with a small cast if required, and brought to lap under a forecastle beam, through which it is bolted with two bolts ; and to small vessels that have no forecastle, or when the forecastle is not sufficiently firm to receive the inner end, it is made to return down the inside of the bows. It has in general two hoops on the outer end, one without and one within the shives, and is supported on the under side by a knee placed nearly vertical, called the cathead supporter, which is bolted in and out through the bow, and up and down through the cathead : when the inner end of the cathead extends down the bow, inside, the in and out bolts pass through it. It is supported, sometimes, on the aft side, by an iron knee lying to the sheer.

The part formed in the bow to receive the cathead is called the bed, and is well caulked and leaded.

CAULK (Swedish, *kalfatra, drifva* ; Danish, *kalfatre, digte* ; Dutch, *kalfaaten* ; German, *kalfaten, kalfatern* ; French, *calfater* ; Italian, *calafatare* ; Spanish, *calafatear* ; Portuguese, *calafeter*). Caulking is the operation of forcing oakum into the seams, rents, and butts, by means of a mallet and iron ; this operation is the same as the force of the wedge, when acted on by impact, to close all the smaller rents, and to make the different parts as one body,

Q

in opposing the passage of the water. In caulking, the thickness of the planking and the parts to be caulked determine the quantity of oakum that is to be driven into each joint. *New weather-decks*, of two inches in thickness, have one thread of white and one of black oakum; 2½ and 3 inches, one of white and two of black: *gun decks* of three inches in thickness, one of white and two of black; and four inches, one of white and three of black: *sides* have, to 2½ inches in thickness, three of black; and to 3-inch, four. *New bottoms, wales, &c.* have sometimes, to all thicknesses, two threads of spunyarn, and to 4 inches in thickness five threads of black, to 5-inch six, 6-inch seven, 7-inch nine, 8-inch ten, 9-inch eleven, 10-inch twelve, 11-inch thirteen, and to 12-inch fourteen threads. And that the proper quantity may be got into the joints, they are made close at the inner part, and left open at the outer, about half an inch in ten inches. This is called allowing seam. The progressive manner of performing the caulking is by first caulking the treenails, if any; then by driving wedge-like irons into the seams (except to fir decks), to close the rents or shakes, and open the seams. This operation is called raiming or reeming. After this, the spunyarn or white oakum is driven, if any, and then the number of black threads, which are then (except to fir decks, and some other parts, when the caulking is not of much importance) hardened, or what is called horsed up; this is done by one man holding, in the seam upon the oakum, an iron fixed in a handle, called the horse iron, and another driving upon it with a large mallet, called a beetle, that the oakum may be made as firm as possible, and be within the outer surface of the plank. It is of importance, in order to give firmness by the caulking, and to prevent decay, that the threads, as they are driven into the seam, should be got in as far as possible, or driven home, and not choaked, as is sometimes the case, and mostly by foreign nations; but that the whole of the oakum driven should form as a wedge, as far in as the thickness of the plank, or what is called be well bottomed.

CENTER OF DISPLACEMENT (see DISPLACEMENT).

CIELING or FOOTWALING (Swedish, *vägare*; Danish, *væger*; Dutch, *waager of weeger*; German, *weger, wegering oder weigering*; French, *vaigres*; Italian, *fasciame di dentro, fiube, ferretle, verzene*; Spanish, *carretas, cinglones*; Portuguese, *escoas*) (114).

CELLS (see SILLS).

CHAINS, iron links that secure the dead-eyes connected with the channels to the side; the part which circumscribes the dead-eye is called the binding: the links of the chain are called the upper, middle, and toe links.

CHAIN BOLTS, the bolts that pass through the toe links and secure the chains to the side; they are formed in general with large and strong heads, called T heads (see BOLTS), that the chain and dead-eyes may be taken down without driving them out. The main and fore channels to all vessels above the small class of brigs have a preventer plate to support the chain bolt; this plate has a hole in each end, the upper one for the chain bolt, and the lower one for a bolt called the preventer bolt. The upper hole in the plate is made to the form of the head of the chain bolt, that when the plate is turned to a right angle from its proper position it may be taken off the bolt, and to allow its lower end to be brought over the point of the preventer bolt, which is driven from the inside, and forelocked upon the plate. A thin plate of iron is placed under the head of the chain bolt, upon the upper part of the preventer plate, which has a hole in it to the form of the bolt, that it may be first turned round and then taken off.

CHANNELS (Swedish, *rustar*; Danish, *ryster eller röster*; Dutch, *rusten*; German, *rusten oder rüster*; French, *porte-haubans*; Italian, *parasarehie*; Spanish, *mesas de guarnicion*; Portuguese, *mesas das emxarcias*), an assemblage of planks lying horizontally in and out, and to the sheer longitudinally, and projecting outwards from the side of the ship. They are placed to each mast, with their fore ends as much before the mast as to have one dead-eye rather before the center, and of sufficient length to receive as many dead-eyes as may be necessary. The fore channel has in general the top-mast and top-gallant back-stay dead-eyes affixed to it; but to the main and mizen channels, there are in general separate stools for them, called the back-stay stools.

The channels are for giving a greater spread to the shrouds, and are of a breadth sufficient for the shrouds to clear the barricading or hammock stantions at least six inches. The fore channel is narrowed at the after end, to allow the spare and sheet anchors to be stowed, that the shank may lie without the shrouds, and for the palm to come within the chock; to obtain this, their outer edges are curved in. Their fore end extends in general sufficiently before the fore-mast dead-eye to receive the anchor lining.

The channels are placed commonly with their lower sides about 1 inch above the lower edge of the upper sheer strakes of ships that have them; except the mizen channel of two-deck ships and upwards, which is placed above the quarter-deck ports, about one inch above the first seam: they are in general from 4 to 5 inches in thickness at the inner edge, and from 1 inch to 1½ inch less on the outer edge.

The planks that compose the channel have their edges coaked together with coaks about three feet apart, and the channels are bolted to the side with bolts from 3 to 4 feet apart, except the stools or channels cut off by the ports, when there is never less than two bolts, and supported by two knees, commonly called knee plates, or T plates, between each port, generally on the timber next the port timber; and when the ends of the channels extend beyond the ports far enough, one is placed from 12 to 18 inches from the ends. These knee plates have their upper ends let through the channel, and have an arm under the channel extending sufficiently within the arm that is connected to the side, to have two or three up-and-down bolts, and out, to receive one up-and-down bolt: the up-and-down arm that forms a prop or tie from the side to the channel is bolted to the side with one collar-headed bolt. The up-and-down bolts, which are eye-bolts or saucer-headed, pass through a plate that is let into the upper part of the channel directly over the channel arm of the knee, and the upper end of the knee that projects above the channel has a hole for a span shackle.

The dead-eyes are placed for the chains to clear the ports below the channel; and the ports above are placed to clear the shrouds. The binding of the dead-eyes is let in, to be well with the outer part of the channel, and a rail is brought over them, called the channel rail; this rail is as deep as the channel is thick at the outer part, and in breadth a half-inch less than its depth; it is fastened in general with saucer-headed bolts, driven between the dead-eyes about twice the breadth of the rail into the channel; and sometimes strops are placed over the rail, that in the event of the masts being carried away, the rail may keep the dead-eyes up, to clear the shrouds with greater ease.

CHEEK BLOCKS, blocks in general brought upon the side of bitts for fair leaders.

*Cheek Blocks* (see MAST MAKING).

CHEEKS OF THE MAST (Swedish, *kinnbacker på masten*; Danish, *kindbakker paa masten*; Dutch, *klampen of kinbakken aan de masten*; German, *backen der masten*; French, *jottereaux ou flasque des mâts*; Italian, *gaetelle o maschetti degli alberi*; Spanish, *cacholas*; Portuguese, *romaom do mastro*). (See MAST MAKING).

*Cheeks of the Head* (Swedish, *slöy-knän*; Danish, *slöy-knæer*; Dutch, *sloi-knies*; German, *backen-knien, schloi-knien oder schliess-knien des galjons*; French, *courbes de jottereaux*; Italian, *bracciuoli di polena*; Spanish, *curvas bandas*; Portuguese, *curvas do beque*). Cheeks are knees brought on each side of the knee of the head for supporting it, and at the same time forming ornamental mouldings, which terminate at the figure with scrolls (see HEAD).

CHESSTREE (Swedish, *halsklampar*; Danish, *halsklamper*; Dutch, *kalsklampen*; German, *halshölzer, halsklampen*; French, *dogues d'amure*; Italian, *castagnuole della mura*; Spanish, *castannuelas de la amura*; Portuguese, *castanhas ou gornes das amuras*), pieces formerly bolted to the side, outside, at a proper distance before the main mast (see FIXED BLOCKS), for hauling home the main tack.

CHOCKS (Swedish, *klässar*; Danish, *klosser der sættes imellem*; Dutch, *klossen, kalven*; German, *kalben, kalven*; French, *entremises, clefs*; Italian, *incimenti*; Spanish, *entremiches*; Portuguese, *chassos*), pieces brought on different timbers to fashion them out.

*Chocks at the Heads and Heels of Timbers* (48).

*Cross Chocks* (48).

*Bowsprit Chock* (see BOWSPRIT).

CHINE, the part of the waterway (387) left above the deck, and hollowed out to the spirketting.

CHINCE or CHINSE. To chince or chinse, is a slight mode of caulking any seams or butts.

CISTERN (Swedish, *pumpback*; Danish, *pompebak*; Dutch, *pompbak*; German, *pumpenback*; French, *cisterne*; Italian, *cisterna*; Spanish, *caja alta*; Portuguese, *cisterna*), a vessel for holding water, placed in different parts of the ship; as the cistern in the well for washing decks, to chain pumps, &c. (see PUMPS).

CLAMPS FOR THE BEAMS (Swedish, *balkvägare*; Danish, *bielkevægare*; Dutch, *balkwaager*; German, *balkwäger oder balkweger*; French, *bouquière*; Italian, *dormente*; Spanish, *durmente o' durmiente*; Portuguese, *dormente*) (124).

CLEAN. When the ship is sharp or the body acute, she is said to be clean; as a clean run, she is clean forward or aft.

CLEATS or KEVELS (Swedish, *klampar, krampar*; Danish, *klamper*; Dutch, *klampen*; German, *klampen*; French, *taquets*; Italian, *tacchj*; Spanish, *tojinos*; Portuguese, *cunhos*), a frame consisting of four pieces bolted to the side, inside, one lying in the direction of the strakes, and two curved pieces let through it, with kevel heads, for belaying principal ropes to; mostly used in foreign ships.

*Belaying Cleats* (Swedish, *horn-krampar*; Danish, *kryds-klamper, horn-klamper*; Dutch, *kruis-klampen*; German, *horn klampen oder kruis-klampen*; French, *taquets à cornes ou à branches*; Italian, *castagnuole*; Spanish, *manignetas*; Portuguese, *cunhos da mariacaom*), cleats fastened to the side of the ship and to the shrouds, for making fast different ropes. Those for belaying the tacks and sheets are in general called ranges, and are bolted to the side with two bolts, driven considerably within the outer part of the range, to prevent the ropes from catching or being injured.

*Cleats or Brackets under the Cross-piece to the Riding Bitts* (Swedish, *betings-klampar*; Danish, *bedings-klam-*

*par*; Dutch, *klampen onder beeting balk*; German, *beet-ings klampen*; French, *taquets des bittes*; Italian, *tacchj della traversa delle bitte*; Spanish, *tojinos de la cruceta de la bita*; Portuguese, *cunhos da travessaom da abita*), for supporting them (see BITTS).

*Yard-arm Cleats* (Swedish, *năck-klampar*; Danish, *nok-klamper*; Dutch, *nok-klampen*; German, *nock-klampen*; French, *taquets de bout de vergue ou de pointure de ris*; Italian, *conj dei pennoni*; Spanish, *tojinos del penol*; Portuguese, *cunhos do luiz*), cleats fastened on the yards. These cleats are square at the large end, for the slings, from one-seventh to one-sixth of their length; and for the yard-arms, from one-sixth to one-fifth. The cleats to all the yards, except the lower yards, have the same proportions nearly for their length, and are square for the slings from one-seventh to one-sixth; and for the yard-arms, from one-sixth to one-fifth (see MAST MAKING).

*Gammoning Cleats* (Swedish, *vulings-klampar*; Danish, *voulings-klamper*; Dutch, *klampen aan de boegspriet-woeling*; German, *bugspriet-wuhlings-klampen*; French, *taquets de lieures de beaupré*; Italian, *tacchj delle trinche del copresso*; Spanish, *tacos de las trincas del baupres*; Portuguese, *cunhos das trincas do gorupes*), cleats brought on the bowsprit for preserving the gammoning in its position.

CLINCH or CLENCH, TO CLINCH (Swedish, *klinka*; Danish, *klinke*; Dutch, *klinken*; German, *klinken oder verklinken*; French, *river, claveter une cheville sur virole*; Italian, *ribadire, ribattere*; Spanish, *rebater los pernos*; Portuguese, *aninar*), to spread the point, or rivet it upon a ring, to prevent the bolt from drawing (see BOLTS).

CLINCH WORK (Swedish, *bygde på klink*; Danish, *klinke bygning*; Dutch, *zoomwerk*; German, *ein klinker-weise gebauetes fahrzeug, klinkerwerk*; French, *bâtiment bordé à clin*; Italian, *le tavole delle bande l'una sopra l'altra*; Spanish, *barco tinglado*; Portuguese, *barca que tem os costados com tablas*), is when the strakes of the bottom have their lower edges lapping or overlaying the upper, on the outside; and the fastenings passing through the two planks where they lap, between the timbers, from the outside, and turning or rivetting on the inside: where the timbers come, the fastening passes through, and turns or rivets upon them. Vessels that have the plank of the bottom worked in this manner, are said to be clincher-built (see CARVEL WORK).

COAKING (Swedish, *damning*; Danish, *tilsammenföyelse af masternes vangerne*; Dutch, *schaakwerk*; German, *schakwerk*; French, *calleboles*; Italian, *indentamento delle gallapazze nell'albero*; Spanish, *adentamiento de los chapuces al alma del palo*; Portuguese, *adentamento das chumeas a alma do mastro*) sometimes called dowelling ; the placing pieces of hard wood, either circular or square, in the edges or surfaces of any pieces that are to be united together, to prevent their working or sliding over each other. Circular coaking has been introduced instead of tabling, which was by forming one piece into another by alternate projections on each side of the middle to prevent their working lengthways, or from side to side as in putting together made beams, channels, knee of the head, rudder, &c. The circular coaking is performed by placing the surfaces that are to be united together in their proper position, and boring holes through one piece into the other with a small auger, at the center of the station of every coak, which will give the center agreeing at the two sur-faces ; then with a circular engine called a dowell engine, which has a spindle connected to it at the center, corres-ponding to the size of the auger, circular holes are bored into each piece, 1¼ inch generally, which will corre-spond at their circumferences, consequent upon thir cen-ters agreeing, and their being formed by the same engine ; pieces of circular wood, three inches long, frequently of lignum vitæ, or some hard wood, formed from a corres-ponding engine, are then driven into the holes of one of the pieces to be united, and the pieces brought together. Sometimes the circular coaks are made of hollow cylinders of cast iron, filled in with cement.

COMINGS (Swedish, *luck-ramarna*; Danish, *luge, karmer*; Dutch, *hoofden, koppen*; German, *scheerstocken der luken*; French, *vassolles, chambranles*; Italian, *mas-cellaj, mezzanili dei bocaporti*; Spanish, *brazolas*; Por-tuguese, *bracolas*), framings round the hatchways, ladder-ways, and scuttles, to prevent the water of the deck from flowing down; they are therefore of greater height to those decks that are the most subject to the encroachment of the sea. The comings are the pieces that lie fore and aft on each side of the hatchways, &c. There is a carling let down between the beams immediately under them (283), into which they have two or three circular coaks, and are fastened to them with two or three treenails: a rabbet is taken out of their upper edge; when for gratings or hatches, from the inner edge; but when for cap scuttles or companions, from the outer, when they are of a parallel thickness. To the main and after hatchways a rabbet is likewise taken out from their lower and inner edges to allow the gratings to be placed on a level with the deck when they are working the pumps; and to all working hatchways an iron plate is let in flush on their upper and inner sides, with the edges of the plates well with the rabbet. The pieces that lie athwart and form the framing at the fore and after part of the hatchways and ladderways, are called head-ledges; these pieces lap and tail over the comings, and are faced into their sides about half an inch, and are bolted with one bolt at each end, that passes through them, the comings and beams, &c. and one or two besides, that pass through the beam; if one, it is placed at the middle line, and if two, at equal distances on each side of the middle. When the hatchways are covered by gratings, the head-ledges have their upper parts formed to a round, but when for cap scuttles or companions, they are in general straight.

COMPANION (Swedish, *kappa eller ruffōfver akter-trappan*; Danish, *stirresen, ruffet over, agter-trappen*; Dutch, *kap*; German, *kappe der luken*; French, *capot d'échelle*; Italian, *capello della scala*; Spanish, *sombrero de la escalera*; Portuguese, *meia laranja*), the hood or covering, in flush-deck vessels, over the ladder-way to the captain's cabin; also the framing, formed with glass, at the upper parts or sides, over the captain's cabin, ward or mess-rooms, or other officers' apartments, for keeping out the weather and giving light.

COPING, to turn the ends of iron knees, to form a hook in the beams, &c.

CORVETTE (Swedish, *corvette, bevāpnat fartyg*; Dan-

R

ish, *korvette, et slags-fartöy*; Dutch, *korvette*; German, *korvette*; French, *corvette*; Italian, *corvetta*; Spanish, *corveta*; Portuguese, *corveta*), a flush-deck vessel, ship-rigged, or a ship with one entire battery, without a quarter-deck and forecastle, except that it mostly has what is called by seamen a top-gallant forecastle, for the shelter of the crew.

COUNTER. The *Lower Counter* (Swedish, *hvalfvet*; Danish, *den underste gilling*; Dutch, *wulf*; German, *die gilling des schiffs oder die hintergilling, grasse gilling*; French, *voute ou grande voute*; Italian, *fornello, forno da popa, carreca*; Spanish, *babeda ó bobedilla*; Portuguese, *almeida*) is that part of the ship right aft, or the stern immediately above the wing transom; it is formed by a curve, arched upwards from the upper and aft side of the wing transom to the first or lower counter rail (65). The *Upper Counter* (Swedish, *öfra hvalfer*; Danish, *överste gilling*; Dutch, *knik-wulf*; German, *die kleine gilling des schiffs über der grossen*; French, *contre-voute*; Italian, *contra carreca, seconda carreca*; Spanish, *segonda bobeda, contra-bobeda*; Portuguese, *contra-almeida*), sometimes called the second counter, is immediately over the lower counter, or between the lower counter and lights; the upper part is formed by the upper counter rail, and lower part by the lower counter rail. The plank of the lower counter is in general the same thickness as the plank of the bottom, and fastened to the counter timber by treenails or nails; sometimes, each strake has one treenail and one nail in every timber. The upper counter is in general from $2\frac{1}{2}$ to 3 inches in thickness, and if in more than one breadth of plank, they rabbet together. This counter rabbets into the rails.

*Counter Timbers* (Swedish, *hvalfvets knäna*; Danish, *gilling knæer*; Dutch, *wulf-knies*; German, *gillinghölzer oder gillingknien*; French, *courbes de voute*; Italian, *carreche*; Spanish, *gambotes*; Portuguese, *cambotas*) (65).

COVE (Swedish, *hvalfvet öfver altanen*; Danish, *gillengen boven galleriet*; Dutch, *plantsier*; German, *plantsier*; French, *route de la galerie*; Italian, *volta sopra la gallerie*; Spanish, *bobedilla del corredor*; Portuguese, *almeida do jardim*), an arch formed immediately over the upper lights of the stern, springing formerly from a bracket or truss, in general called terms or term pieces, brought on the side counter timber, or upon the munion that covers it ; but now it springs from the outside of the outer lights, and terminates on a plain moulding. The upper and lower part of the cove is formed by mouldings, mostly astragals ; the lower one is called the necking.

CRAB (Swedish, *lös spel, krypple-spel* ; Danish, *kröbbel-spil* ; Dutch, *los spil, kreupel-spil* ; German, *loses spill, loses gang-spill* ; French, *cabestan volant* ; Italian, *argano volante, (b) piccolo mulinello di ferro* ; Spanish, *cabrestante volante* ; Portuguese, *cabrestante volante*), a small capstan fixed in a frame, and made portable, that it may be used for different purposes ; likewise a wooden spindle, with its lower end working in a socket, and circumscribed at a convenient distance from the upper part by pieces similar to the partners of a capstan ; and having, at a proper height from the lower end, two holes, at right angles to each other, which pass quite through the spindle, for receiving the bars. This machine, which is simple in its construction, and has great mechanical power, on account of the length of the bars and smallness of the spindle, is used principally while the ship is building ; and a similar one on board of ships in ordinary, for hoisting their water, &c. on board.

CRADLE (Swedish, *aflöpnings-slade* ; Danish, *slæde* ; Dutch, *slede* ; German, *schlitten worauf ein schiff abläuft* ; French, *berceau* ; Italian, *l'invasure* ; Spanish, *cuna* ; Portuguese, *berco*), a strong frame made under the bottom of the ship, for supporting her when launching ( see LAUNCH).

CRANKS, iron rods bent at each end, and generally attached to the beams, at different parts of the ship, for stowing capstan bars, spunge rods, &c. : likewise the iron frame that supports the poop lanthorns.

CROAKY. When plank or timber forms sudden and and inflected curves it is said to be croaky.

CROSS CHOCKS (see CHOCKS).

CROSS-JACK YARD (see YARDS).

CROSS-PIECE TO BITTS (see BITTS).

CROSS-SPALLS, pieces of fir plank that keep the

frame of the ship to its proper breadth until the beams are in, when they are removed (52).

CROSSTREES (Swedish, *tvärsalningar*; Danish, *tvær-salinger*; Dutch, *dwars-zaalingen*; German, *dwars sah-lingen*; French, *barres traversières de hune et de perro-quet*; Italian, *crocette*; Spanish, *crucetas*; Portuguese, *curvatois*). (See MAST MAKING).

*Top-mast Crosstrees* (Swedish, *salningar*; Danish, *salingar*; Dutch, *zaalingen*; German, *sahlingen*; French, *barres de hune*; Italian, *crocette*; Spanish, *crucetas*; Portuguese, *vaos e curvatoes*). (See MAST MAKING).

CRUTCHES (Swedish, *resande botnstockar*; Danish, *pigsuer*; Dutch, *sogstukken*; German, *piekhölzer, piek-stucke*; French, *fourcats*; Italian, *forcazzi*; Spanish, *piques*; Portuguese, *enchimentos*), timbers aft, lying square to the body, and extending equally on each side of the keelson, for uniting the two sides abaft the floors. The crutches are now formed of two pieces and an iron brace (fig. *b*, 29), to save the crooked timber; and when with a diagonal frame, the ends of the timbers extend down, and meet at the middle line, where they are combined by an iron brace.

CUTTER (Swedish, *kutter*; Danish, *kutter*; Dutch, *kutter*; German, *kutter*; French, *cutter*; Italian, *balan-dra, cutter*; Spanish, *balandra, cutter*; Portuguese, *chalupa cutter*), a small vessel, vessel-rigged as a sloop; they are frequently distinguished in his Majesty's service by king's cutters and revenue cruizers; the former is em-ployed against a foreign enemy, to carry dispatches, &c. while the latter is employed against an illicit trade.

*Cutter* (see BOATS).

CUTWATER (Swedish, *skiägg*; Danish, *skiægget*; Dutch, *schagt, schegge*; German, *schaft oder scheg des schiffs*; French, *taille mer, la guibre*; Italian, *tagliamare*; Spanish, *tajamar*; Portuguese, *talha mar*), a name given by seamen to the knee of the head (see HEAD).

DAGGER, a term given to all timbers lying diagonally, as dagger-knees (185) (*e*, fig. 23).

PUMP-DALE (Swedish, *pump-ränna, dala*; Danish, *pomperende, pomp-dæle eller pompedale*; Dutch, *daal van de pompe*; German, *daal, pumpendaal*; French, *dale de pompe*; Italian, *dala*; Spanish, *adala ó dala*; Portuguese, *dala*), a conducter for conveying the water from the cisterns to the pumps overboard, when the ship is pumped out. It fixes in a groove at the cistern, and in a cleat at the side. The hole through the side is called the pump-dale scupper; it is formed of lead, and has an iron flap or valve outside, to prevent the sea entering the ship.

DAVIT (Swedish, *penterbalk, dävert*; Danish, *dœvis, bielke*; Dutch, *pentcrbalk*; German, *penter-balken*; French, *davit ou minot pour les ancres*; Italian, *pescante per traversare l'ancora*; Spanish, *pescante*; Portuguese, *pao de ferviola*), a beam used similar to a crane, for what is called fishing the anchor, or bringing up the flukes, after it is brought up to the cathead, or catted, so as to clear the side. It mostly steps on the fore-channel in cleats, fixed there for that purpose. These davits are from 9 to 17 feet 6 inches in length, according to the class of ship, and from $8\frac{1}{2}$ to $15\frac{1}{2}$ inches square at the lower end, and from $1\frac{1}{2}$ to 2 inches less at the upper end. They are left square from the lower end $2\frac{1}{4}$ diameters, above which they are eight-squared; one diameter up from the lower end, they are snaped, and have a necking at the upper end one diameter down.

*Boats' Davits*, outriggers fixed right aft on each side, at the upper part of the stern, for hoisting the stern boat; and sometimes on each side, opposite the mizen channel, for hoisting the quarter boats; those right aft project beyond the stern rather more than the half-breadth of the boat; they extend along the side forward, and are bolted with from three to four bolts. At the outer end are placed two shive holes for the boat falls, and one hoop for strengthening it; and on the under side is driven one eye-bolt for lashing the boats when up. The quarter davits are fixed to the side between two iron plates, which have a collar-headed bolt to pass through them and the davit, and to forelock, upon which it turns to bring the boats more into the ship when hoisted. Their outer ends have a necking for the pendants, two shives for the falls, and four eye-bolts, one on each square, for the guys, and for lashing the boats, or bringing the stopper to; and frequently a hoop just without the shives. Sometimes a hoop is likewise driven on the inner end for the bolt to pass through.

DEAD-DOORS; these doors are used when the quarter galleries are carried away, to prevent the encroachment of the sea through the gallery doors; they are in general made of deal of 1¼ inch in thickness, called whole deal, and lined with deal of about five-eighths of an inch in thickness, called slit deal, and fixed in a rabbet taken out on the outside of the gallery doors; to keep them in their places they have sliding bolts on the inside.

DEAD-EYES (Swedish, *jungfru*; Danish, *jomfru*; Dutch, *juffer*; German, *jungfer*; French, *cap-de mouton*; Italian, *bigotta*; Spanish, *bigota*; Portuguese, *bigota*), pieces of elm, of an oblate form, for receiving the lanyards for setting up the shrouds through; those attached to the ship are fixed to the outer edges of the channels, (see CHAINS (Swedish, *puttinger*; Danish, *puttinger, patenter, pytling-kœtinger*; German, *puttingen oder pyttingen*; French, *chaines de haubans*; Italian, *lande*; Spanish, *cadenas de las bigotas*; Portuguese, *cadèas da abotucadura*): they have three holes through each, the two upper are perpendicular to the center of the chain about the center up, and the lower one is placed so as to form nearly an equilateral triangle; they are placed so as for the chains to clear the upper deck ports; but the quarter-deck and forecastle ports are placed to clear them. The foremost is placed in general nearly opposite the center of the mast; and it is desirable that there should be, for giving the best support to them, two or three at equal distances abaft it, before the distance is increased by the ports intervening.

DEAD-LIGHTS (Swedish, *blind luker*; Danish, *blind luger, lendse-skoder eller lemmer for kahyts vinduerne*; Dutch, *blinden*; German, *blinden oder blinde-luken vor den fenstern der kajute*; French, *faux sabords ou faux mantelets pour les fenêtres de la poupe*; Italian, *contra portelli o finestre oscure*; Portuguese, *pastigos de pao*), shutters made as the dead-doors, and fixed outside of the stern lights, in tempestuous weather, to prevent the encroachment of the sea through the windows.

DEADWOOD (Swedish, *kläffar*; Danish, *det döde træe*; Dutch, *kielklosten*; German, *kielklotze*; French, *massif*;

Italian, *legno che forma il fondo del taglio della nave*; Spanish, *dormidos*; Portuguese, *coral*), a range of timber placed on the upper part of the keel (35 to 41).

DEAD-WORKS (Swedish, *öfver skepp*; Danish, *over, skibet*; Dutch, *dood werk huising boven-schip*: German, *ober-schiff, oberwerk ober todte werk*; French, *œuvre morte*; Italian, *opera morta*; Spanish, *obra muerta*; Portuguese, *obra morta*), the upper or supernatant part of the body.

DEAL (Swedish, *bräde*; Danish, *dæle*; Dutch, *deel*; German, *diehle*; French, *bordage mince*; Italian, *tavola di poco grossezza*; Spanish, *tabla poco gruessa*; Portuguese, *taboinha*), fir similar to planks (see TIMBER).

DECK (Swedish, *dack*; Danish, *dæk*; Dutch, *dek*; German, *deck*; French, *pont*; Italian, *coperta*; Spanish, *cubierta*; Portuguese, *cuberta*), the different platforms in ships for supporting the artillery, for the accommodation of the officers and crew, and for placing the stores. They are distinguished by different names according to their situation and purpose.

*Upper Deck* (Swedish, *öfra däck*; Danish, *överste dæk*; Dutch, *het bovenste dek, het boevenet*; German, *das dritte deck*; French, *troisième pont*; Italian, *terza coperta*; Spanish, *tercera cubierta*; Portuguese, *terceira cuberta*).

*Gun Deck* (Swedish, *underdack*; Danish, *förste eller underste dæk*; Dutch, *het onderste dek*; German, *das erste oder unterste deck*; French, *premier pont*; Italian, *prima coperta*; Spanish, *primera cubierta, cubierta principal, cubierta de la bordega*; Portuguese, *primeira cuberta*).

*Middle Deck* (Swedish, *mellan däck på tredäckare eller öfra på tvädäckare*; Danish, *mellemste dæk paa en tredække*; Dutch, *het tweede dek*; German, *das zweyte deck*; French, *second pont*; Italian, *secondo coperta*; Spanish, *segonda cubierta*: Portuguese, *segunda cuberta*).

*Quarter-Deck* (Swedish, *halfdäck*; Danish, *half dækket, skandsen*; Dutch, *half dek*; German, *halb deck*; French, *demi-pont*; Italian, *cassaro*; Spanish, *alcazar*; Portuguese, *tolda*).

*Forecastle* (Swedish, *back*; Danish, *bak*; Dutch, *bak*; German, *back*; French, *chateau d'avant*; Italian, *castello*; Spanish, *castillo*; Portuguese, *castello de proa*).

*Poop* or *Round-house* (Swedish, *hyttan*; Danish, *hytten*; Dutch, *hutte*; German, *hütte*; French, *dunette, poupe*; Italian, *casseretto da poppa*; Spanish, *toldilla*; Portuguese, *tombadilho*).

*Orlop* (Swedish, *trässbotton*; Danish, *banierne*; Dutch, *koebrug*·; German, *kuhbrücke unten im schiff*; French, *faux pont*; Italian, *falso ponte*; Spanish, *sallado*; Portuguese, *baileos do poraom*).

*Flush-Deck* (Swedish, *glatt däck*; Danish, *glat dæk*; Dutch, *glud dek*; German, *ein glattes deck*; French, *pont entier*; Italian, *coperta intera*; Spanish, *cubierta de punta al oreja*; Portuguese, *cuberta corrida*), is when it extends the whole length of the ship without drops or intervals. Cutters, brigs, and corvettes are said to be flush-deck vessels, by their not having the regular quarter-deck and forecastle, as to frigates, &c.

DECK PLANKS (Swedish, *däckplanker*; Danish, *dæk-planker*; Dutch, *dekplanken*; German, *deckplanken*; French, *bordages des ponts*; Italian, *tavole di coperta*; Spanish, *tablas de las cubiertas*; Portuguese, *assoalhado das cubertas*), the flooring or covering of the beams (29).

TWO-DECK SHIP (Swedish, *tvädäckare*; Danish, *en todœkker*; Dutch, *tweedecker*: German, *ein zweydecker*; French, *vaisseau à deux ponts*; Italian, *nave di due ponti*; Spanish, *navio de dos puentes*; Portuguese, *navio de duas cubertas*), ships of war having two entire batteries.

THREE-DECK SHIP (Swedish, *tredäckare*; Danish, *tredœkker*; Dutch, *driedekker*; German, *ein drey-decker*; French, *vaisseau à trois ponts*; Italian, *nave di tree ponti*; Spanish, *navio de tres puentes*; Portuguese, *navio de tres cubertas*), ships of war having three entire batteries.

DECK TRANSOM (Swedish, *däckvarporna*; Danish, *dœkwarperne*; Dutch, *dekworpen*; German, *deckworpen, deckwrangen*; French, *barres d'arcasse, barre du premier et du second pont*; Italian, *gue*; Spanish, *yugos de las cubertas*; Portuguese, *gios*), a timber or beam extending across the ship for supporting the after extremity of the decks, having both the round aft of the stern and round up of the beams. They score and face upon the counter timbers, and are bolted through them with one or two bolts: each end of this transom has an iron knee, called the transom knee affixed to it, with one arm extending a certain distance along their fore side, and the other against the side of the ship; if a shelf (211), the side arm is brought down and extends along the front; if not, this arm is brought in front of the clamp (124).

*Deck Transom.* When the ship has a stern frame, one of the transoms in this frame is made to support the after ends of the lower or gun deck (19).

DEPTH OF HOLD (Swedish, *djup i rummet*; Danish, *lastens dybhed*; Dutch, *holte van het ruim*; German, *hohl oder holl des raums*; French, *creux de calle*; Italian, *pontale della stiva*; Spanish, *puntal con que se debe arquear*; Portuguese, *pontal do poraom*), one of the principal dimensions of a ship; it is the depth in midships, from the upper side of the upper deck beams, in flush-deck vessels, and lower deck beams in all others, to the upper part of the limber strake.

DISPLACEMENT. The displacement is the volume of water displaced by the immersed part of the body, and which is always equal to the weight of the body. The light displacement equals the weight of the hull only, while the load displacement equals the weight of the hull and all it contains.

A certain displacement is therefore given to different vessels according to their rate and employment, and which can only be deviated from by increasing or diminishing the ballast; since the weight of the hull, stores, ordnance, &c., will be determined by the class of ship, and will be always constant. (See Architectura Navalis Mercatoria, by Frederick De Chapman: translated by the Rev. James Inman, D. D.).

DOCK (Swedish, *däcka*; Danish, *dokke*; Dutch, *dok*; German, *docke, schiffs-docke*; French, *bassin de construction*; Italian, *baccino*; Spanish, *dique bise, bacin*; Portuguese, *dique*), a basin for repairing ships, fitted with floodgates, to prevent the flux of the tide from having a passage into it.

*To Dock the Ship* (Swedish, *at docka*; Danish, *at dokke*; Dutch, *ein schip dokken, of in een dok brengen*; German, *docken ein schiffs docken*; French, *mettre un vaisseau dans un bassin*; Italian, *mettere una nave in un*

s

*bacino*; Spanish, *meter un navio en un bacin ó dique*; Portuguese, *meter hum navio em hum dique*).

*Wet Dock* (Swedish, *den innersta delen af en hamn*; Danish, *det inderste af en söe-havn*; Dutch, *kom*; German, *docke*; French, *darsine, darse, bassin*; Italian, *darsena*; Spanish, *darsena*; Portuguese, *darsena*), a basin for containing ships afloat.

DOWSING CHOCK, a chock that crosses the apron, and laps on the inside plank, for receiving the messenger rolls when there are no hooks to receive them.

DRAUGHT (Swedish, *ritning, tekning*; Danish, *tegning, plan*; Dutch, *plan, tekening*; German, *riss oder abriss eines schiffs*; French, *plan d'un vasseau*; Italian, *disegno*; Spanish, *proyeccion*; Portuguese, *plano*), designs given on paper for the several parts of the ship; they consist of the *Sheer Draught* (Swedish, *sido-ritning*; Danish, *side-tegning*; Dutch, *zyde tekening*; German, *seiten-riss eines schiffs*; French, *plan d'élévation*; Italian, *disegno d'élévazione*; Spanish, *proyeccion longitudinal*; Portuguese, *plano da elevaçaom*), which has the *Half-breadth Plan* (Swedish, *vattenpass eller horisontel ritning*; Danish, *vaterpasse tegning*; Dutch, *waterpasse tekening*; German, *wasserpasser riss senten-riss*; French, *plan horizontal*; Italian, *disegno orizontale*; Spanish, *proyeccion horizontal*; Portuguese, *plano horizontal*) and *Body Plan* (Swedish, *spant-ritning*; Danish, *spant-tegning*; Dutch, *spant-tekening*; German, *span-riss*; French, *plan vertical, plan de projection*; Italian, *disegno verticale*; Spanish, *proyeccion transversal*; Portuguese, *plano vertical*) connected with it, profile, and plans of the decks.

The sheer draught gives the vertical longitudinal form, and has delineated upon it all the out-board works, projected upon a plane passing through the middle line of the keel, stem, and post, as the elevation of the head and quarters, place and sheer of wales, place of the channels, dead-eyes, &c.; and place of the ports, drifts, &c. From this plan lines are transferred to the half-breadth plan as to length, and to the body as to height. The body plan is that in which the form of the ship is shewn by transverse sections, perpendicular to the keel, which are transferable to the half-breadth plan as to breadth, and to the sheer plan as to height. The half-breadth plan is that in which is shewn the form of the body by horizontal and diagonal longitudinal sections. The profile is a draught upon which is delineated upon a plane of elevation the whole of the in-board works ; it shews the vertical longitudinal section of the ship the same as the sheer draught, and has upon it the height and sheer of decks and ports. The plans of the decks shew the disposition of the in-board works upon the surface of the decks, with their distances from the middle line.

DRAUGHT OF WATER (Swedish, *et skeppes djupgäende*; Danish, *so mange fod vand et skib stikker dybt*; Dutch, *waterdragt*; German, *wassertracht eines schiffs*; French, *tirant d'eau*; Italian, *il pescare della navio*; Spanish, *lo que cala el návio*; Portuguese, *o tirante de agua*), the depth that the body is immersed. Where the surface of the water cuts the body, when the hull is entirely clear, is called the light water line ; and the draught of water to this line, the light draught of water ; and when every thing is on board, the load water line ; and the draught of water, the load draught of water. The depth that the ship swims is shewn by marks placed on the stem and stern post ; the lower part of the mark shews the feet, and the upper part six inches.

DRIFTS (Swedish, *fortynning* ; Danish, *fortönningen* ; Dutch, *vertuinning* ; German, *zerbrochenergang* ; French, *rabattues* ; Italian, *risalto del cassaro* ; Spanish, *medias hiladas de los castillos* ; Portuguese, *alcacha* (90).

DRIFT PIECES, pieces that formerly formed scrolls at the drifts, but are now face pieces placed at the termination of the round-house, and quarter-deck and forecastle barricading (192).

DRIVER BOOM (see MAST MAKING).

DROPS, carved ornaments, festoons of foliage, or flowers entwined by ribbands, &c. placed on the munions between the lights to the stern and quarters.

DRUMHEAD (see CAPSTAN).

DRUXEY (Swedish, *fyr i tra*; Danish, *fyr i træ*; Dutch, *vuur in't hout* ; German, *das holtz hat das feuer* ; French, *le bois est cani*; Italian, *legno marcito*; Spanish, *madera que ya está podrida ó blanca* ; Portuguese, *ma-*

*deira apodrecida*), a decay in timber, which has a dark appearance, with white spungy veins.

DUMB PINTLE, when the pintle is short and works in a socket brace.

DUNNAGE BATTENS, strips of fir or oak nailed across the cable tier, sail-rooms, and magazines, to prevent the cables, sails, and powder, from being damaged, by admitting air under them. Dunnage battens are likewise placed behind the lining of the bread room, sail-room, magazine, &c. to keep the lining from the side. Dunnage likewise signifies, generally, battens or other light pieces used in different stowages to keep the tiers clear of each other.

EKEINGS, pieces brought on to make good the length of any principal timbers, or abutting against their ends, as to the cheeks, knees, and the deck hooks. Ekeings are now brought over the stemson, and extend from the middle line to the first beam, and the deck hook is placed upon them, to prevent the consumption of large timber. The hook is coaked to the aft side of them, the quoif on the upper part, so as to cross their abutments at the middle, and the shelf to the lower part, so as to extend four or five feet beyond their after end.

ELM (Swedish, *alm*; Danish, *alm*; Dutch, *olman, ypen-hout*; German, *ulmen oder ipern holz*; French, *bois d'ormeau*; Italian, *olmo*; Spanish, *olmo*; Portuguese, *olmo*), a timber used but for few purposes in ship building; principally for the keel, on account of its toughness, through which it is not so liable to be injured when the ship takes the ground; nor split by the number of bolts that pass through it, in the same range of fibre, and lower strakes of the bottom. The two species in common use are the *ulmus campestris* and *montanus*. The *campestris*, or wych, is very free grained, and therefore seldom used for keel pieces.

ENSIGN STAFF (Swedish, *flagstaken*; Danish, *flagstangen*; Dutch, *vlag-stok, vlag-staf*; German, *flaggstab oder flaggenstock*; French, *bâton de pavillon, mât de pavillon*; Italian, *asta della bandiera*; Spanish, *asta de bandera*; Portuguese, *asta da bandeira, paó da bandeira*), the staff placed upon the taffrail, for displaying the ensign; it is secured generally by a step at the lower end, and a strap at the upper part of the taffrail or fiferail.

Even Keel, when the ship has the same draught of water before as abaft.

Eye-Bolt (see Bolts).

Face-Piece (see Bitts).

Facing, the letting of one piece into the other, as the facing taken out of the side of the post (26) for the transom, and out of the deadwood for the floors (44), (see *i*, Fig. 6, and *k*, Fig. 11).

Falling Home, sometimes called tumbling home, what the top side falls in from a vertical line, from the main breadth.

False Keel (Swedish, *lösköl, stäköl*; Danish, *straae kjöl*; Dutch, *loose kiel*; German, *loser kiel, falscher kiel*; French, *fausse quille*; Italian, *sapata della colomba*; Spanish, *zapata de la quilla*; Portuguese, *sobresano inferior ou exterior*), is a keel brought on the under side of the main keel with short bolts or nails, about 4 feet apart on alternate edges, and staples driven into the side, and let in flush, called keel staples, about 2 feet 4 inches apart. The false keel is from 2 to 6 inches in thickness, and but slightly fastened, that in the event of the ship taking the ground it may readily clear itself, and help to free the ship. When false keel is wanted for making the ship hold a good wind, there are frequently more than one, to increase the lateral resistance. The main keel is coppered on the under side, and between the false keels, if more than one; and on the under side of the lower false keel, where a groove or channel is taken out for the butts and edges of the sheets of copper, that should the ship touch the ground lightly, they may not be rubbed off so easily. The under side of the false keel forward has thick lead brought under it, as far aft as there is danger of the cables rubbing.

False Post (Swedish, *följare utan pa ackterstäfven*; Danish, *bagkanten af agterstœvnen*; Dutch, *buitensteven, loose agter-steven*; German, *loser hinter-steven, buten-steven*; French, *contre-étambot extérieur*; Italian, *contraasta esteriore di poppa*; Spanish, *contracodaste exterior*; Portuguese, *contracadaste exterior*), a piece brought on the aft side, at the lower part of the stern-post, to make good any deficiency of wood, or to allow a smaller piece of timber to do; and should the ship take the ground, it may defend the main post. This piece is either tabled or coaked to the main post; tabling is most to be recommended, as the edges between the false and main posts are caulked. The coaks in the tablings are about 20 inches in length, and brought with their edges from about $2\frac{1}{2}$ to $3\frac{1}{4}$ inches from the edge of the post; the upper and lower ones are brought on the middle line, and about 10 inches in length: if circular coaks, they are placed from 18 inches to 2 feet apart, with their outsides the same distance as the tabling from the side of the post. The false post in most foreign ships extends the whole length of the post, and may be considered as a backing.

FALSE RAIL, a piece brought on the upper part of the main head rail to strengthen it: it is bolted through the main rail with bolts about 2 feet apart (see HEAD).

FASHION-PIECE (Swedish, *ransoms timmer*; Danish, *ransonholter*; Dutch, *randsoenhouten*; German, *randsomholzer*; French, *estains*; Italian, *alette*; Spanish, *aletas*, *brazales*; Portuguese, *mancos*), timbers that give the form or fashion of the after extremity, below the wing-transom, when they terminate the tuck (32); and with a stern frame partake of the form of the body with the transoms at their ends (27).

FAY, to fit close or to bring two surfaces to conform to each other, so that there may not be any perceptible space between them.

FID (Swedish, *sluthult*; Danish, *slutholt*; Dutch, *slothout*; German, *schlosholz oder schlotholz der stengen*; French, *clef du ton du mât*; Italian, *cassacavallo*; Spanish, *cunna*; Portuguese, *cunha dos mastareos*), a bar of wood or iron used to support the weight of the top-masts and top-gallant-masts when erect, and to keep the bowsprit, in cutters, out, &c.

FID-HOLE (Swedish, *slutgatt*; Danish, *slutgat*; Dutch, *slotgat*; German, *schlosgat, oder schlotgat der stenge*; French, *trou pour le clef du ton de mât*; Italian, *pertuso o ribasso delllalbero*; Spanish, *buraco ô ojo de la cunna*; Portuguese, *buraco de cunha*), mortises in the heels of top-masts, top-gallant-masts, &c. (see MAST MAKING).

FIFE RAIL, a rail formerly above the planksheer,

let on timber heads, at the quarter-deck and forecastle, and above the taffrail (92) (see RAILS).

FIGURE (Swedish, *skepps bild*; Danish, *löven eller figuren af skibet*; Dutch, *leeuw van het schip*; German, *bild des schiffs*; French, *la figure*; Italian, *figura di prua*; Spanish, *el leon, ln figura de proa*; Portuguese, *a figura de proa*), the principal ornament of carved work at the head of the ship.

FILLINGS, pieces of timber placed wherever solidity is required, as pieces between the timbers of the frame (42) for the chain and preventer bolts to pass through at the ends of beams, &c.

*Fillings between the Cheeks* (Swedish, *kam*; Danish, *kam*; Dutch, *kam*; German, *kam zwischen den schliessknien des galjons*; French, *remplissage entre les jollereaux, frise de l'éperon*; Italian, *riempimenti frà gli scarmoti della polena*; Spanish, *taco'ó moldura entre las curvas bandas*; Portuguese, *ornato del talha*), pieces of fir worked so as to fill up between the cheeks. When the bolsters of the hawse or naval hoods are between the cheeks, these fillings extend from them to the block of the figure; if not, the fillings extend to the after end of the cheeks.

*Fillings in the Openings*, between the timbers of the frame (255).

FILLING TIMBER, or FILLING FRAMES (Swedish, *timmer*; Danish, *fyllings-spant*; Dutch, *vulling spant*; German, *füll-spann füllungs-spann*; French, *couple de remplissage*; Italian, *quaderno di riempimento*; Spanish, *cuaderna de enchimiento, cuaderna intermedia*; Portuguese, *baliza de encher, madeira de encher* (46).

FILLING TRANSOM (see TRANSOM); this transom is now done away with, as an unnecessary consumption of scarce timber (25).

FINISHING, ornamental work for forming a finish to the upper and lower parts of the quarter gallery; those below are called the *Lower Finishings* (Swedish, *nedre delen af gallerien*; Danish, *det underste af en side-gallerie*; Dutch, *voet van de zyde-galderyen*; German, *schwanz der seiten gallerie*; French, *cul de-lampe des bouteilles*; Italian, *pié dei giardini*; Spanish, *pié del jardin*; Portuguese, *pé do alforge*); and those above, the *Upper Finishings*.

FILLET, a small square moulding which accompanies or crowns a larger. Also a strip of fir nailed to stop the different bulkheads of the cabins in their places.

FIR (Swedish, *furu*; Danish, *fyrr*; Dutch, *vuurenhout*; German, *fohren-holz, tannen-holze, fichten-holz*; French, *sapin*: Italian, *pino*; Spanish, *pino*; Portuguese, *pinho*), timber used for many purposes in ship building, and for making masts and yards. This timber is of various species, as the *Pinus Sylvestris*, the wild pine or Scotch fir; it grows principally in Denmark, Norway, and Sweden, and is that timber from which the white deal is cut. The *Pinus Strobus* or Weymouth pine, commonly called the white or masting pine; it grows in North America, and from it the single-tree masts and bowsprits are principally made, on account of the size to which it grows. The *Pinus Larix*, or the larch: this timber is of quick growth, and is a native of the Alps and Appenine mountains, though a considerable quantity of it is grown in Scotland, and has been used in ship building. The *Pinus Picea*, the silver fir tree or pitch tree: this timber is most common in Norway, and in some of the mountains of Scotland; from it the yellow deal is cut. The *Pinus Abies*, or spruce fir: this timber is one of the principal productions of the woods in Norway and Denmark, and is of close texture; the white deal is cut from it. This species of fir has likewise been grown in Scotland, and been used in ship building. And the *Pinus Canadensis*, or Canada spruce: this timber grows to a considerable size, and is a native of North America.

The fir from Prussia, Dantzic, Norway, and especially that exported from Riga, is much esteemed; the Prussian and Dantzic for the flats of weather decks, and the Norway and Riga for masts. Though the red pine from North America is considered but litttle inferior, Riga is now principally used for topmasts, while the North American fir, as the red, white, and yellow pines, are used for standing masts.

FIRE BOOM (see BOOMS).

FIRE HEARTH, a machine placed in the galley for the convenience of cooking. It is composed of a grate, oven, and boilers.

FIRE SHIP (Swedish, *bränuare*; Danish, *brander*;

Dutch, *brander, brandschip*; German, *brander*; French, *brûlot*; Italian, *brulotto*; Spanish, *brulote*; Portuguese, *brulote*), a ship having combustible materials on board, that they may be readily set on fire, to produce a conflagration in the enemy's fleet, &c. ; and that they may be easily entangled with the enemy's rigging, the yards are fitted with grappling irons and sheer hooks.

FIRE-ROOM, the room that contains the combustible materials, fitted between the upper most deck and the deck below. This room has funnels connected with it, for communicating the fire to the rigging ; the port lids on each side are hung on the lower part, and have placed against them iron chambers, which at the time of the firing of the ship blows them out. A sally-port on each side is placed abaft the after bulkhead of the fire-room ; it is formed for the retreat of the officer after the train is set on fire.

FISHES, fore and after, and side fishes, or side trees, (Swedish, *skalar* ; Danish, *vanger*; Dutch, *zwalpen* ; German, *schwalpen* ; French, *jumelles d'assemblage* ; Italian, *galapazze* ; Spanish, *jimelgas* ; Portuguese, *chumeas meas de uninom*), the components of made masts.

FIXED BLOCKS (see BLOCKS).

FIXED BOLTS (see BOLTS)

FLAT-SOLED FISH, when the faying surface is made flat.

FRONT FISH, a fish brought on the fore side of the mast.

FISH-ROOM, a room in the after hold, used in general for stowing spirits. It lies between the spirit and powder-room, or after magazine.

FLAIRING, to fall out from the main breadth, the reverse of falling or, tumbling home (see BOW).

FLATS. The frames that have the same area as the greatest transverse section, are called flats, and the greatest transverse section is called dead flat (50).

FLIGHT, to rise suddenly ; as what the cathead is above a horizontal line is called the flight of the cathead ; or what the cheeks curve above the sheer before the stem, is called the flight of the cheeks ; or what the transoms, at their ends, are from an athwartship line at their breech, is called the flight of the transoms ; whereas what the floor rises above a horizontal line, is called the rise of the floor.

T

FLOOR. The floor is considered that part of the ship, on each side of the keel, that would be in contact with the supporting surface when inclined ; and according as the floor will allow her to incline, it is said to be *Flat* (Swedish, *flat bätnstäck* ; Danish, *plat bundstok* ; Dutch, *buikstuk i·'t vlak* ; German, *ein flaches oder plattes bauchstück* ; French, *varangue platte* ; Italian, *matera piana, majer piano* ; Spanish, *varenga llana* ;· Portuguese, *caverna chata ou plana*), or *Rising* (Swedish, *resande bätnstäck* ; Danish, *reisende bundstok* ; Dutch, *twill, pickstuk* ; German, *eingezogenes bauchstük* ; French, *varangue acculée* ; Italian, *matera levata* ; Spanish, *varenga de levanta* ; Portuguese, *cavernas que ficaom perto da roda de próa e cadaste*) (43).

FLOOR TIMBERS (Swedish, *bätten-stäcken* ; Danish, *bundstokken* ; Dutch, *buikstuk* ; German, *bauchstück* ; French, *varangue* ; Italian, *matera, legno di piano, piana (gen majera)* ; Spanish, *un plan, una varenga* ; Portuguese, *caverna*) (43 and 44).

MADE FLOORS. Floors are said to be made when formed of more than one principal piece. The difficulty and expense of providing timber suited for floors, especially in the acute parts, or where they have a great rising, which require timbers with a great bend, and frequently make it necessary to provide them out of knee timber, have led to different methods of making them of several pieces, both by the French (Fig. 14) and English. The English method now in general use, in the new system of building (Fig. 13), the floor is composed of three pieces, two pieces that are called half-floors (*b* and *d*), and one piece called a cross piece (*a* and *e*), which unites them. The half-floors scarph to each other, or abut with a circular coak at the middle, and the cross piece preserves their union by having circular coaks, and from two to three bolts to pass through each : but when the rising of the floor is considerable and there is a great cutting down, two cross pieces (Fig. 13, *ee*) are placed to each, and the half-floors, in the room of scarphing, butt against each other*.

---

* The flat floors now, as well as the rising, have the half-floors to abut against each other, and have a circular coak in their abutment.

The half-floors and cross pieces, when the timber will admit, have frequently now their siding so as to make together the room and space, so as to prevent the necessity of having any openings to fill in.

FLOOR HEADS (Swedish, *kimming*; Danish, *kimmingen af et skib*; Dutch, *kim, kimming*; German, *kimm oder kimming des schiffs*; French, *fleurs de vaisseau*; Italian, *fiori della nave, intiunte*; Spanish, *cantos del pantoque*; Portuguese, *cantos do fundo do navio*), sometimes called rung heads, the outer ends of the floors.

FLOOR RIBBAND, the ribband next below the floorhead (70), (see RIBBANDS).

FLOORS, MADE.

FLUSH, to be fair, or any parts being on the same surface.

FLUSH-DECK (see DECK).

FOOT SPACE RAIL, the lower rail of the balcony, or stern gallery, or the rail into which the ballustrades step, when there is no pedestal rail (see BALCONY).

FOOTWALING or FUTTLING (see CIELING).

FORE, distinguishes the several parts of the ship that lie towards the stem.

FORE AND AFT, in direction of the ship's length, ranging from end to end.

FORECASTLE (see DECK).

FORE FOOT (11).

FIRELOCKS (Swedish, *knapar*; Danish, *knapper*; Dutch, *knaapen*; German, *knapen*; French, *taquets de clous*; Italian, *tacchetti dei chiavi*; Spanish, *taquets ó tojinos por los clavos*; Portuguese, *tacos ou cunhos dos cravos*), a thin circular or straight wedge of iron, made to pass through a mortise at the point of a bolt, to prevent its drawing when a direct strain is brought upon it (see BOLTS).

FORKED BEAMS, beams formerly placed in the wake of the hatchways and masts, on account of the great space between the main beams in these places. They formed an inflected curve, so as to be united to the side of the beam, at the midship end; and to have their side ends in the middle, between the two beams, they were placed between.

FRIEZE, thin deal placed between the beams, over the fore and aft bulkheads of the cabins.

FRAME (Swedish, *spant rigtspant*; Danish, *rigtspandt*; Dutch, *rigt-spant, scheer-spant*; German, *richtspann, scheer-spant*; French, *couple de levée*; Italian, *quaderno principale*; Spanish, *cuaderna principal*; Portuguese, *baliza principal*) (42), without the filling frames.

FRAMING (see BULKHEADS).

FURRENS or FIRRINGS, pieces brought on to fashion, or make up the deficiency of timber, the moulding way.

FUTTOCKS, single timbers in the frame (66) : as the *First Futtock* (Swedish, *ziltror*; Danish, *ziters*; Dutch, *zilters*; German, *sitzer*; French, *genoux*; Italian, *foreami del fondo, stamenali*; Spanish, *estemenaras*; Portuguese, *bracos primeiros*), *Second, Third, and Fourth Futtocks* (Swedish, *uplängor*; Danish, *oplanger*; Dutch, *oplanger*; German, *auflanger in einem spann*; French, *allonges*; Italian, *stamenali, slongatori*; Venetian, *forcameli*; Spanish, *jenoles, ligazones de los cuadernas*; Portuguese, *os bracos segundos, terceiros, &c. das balizas* (45).

FUTTOCK RIDERS (Swedish, *katsporets uplangor*; Danish, *katsporenes oplanger*; Dutch, *de oplanger van de katspooren stuinders*; German, *auflanger der katspuhren*; French, *allonges de porques*; Italian, *stamenali delle porche*; Venetian, *forcamli dei raisoni*; Spanish, *jenoles de lias bularcamas*; Portuguese, *bracos dos prodigos do poraom*) (242).

GAFF (Swedish, *gaffel*; Danish, *gaffel*; Dutch, *gaffel*; German, *eine gaffel*; French, *vergue à corne*; Italian, *pico*; Spanish, *pico*; Portuguese, *carangueia*.

*Trysail Gaff* (see MAST MAKING).

GALLERY. The stern gallery is a balcony projecting from the stern, mostly formed by ballustrades which extend from side to side, fixed in two rails; the upper, called the breast-rail, and the lower one the footspace. This gallery, sometimes called the stern walk, is limited on the fore part by a partition, called the screen bulkhead, which is a framed bulkhead, and has lights and doors fixed in it (see BALCONY).

*Quarter Galleries* (Swedish, *gallerie*; Danish, *side*

*gallerie*; Dutch, *zyde-gallery*; German, *obere oder offene seiten-gallerie*; French, *les clavecins de la galerie*; Italian, *giardino*; Spanish, *jardin*; Portuguese, *alforgee*), are on the side of the ship connected with the stern : they are principally for the convenience of water closets and for ornament. In three-deck ships, they are called the upper, lower, and middle gallery.

The galleries are formed by rails, stools, munions, birthing, finishing, and the lights. The *Rails* are distinguished, those immediately under the lights, by the rim rails, as the lower, which is connected with the upper counter rail of the stern, middle, and upper rim rails ; the rail next below the lower rim is called the lower stool rail, and is connected with the lower counter rail of the stern ; those above the lights are called stool rails, according as they are placed, as upper and middle stool rails ; the rails over the the upper finishing are called upper finishing rails, or rails to fret work, as the two small rails and part between them is called the fret work ; the rail below the lower stool is called the lower finishing rail. The *Stools* are several breadths of plank bolted to the ship's side, for giving the form of the outer part of the galleries, and forming the flooring of each gallery ; their outer part is an arc of a circle, for the convenience of sliding the lights, the fore and aft line being a tangent to it at the after part of the gallery, and intersecting the line of side at the length of the gallery forward. The *Munions* are the pieces that pass between the lights and form the side of them ; their upper ends let into the stools, and to the lower gallery, rests upon the water table that is brought upon the upper part of the rim rail. The *Birthing* is the part that incloses the quarter, except in place of the lights. The *Lights* are formed into sashes and mock lights ; the sashes have glass in them and slide, the mock lights are blank parts to make the quarter uniform outside. The finishings are the upper and lower parts (see FINISHINGS).

GALLEY (Swedish, *cabbysan* ; Danish, *kabyssen* ; Dutch, *kombuys* ; German, *kombüse* ; French, *cuisine* ; Italian, *fogone, fuocone* ; Spanish, *fogon* ; Portuguese, *cozinha*), the place appropriated for the fire hearth and cooking (see FIRE HEARTH).

Row GALLEY (Swedish, *gallere*; Danish, *galeje*; Dutch, *galey*; German, *gallere*; French, *galère*; Italian, *galera*; Spanish, *galera*; Portuguese, *galè*), a flat-built vessel, in general with one deck, and navigated both with oars and sails; they are most common in the Mediterranean.

GALLEY (see BOATS).

GALLIOTE (Swedish, *galliot, galliotte eller galleoth*; Danish, *galliot*; Dutch, *galjoot*; German, *galjote, galjotschiff*; French, *galiote Hollandoise*; Italian, *galeota Ollandese*; Spanish, *galeota del norte*; Portuguese, *galeota do norte, huma fandarga*), a Dutch ship with a lofty and round stern.

GAMMONING-HOLE, the hole for the gammoning of the bowsprit to pass through; it is placed between the cheeks. When there are two gammoning-holes, one is in general placed above the upper cheek under the lacing of the knee.

GANGBOARD (Swedish, *ställning*; Danish, *stilling, stilladse*; Dutch, *jok, juk*; German, *jock oder joch*; French, *échaffaud*; Italian, *ponte, bazigo*; Spanish, *andamios*; Portuguese, *andaimes*), several breadths of deal bolted together, formerly used for a passage on each side from the quarter-deck to the forecastle; likewise a board used to pass in and out of a boat.

GARBOARD STRAKE (Swedish, *sandbords-planka*; Danish, *spunningsplanken, kiölplanken*; Dutch, *kielgang*; German, *kielgang*; French, *gabord*; Italian, *toello*; Spanish, *primera tabla del bordo exterior, tabla de la quilla*; Portuguese, *taboa do resbordo*), the lower strake of the plank of the bottom (111).

GARLAND, or SHOT GARLAND (Swedish, *kulräckar*; Danish, *kugle-rekker*; Dutch, *kogel-rekken*; German, *kugel-recken*; French, *petit parquet pour les boulets dans les entre deux de sabords*; Italian, *latas de baleria*; Spanish, *rastrelliera da palle*; Portuguese, *cheleira de balas*), pieces of oak or beech plank, with holes formed in them, fastened round comings and head ledges of the hatch and ladderways; and sometimes between the ports, and in other parts of the ship, for placing the shot for immediate use.

GOOINGS or GUDGEONS (Swedish, *fingerlingar*;

Danish, *roer lykkar, fingerlingar*; Dutch, *duimelingen*; German, *fingerlinge*; French, *femelles ou femelots*; Italian, *femine*; Spanish, *hembras*; Portuguese, *fêmeas do leme*), the hinges upon which the rudder turns; those fastened to the rudder are called pintles, and those to the ship, braces; they are made of mixed metal*.

Goose-neck (Swedish, *svanhals*; Danish, *svanehals*; Dutch, *zwaanenhals*; German, *schwanenhals, an einem gieck-baum*; French, *crochête de fer fixé au bout intérieur d'un gui, et par le moyen duquel le gui tient à son mât*; Italian, *gancio della boma d'una randa*; Spanish, *gancho de la botabarra*; Portuguese, *gancho do bome*), an iron hook, placed at the after end of the main channel, with a strap to clasp it, for stowing the swing boom or a top-sail yard.

Goose-Neck is likewise an iron cleat placed on the fore end of the tiller to support it.

Gratings (Swedish, *trall*; Danish, *röstverket*; Dutch, *roosterwerk*; German, *rosterwerk*; French, *caillebotis*; Italian, *quartieri*; Spanish, *jareta, cuartel de enjaretado*; Portuguese, *xadrezes des escotilhas*), the covering of the hatchways, with a lattice covering to admit light and air; they are formed by ledges that lie athwart, and battens let into them, lying fore and aft.

Gripe, a piece of elm or beech scarphed to the lower end of the knee of the head (Fig. 5 and 11, *d*), to make a finish with the fore foot; it forms an abutment (27) against the foremost piece of keel, and is fastened with bolts, that pass no further into the stem than the rabbet, and a mixed metal plate (Fig. 5, *c*), brought on each side, called the horse shoe, on account of its form.

Gunwale (Swedish, *skandäck*; Danish, *skankdækket*; Dutch, *schamdek, schandek*; German, *schanddeck oder schanddeckel*; French, *plat-bord*; Italian, *orlo della nave*; Spanish, *regala, solera*; Portuguese, *alcatrate*) (92).

Hair Bracket (see Brackets).

Half Breadth Plan (see Draught).

---

\* Mixed metal is a compound of copper and zinc, mixed with grain tin to give it sufficient rigidity.

HALF-PORT (Swedish, *lösa stykepotar*; Danish, *löse stykporter*: Dutch, *uitvoering van de stukpoorten*; German, *ausfutterung der stückpforten*; French, *faux mantelets, faux sabords*; Italian, *falsi portelli*; Spanish, *arandelas de la artilleria*; Portuguese, *oculos das portinholas das pessas*), shifting shutters fixed in the stops of those ports, which have no hanging lids. Those to the quarter-deck and forecastle ports are in general in one, and made of two thicknesses of slit deals, and to the ports for the long guns have holes in them for the gun to run out; and those to the upper deck, in two parts called buckler half-ports; for long guns, the lower part is to the center of the gun, when run out and levelled, as they have a hole in them that fits close round the guns; and to carronades, to the under side of the gun, if not too low, that they may be fixed over them. The lower piece of these half-ports is of fir, and in one piece, to fill up the stops; with a rabbet taken out of its upper edge, to receive the upper part, and with two strengthening bolts driven up and down through it. This piece is in general hung with hinges at the lower part, and kept in its place by sliding bolts. The upper part is made commonly of whole and slit deal, the whole deal up and down, and the slit deal, to cross it, fore and aft.

HALF TIMBERS, the short timbers before and abaft the floors, in the cant bodies, which correspond with the shift of the heads in the square body.

HAMMOCK RACK, battens, with scores taken out of them at 14 inches distance, or with stops fixed to them; they are nailed to the side of the beams, for the sailors to hang their hammocks to.

HAMMOCK STANCHIONS, iron stanchions fixed in the waist between the drifts and upon the barricadings, for stowing the hammocks between; they are in general made with horns at their upper ends to receive a small rail; if not, they have an eye for a ridge rope. The two arms of these stanchions are made to spread, according as they are to stow one or two hammocks abreast.

HANCE, the sudden breaking in from one form to another, as when a piece is formed, one part eight square, and the other part cylindrical; the part between, where these different forms terminate, is called the hance, or the parts of any timber where it suddenly becomes narrower or smaller.

HANGING, the same as sheer, or a bending down (81).

HANGING KNEE (see KNEES).

HARPINS, pieces formed to the shape of the body, and fixed at each extremity, for keeping the frames in their proper position until the planking is brought on (53).

HARRIS or ARIS PIECES, are pieces cut to a triangular form.

HARRIS EDGE, the same as cypher edged, or when the edges are cut to form an acute angle with the sides, as the plank to the well and shot-locker bulkheads (see BULK-HEAD).

HATCHES (Swedish, *stulplucka*; Danish, *stulp luge*; Dutch, *stulp luik*; German, *stulp-luken*; French, *panneaux à boite*; Italian, *boccaporta da incassare*; Spanish, *escotilla ó cuartel a encaje*; Portuguese, *quartel que encaixa*), the coverings of the hatchways; or, if made with ledges (Swedish, *lucka falldör eller locket af en lucka*; Danish, *luge som paalægges*; Dutch, *luik, lucken-dekzel*; German, *luke, lukendeckel, lukenklappe*; French, *panneau d'écoutille*; Italian, *coverchio della boccaporta*; Spanish, *cuartel de la escotilla*; Portuguese, *quartels das escotilhas*); and when the comings and head ledges have a rabbet on the outer parts, and the covering has a rim that circumscribes them, in this rabbet, they are called *Cap Scuttles* (Swedish, *spring lucka*; Danish, *spring luge*; Dutch, *spring luik*; German, *spring luke oder lose luke*; French, *écoutillon à panneau*; Italian, *piccola boccaporta nella grande*; Spanish, *escotillon en un cuartel*; Portuguese, *escotilhaom*).

HATCHWAY (Swedish, *lucka*; Danish, *luge*; Dutch, *luik*; German, *luke*; French, *écoutille*; Italian, *boccaporta*; Spanish, *escotilla, boca de la escotilla*; Portuguese, *escotilha*), passages from one deck to the other, and into the hold of the ship. The principal hatchways are the *Main Hatchway* (Swedish, *storluckan*; Danish, *stor lugen*; Dutch, *het groot luik*; German, *die grosse luke*; French, *grande écoutille*; Italian, *boccaporta maestra*; Spanish, *escotilla mayor*; Portuguese, *escotilha grande*): *Fore Hatchway* (Swedish, *forluckan*; Danish, *forlugen*;

U

Dutch, *het voor luik*; German, *vor-luke, kabelgats-luke*; French, *écoutille de la fosse aux cables*; Italian, *boccaporta della fossa delle gomene*; Spanish, *escotilla de prua, del pannol de los cables*; Portuguese, *escotilha de proa*): and *After Hatchway* (Swedish, *akterluckan*; Danish, *agter lugen*; Dutch, *agter luik*; German, *hinter-luke*; French, *écoutille de l'arrière*; Italian, *boccaporta di popa*; Spanish, *escotilla de popa*; Portuguese, *escotilha de popa*). The other passages that do not communicate with the hold, are called ladderways.

HAWSE HOOK (Swedish, *klysband*; Danish, *klysbaand*; Dutch, *kluisband*; German, *klus-band*; French, *guirlande des écubiers*; Italian, *busarda della cobie*; Spanish, *busarda de los escobenes*; Portuguese, *busarda dos escovoens*), the breast hook at the hawse holes.

HAWSE HOLES (Swedish, *klys, klysgatorna*; Danish, *klyds-huller*; Dutch, *kluisgaten*; German, *klusen order klusgaten*; French, *écubiers*; Italian, *cobie, occhj*; Spanish, *escobenes*; Portuguese, *escovoens*), the holes at the fore part of the ship through which the cables pass. The size of these holes is determined by the size of the cables, and thickness of the pipes. If for iron cables, the hole before it is defended, must be larger, since they are lined with both a lead and iron pipe, and are left sufficiently large to work the hempen cables when required.

For hempen cables, the holes are lined with a leaden hawse pipe, which is cast thicker at the lower part than the upper, to bear the rub of the cable. For the iron cables, the holes are first lined with a leaden pipe through the bow, of about ¼ of an inch in substance; and when the bolsters of the hawse are in, an iron pipe is let in from the outside, with its inner end square, as far aft as the joints, between the bolster and the bow, at the after part of the hole, with a flange or lap on the bolster; and another pipe is let out from the inside to meet it, nearly, with a lap or flange on the spirketting. These two pipes are united together with four bolts that pass through the bolster, bow, and the laps. Should there be any opening at the joint of the two pipes, it is filled with Roman cement (see Table I).

HAWSE PIPES (Swedish, *klysbussar*; Danish, *klysbösser*; Dutch, *kluisbossen*; German, *klüs-buchsen*; French, *une boîte ou tuyau de plomb dans les écubiers* ; Italian, *il piombo delle cobie* ; Spanish, *el forro ó canal de plomo en los escobenes* ; Portuguese, *o forro de chumbo nos escovoens*), thick lead pipes that line the hawse holes.

HAWSE PLUGS (Swedish, *klys proppar* ; Danish, *klyds-propper* ; Dutch, *kluis proppen, teersjes* ; German, *teersjen zu den klüssen* ; French, *tampons d'écubier* ; Italian, *tappie delle cobie* ; Spanish, *tacos de los escobenes* ; Portuguese, *tacos dos escovens*), plugs made to fit the hawse holes, to prevent the passage of the sea through them when the cables are unbent.

HAWSE PIECES (Swedish, *bogtimmer* ; Danish, *bovstykkërne* ; Dutch, *boegstukken, aposteln* ; German, *bagstucke oder bugholzer* ; French, *alonges d'écubiers* ; Italian, *apostoli* ; Spanish, *astas de proa* ; Portuguese, *columnas de proa* (55).

HEAD, the upper end of any piece of timber, as the heads of the timbers of the frame*, bitt heads, timber heads (Swedish, *pållar* ; Danish, *pullerter* ; Dutch, *polder* ; German, *polder oder pöller* ; French, *têtes des alonges de revers* ; Italian, *bittoni* ; Spanish, *posturas escalamotes* ; Portuguese, *cabecos*), bollard heads, &c.

HEAD (Swedish, *gallian* ; Danish, *gallion* ; Dutch, *galjoen* ; German, *das galion oder galjon eines schiffs* ; French, *poulaine* ; Italian, *polena* ; Spanish, *las alas de proa* ; Portuguese, *beque*), the whole of the fore part of ship, with the bows, when used in the enlarged sense of the word, but here it is intended to signify the finishing of the fore part, which consists of the knee of the head (see CUTWATER), figure (see FIGURE HEAD), head rails (Swedish, *gallions ziegler* ; Danish, *gallions reilinger* ; Dutch, *regelingen van het galjoen* ; German, *regelingen des galjons* ; French, *lisses de herpes* ; Italian, *soggie dello sperone* ; Spanish, *perchas* ; Portuguese, *perchas*), and cheeks (see CHEEKS).

The knee of the head (Fig 11, A B C) is an assemblage of pieces tabled or coaked together, and brought on

---

* The heads and heels of the timbers are the parts that form their abutments against each other ; the head being the upper part, and heel the lower part of the timber.

A

the fore part of the stem, projecting forward from about 1-13th to 1-11th of the length on the deck; it is composed in general of three principal pieces, the stem-piece (A), main or lacing-piece (B), and bobstay-pieces (C). The *Stem-piece* extends from the lower end of the knee, where it has a scarph for the gripe, and sufficiently up to have a hole cut in it for the collar of the main-stay: *the Main or Lacing-piece* has its upper part forming the lacing for the back of the figure, and in general extends down to form an abutment into the stem-piece, and to give the form to some distance up, of the fore part of the knee: the *Bobstay-piece* has an abutment in the main piece and extends up to the under side of the figure, and has its fore edge to the form of the fore part of the knee. The other pieces that make up the breadth and form of the knee are of a size and form as most convenient. As the several pieces are placed in their position, two or three treenails are driven into each, to keep the knee together till the bolts are driven.

Upon the upper part of the knee a timber is brought, called the lacing (D), which abuts against the stem-pieces, and has a tenon into it; this piece extends forward so as to have one or two bolts through it from the fore part of the knee. *The Figure* is the carved ornament at the extremity of the knee, in general having an allusion to the ship's name. *The Head Rails* are called the main and small, or middle rails; the main rails extend from the back of the figure to the bow of the ship; sometimes to the supporter of the cathead, or snaping against the bow, when they are called straight or sheer rails, according as they are formed; at other times, which was common formerly, they have a sudden curve at the after end, and return against the fore side of the cathead, when they are called circular rails. The main rails are supported by a piece brought upon each, called a false rail, and secured, at the fore end, by an iron knee which bolts through the two rails and the lacing of the figure; and at the after end, by being bolted to the bow. They are likewise secured by cross-pieces, that lie from side to side and lap on each rail. The after cross-piece has on each end a knee against its aft side; and to the inside of the rail, between the cross-pieces, are placed pieces in a fore and aft direction, something less than half the diameter of the bowsprit from the middle line, when the bowsprit is above them, called fore and aft carlings ; they score into the cross-pieces, from about 1 inch to 1½ inch ; and from the fore and aft carlings to the rails, and from the bow to the rails, abaft the after cross-pieces, are let down small ledges to form the platform, having their lower edges made to a sharp, that they may oppose as little resistance as possible when the sea strikes them ; and to keep them down, an iron plate is fastened over their upper ends.  The small or middle rails are one or two in number, according to the size of the ship ; they are placed at equal distances between the lower side of the main rails and upper side of the cheeks ; their fore end abuts against the hair bracket (see BRACKET), and their after end against the bow ; they are let into the pieces called the head timbers, which are placed up and down in the direction of, or with a little more rake than the stem, and which extend from the lower side of the main rail to the upper part of the upper cheek, and are bolted through them with one bolt.   *The Cheeks* are two or three on each side for supporting the knee of the head ; they have one arm bolted to the bow and the other through the knee.   The bolts through the bow go through, and are clenched on the inside, and those in the knee go through each cheek and its opposite ; they are driven from each side alternately, and are clenched on the opposite side. The cheeks have ornamental mouldings struck on their outer edges.   The fore end of the upper one, which terminates with a scroll or volute, at the back of the figure, is called the hair bracket ; and the fore end of the middle, if three, or the upper, if two, terminates with a scroll or volute under the figure.

HEAD LEDGES (see COMINGS).

HEAD RAILS (see HEAD).

HEAD TIMBERS (see HEAD).

MAST HEAD (see MAST MAKING).

HEEL, the lower end of any piece of timber, as the heel of the timbers, *Heel of the Mast* (Swedish, *mastfot* ; Danish, *mastfod* ; Dutch, *hiel van een mast* ; German, *hiel eines masts* ; French, *pied d'un mât* ; Italian, *pié d'un albero*; Spanish, *mecha*; Portuguese, *pé do mastro*), *Heel of the Topmast* (Swedish, *stängens, hål eller fot*; Danish, *fod eller, hål af en stæng*; Dutch, *hieling van de steng*; German, *hiel oder hieling der stenge*; French, *talon d'un mât de hune*; Italian, *cogion d'un albero di gabia*; Spanish, *coz del mastelero*; Portuguese, *coz do mastaroe*), &c.

HEEL, to incline.

HELM (Swedish, *roder, ror, styre*; Danish, *roer eller ror*; Dutch, *stuur, roer*; German, *steuer oder ruder*; French, *gouvernail*; Italian, *timone*; Spanish, *timon*; Portuguese, *leme*), the rudder, tiller, and wheel, or the machine that steers the ship.

HELM PORT (Swedish, *hål för roderpinnen*; Danish, *hennegat eller hul for roerpinden*; Dutch, *hennegat*; German, *hennegat*; French, *jumière*; Italian, *pertuso della manovella*; Spanish, *limera del timon*; Portuguese, *abertura por onde entra a cabeca do leme na almeida*), the hole through which the head of the rudder and the tiller pass.

HELM PORT or COUNTER TRANSOM (Swedish, *bofven hackbalk*; Danish, *ovre hækbialke*; Dutch, *boven hekbalk*; German, *obenheck-balken*; French, *barre d'écusson ou barre ou bout de l'étambot*; Italian, *controtriganto*; Spanish, *contrayugo, sobreyugo, crus*; Portuguese, *barra que forma o batente superior das portas da praia de armas*), a transom between the wing and middle or upper deck transom, with a cast to bring it below the helm port. This transom was bolted through the counter timbers, and was kneed at each end. It is now left out, on account of the large timber required to make it, and iron braces are placed instead.

HOGGING, the arching up of the body, occasioned frequently by the unequal distribution of the weights upwards with the pressure of the fluid (see NOTE to page 6).

HOLD (Swedish, *rummet*; Danish, *lasten*; Dutch, *ruim*; German, *raum eines schiffs*; French, *la cale*; Italian, *stiva*; Spanish, *bodega*; Portuguese, *poraom*), the part of the interior cavity of the ship below the lower deck or orlop, which is reserved for the ballast, water, and provisions.

HOOD. The foremost and aftermost plank in each

strake, both inside and out, are called the fore and after hoods (78).

*Hood*, the covering over the chain pumps.

HOODING ENDS (78).

HOOKS. *Breast Hooks* (Swedish, *bogband*; Danish, *bogbaad*; Dutch, *boegbanden*, *kropwrangen*; German, *banden im bug oder bug-banden*; French, *guirlandes*; Italian, *busarde*; Venetian, *zogie*; Spanish, *busardas*; Portuguese, *busardas do poraom*). Hooks are breast or deck hooks. The *Breast Hooks* are large compass timbers, lying across the apron or stemson inside, at an equal distance on each side, for uniting and supporting the bows. They are in length from about 10 to 18 feet, and bolted through both bows with from about 7 to 13 bolts, according to their length or class of ship; the bolts in the throat are placed nearer to each other than those towards the arm, and sometimes they are made to cross, that is, the two middle bolts are placed from about 6 to 12 inches apart, and are so disposed, as to their direction, to come outside the bow, on the side opposite to which they are placed upon the hook. The breast hooks are now in general made, so as to avoid great consumption of large and scarce timber. They are composed (Fig. 29) of two pieces (*a*) scarphed together at the middle, and united by an iron brace (*b*). The breast hooks are placed between the different decks, and below the lowest deck, and are sometimes named according to their situations; as the *Hawse Hook* (see HAWSE HOOK and HOOK UNDER THE BOW-SPRIT) (Swedish, *bogsprotband*; Danish, *bogsprytbaaud*; Dutch, *boegsprietband*; German, *bugspriet-band*; French, *guirlande du beaupré*; Italian, *busarda del copresso*; Spanish, *busarda del baxpres*; Portuguese, *busarda do gurupes*). The breast hooks below the lowest deck are placed nearly square to the body, and those between the decks, after the sheer of the decks. *Deck Hooks* are those upon which the fore ends of the deck rest; they have the round-up of the deck as well as the form of the inside of the bow (see EKEING).

HOOKING or HOOK AND BUTT, is when the edges of the different planking work into each other, with a small abutment of about 1 inch to 1¼ inch, sometimes called tabling, to prevent extension (127 and 134).

HOOP. Hoops are used for different purposes; as bands, as the *Hoops of the Masts* (Swedish, *mastböglar*; Danish, *mastboyler*; Dutch, *bengels om de mast*; German, *masten-bugel oder bügel um die masten*; French, *cercles de mât*; Italian, *cerchj degli aberi*; Spanish, *sunchos de las palos*; Portuguese, *chapas dos mastras*), *Hoops on the Pumps* (Swedish, *pumpboglar*; Danish, *pompböyler*; Dutch, *beugels tot de pomp*; German, *pumpen-bügel*; French, *cercles de pompe*; Italian, *cerchj della tromba*; Spanish, *sunchos de la tromba*; Portuguese, *chapas de bomba*) (see PUMPS).

*Hoops of the Capstan*, and in the Partners of the Capstan, (Swedish, *bogel i gângspels fiskar*; Danish, *boylen*; Dutch, *beugel in de vischer*; German, *bügel in den fischen des gangspills*; French, *cercle d'étambrai de cabestan*; Italian, *cerchio nelle fogonature dell'argano*; Spanish, *suncho en la fogonadura del cabrestante*; Portuguese, *chapa da ennora do cabrestante*) (see CAPSTAN).

*Clasp Hoops.* Joint or clasp hoops are used where it is impracticable to drive hoops; they have sometimes a joint, which is placed on the aft side of the mast, but mostly the spring of the iron is sufficient to allow them to open, and on the fore side, with the two parts to clasp each other, with mortises, which have wedge-like keys driven in to set them tight; these keys when hot are formed close to the mast, and are mostly covered with lead to prevent any ropes catching under them.

*Joint Hoops.* These hoops are similar to clasp hoops, excepting that they have joints on the opposite side to the clasp, to allow them to be opened for the ease of placing them on the mast before they are set up; as in some cases, if there were no joint, the hoop would be strained too much in placing it.

HORSE, a cylindrical bar of iron, extending from the fore side of the after end of the main rail of head, or from the bow, to the back of the figure, with one or two iron stanchions for support. It was intended formerly as a guard, and had a rope netting or canvass attached to it, but now a rail, called the birthing rail, is brought above the horse, and the head is birthed in with rabbetted deal of 1½ inch in thickness.

HORSE SHOE, straps of mixed metal, in the form of a horse shoe, used for securing the gripe to the stem; there is one on each side placed immediately opposite to each other, that the bolts that fasten them may pass through both (Fig. 5, c) (see GRIPE).

HOUNDING, the length of the mast from the heel to the lower part of the head (see MAST MAKING).

HOUND-PIECES, pieces fixed to standing masts, cutters' masts, and topmasts, for supporting the cross and trestle-trees for fixing the mast above.

HOWKER (Swedish, *hukare*; Danish, *huker*; Dutch, *hoeker*; German, *huker*; French, *heucre*; Italian, *sapata*, *ucaro*; Spanish, *ucaro*; Portuguese, *huquer, gangorra, charrua*), a Dutch vessel, from about 60 to 200 tons burthen, or more; they are rigged with a main and mizen mast.

HOY (Swedish, *hoy*; Danish, *hoy*; Dutch, *heu*; German, *heu*), a vessel usually rigged as a sloop, but sometimes with a main-sail without a boom, and in Holland with two masts; they are mostly used for carrying stores, water, &c. to ships in bays and roads, and for carrying passengers and luggage from one place to another, along the sea coast. Small vessels thus defined are in some places called sloops; and in others, smacks, &c.

HULL (Swedish, *skräf*; Danish, *skrov*; Dutch, *hol van't schip, lighaam*; German, *rumpf eines schiffs*; French, *corps*; Italian, *scaffo*; Spanish, *buque, casco*; Portuguese, *casco*). The part of the hull below water is called the bottom or *Quick Works* (Swedish, *under skepp*; Danish, *under skibet*; Dutch, *onder schip, het schips onder water zynde deel*; German, *unter-schiff*; French, *œuvre vive*; Italian, *opera viva*; Spanish, *obra viva*; Portuguese, *obra viva*), and upper or *Dead Works* (Swedish, *öfver skepp*; Danish, *over-skibet*; Dutch, *dood werk, huising, boven-schipt*; German, *ober schiff, oberwerk oder todte werk*; French, *œuvre morte*; Italian, *opera morta*; Spanish, *obra muerta*; Portuguese, *obra morta*) (see page 2).

HUTCHUCKS, small pieces of elm or oak, with a sin-

X

gle hole in each for a nail to pass through, used for the temporary fastening of any works, that the nails may easily be drawn.

JAMBS, broad pieces of oak fixed up and down on each side the captain's stove, in flush-deck vessels; likewise, formerly, pieces for fixing the lights in the magazine.

JEER BITTS (see BITTS).

JEER CAPSTAN (see CAPSTAN).

JIB BOOM (see BOOM).

IN-AND-OUT. The bolts that are driven through the ship's side, are said to be in-and-out bolts (206 and 207).

INBOARD, within the ship. The profile is the elevation of the inboard work (see DRAUGHT).

INNER POST (Swedish, *folgare innan på ackterstafven*; Danish, *indenstevnen paa agterstevnen*; Dutch, *binnenagtersteven*; German, *binnensteven hinten, oder binnenhintersteven*; French, *contre-étambot intérieur*; Italian, *contra-asta interiore di poppa*; Spanish, *albitana del codaste*; Portuguese, *contracadaste*) (24).

JOINT, where two edges or surfaces unite.

IRONS, *Studding-sail Boom Irons* (Swedish, *böglar til läseglets spiror*; Danish, *læsejlenes böyler*; Dutch, *lyzeils beugels*; German, *bügel der leesegelspieren*; French, *cercles des boutehors des bonnettes*; Italian, *cerchj die bastoni dei cortellazzi e scopamere*; Spanish, *sunchos de los botalones de las alas y rastreras*; Portuguese, *arcos dos paos de cutelos e barredouras*.

KEEL (Swedish, *köl*; Danish, *kiöl*; Dutch, *kiel*; German, *kiel eines schiffs*; French, *quille*; Italian, *chiglia*, *primo*; Venetian, *colomba*; Spanish, *quilla*; Portuguese, *quilha*) (2).

*False Keel* (see FALSE KEEL).

KEELSON (Swedish, *kölsvin*; Danish, *kiölsvin*; Dutch, *kolsem, kolswyn, saad-hout*; German, *kolschwein, kolschwinn, kolsem oder saatholz*; French, *carlingue du fond du vaisseau*; Italian, *paramezzale*; Spanish, *carlinga, sobre-quilla*; Portuguese, *sobre-quilha*) (69 to 72).

*Additional Keelson*, a piece of keelson brought on each side, upon the floors, &c. under the main step, to support the body against the stress of the main mast. It is of such a distance from the common keelson as to receive the ends of the step. It is coaked and bolted as the common keelson, except that the bolts pass through the floors or cross timbers, and outside planking.

KNEE (Swedish, *kna*; Danish, *knœ*; Dutch, *knie*; German, *knie*; French, *courbe*; Italian, *bracciuolo, curva*; Spanish, *curva*; Portuguese, *curva*). Knees are timbers formed from the trunk and branch of the tree; they are called *Lodging* (Swedish, *vinkelknä*; Danish, *vinkel-knœ, horizontal leggend knœ*; Dutch, *winkel-knie, waterpas leggende knie*; German, *winkle-knie, schlafende knie, horizontale knie*; French, *courbe horizontale*; Italian, *bracciuolo orizontale*; Spanish, *curva valona, curva diagonal*; Portuguese, *curva de abertona*) (181), *Hanging* (Swedish, *hängande knän*; Danish, *verticale knœer, op og ned staaende knœer*; Dutch, *op en neer staande knies*; German, *auf und neiderstehende knien, hängende knien, stech-knien*; French, *courbes verticales*; Italian, *bracciuoli verticali*; Spanish, *curvas de alto a bajo, curvas de peralto*; Portuguese, *curvas ao alto*) (181), and *Standard Knees* (Swedish, *knän som sitta verticalt på däcket*; Danish, *forkeerte knœer paa dekkene*; Dutch, *verkeerde knies op't dek*; German, *verkehrte knien*; French, *courbes verticales des ponts (dont une branche se cheville sur le pont)*; Italian, *bracciuoli verticali sopra le coperte*; Spanish, *curvas llaves*; Portuguese, *curvas do alto, dos chaves*), (186).

*Dagger Knee* (see DAGGER KNEE).

*Transom Knee* (Swedish, *häck-knän*; Danish, *hœk-knœer*; Dutch, *hek knies*; German, *heck-knien oder knien des heck-balkens und der spiegel-wrangen*; French, *courbes d'arcasse*; Italian, *bracciuoli delle alette e del tragante*; Spanish, *contra-aletas*; Portuguese, *curvas de palmejar*), a knee brought against the side of the ship and the foreside of each transom.

KNEE OF THE HEAD (see HEAD and CUTWATER).

KNIGHT HEADS (Swedish, *klyshultar*; Danish, *judas örne*; Dutch, *boegstukken van de kluisen, kluishouten, judes ooren*; German, *die bugstucke wodurch die klusen gebohrt sind oder die klusholzer*; French, *apôtres*; Italian, *apostoli delle cobie*; Spanish, *astas de proa para los escobenes*; Portuguese, *paos ou columnas dos escovoens*) (15).

KNUCKLE OF THE COUNTER (67).

LACING (see HEAD).

LADDERS (Swedish, *trappor*; Danish, *trapper*; Dutch, *trappen*; German, *treppen*; French, *échelles*; Italian, *scale*; Spanish, *escaleras*; Portuguese, *escadas*), frames used in ships for the convenience of ascending and descending from one deck to the other, similar to the staircases in houses. The ladders are formed of two principal pieces, that extend from one deck to the other, called sides, lying at as great an inclination as the breadth of the ladderway will allow, with proper head room; fitted between the sides, in groves or scores taken out of them, are pieces called the steps, lying after the deck, from 7 to 9 inches apart; what they are above each other, is called the rise, and what the front edge of one step projects beyond the step above, is called the tread, which will be more or less according to the inclination of the sides.

*Accommodation Ladder* (Swedish, *fallerpstrappa*; Danish, *fald-rebs-trappe*; Dutch, *valreeps-trap*; German, *fallreepstreppe*; French, *escalier ou échelle de commandement*; Italian, *scala alla banda della nave*; Spanish, *escala del costado, escala real*; Portuguese, *escada do costado*), a ladder sometimes fixed at the gangway, outside, for the accommodation of ascending and descending the side of the ship.

LADDERWAYS (see HATCHWAY).

LANDING STRAKE, the upper strake but one in a boat (see BOAT BUILDING) (see RAIL).

LARBOARD SIDE (Swedish, *bagbord*; Danish, *bagbord*; Dutch, *bakboard*; German, *backbord*; French, *babord*; Italian, *sinistra della nave*; Spanish, *babor*; Portuguese, *babordo*), the left-hand side when looking forward.

LAUNCH (see BOATS).

LAUNCH, the slip (1) upon which the ship is built, with the cradle and all connected with launching. While the ship is building, she is supported on blocks (1); but when she is to be launched, on an inclined plane laid on each side, to a declivity of from seven-eighths of an inch to one inch and one-eighth in a foot, the smallest declivity to largest ships. These inclined planes are formed in gene-

ral by laying first, lengthways of the slip, one or more
tiers of fir timber, two or more abreast, and upon them laying blocks, from 2 to 4 feet apart, to make up the height,
so as to have the depth of the builgeways at least in the
fullest part of the body, the inclined plane or ways to their
proper inclination, and that the fore foot of the ship may
clear at the bottom of the slip, or the slip where she floats.
Then upon the blocks are laid, lengthways the slip, two or
three breadths of plank, called sliding plank, from 3 to 4
inches in thickness, made even at their upper surface, and
with the butts of the different planks cut to a bevelling, so
that the butts of the upper planks may lie over the lower,
to prevent any part of the builgeways catching as the ship
descends. When the inclined planes or ways are com-
pleted on each side, the builgeways which form the principal, or base for the cradle, are placed upon them, with
their outer parts rather more than one-sixth of the extreme
breadth of the ship from the middle line. In the full part of
the ship, the space from the builgeways to the bottom is
filled up with solid pieces of fir, called fillings, or stoppings
up ; these fillings fit close on the builgeways, on the inside,
but are left about ¼ of an inch up, on the out, for wedge-
like pieces, called slices ; and before and abaft the fillings,
a plank is likewise placed on the builgeways, leaving it up
on the outside the same as the fillings, and for the same
purpose ; then upon these planks, pieces of fir timber, called
poppets, are placed endways up to the bottom, at the lower
end fixing in scores taken out of the plank, and at the upper
end faying to the bottom ; to unite the poppets and fillings
in one mass, a plank of 3 or 4 inches in thickness is
brought on the outside, over their heels, extending to
some distance along the fillings, and one or two others
above, one up to the bottom, and the other in general in
the middle between ; these two planks are commonly called
dagger planks. Between these planks, short pieces of the
same thickness, and in the direction of the poppets, are
fitted, and the whole are fastened with nails and trec-
nails to the poppets and fillings. As far, at each end, as
the poppets extend, and a small distance along the fillings,
a plank is bolted to the bottom, to prevent their being
forced out when they have to sustain the weight of the

ship. The edge of these planks, in general, forms a mitre with the upper edge of the upper dagger planks; and against the outer edge of this plank, and against the fillings, to give additional support, cleats are bolted to the bottom, one over every poppet, or every other one, and one over the butt of each piece of filling, and one or two between. These cleats are fastened with two or three copper bolts at the lower end, and two or three nails at the upper. The holes for the bolts are in general bored the thickness of the cleats more than their length, into the bottom, in case it should be required to drive them up, after the cleat is off. A cleat is likewise placed on the fore side of the foremost poppet on the builgeways, and one against the bottom; the same is placed against the aft side of the after poppet.

When the whole of the cradle is fitted, it is taken apart, and the upper surface of the sliding plank and lower side of the builgeways are greased, by first paying it over with hot tallow, and then with train oil, after which with small portions of soft soap, at small distances apart. The cradle is then again refitted, and the wedge-like slices placed close together, between the filling and builgeways and the plank under the poppets and builgeways, and set in tight, so as to bring the weight of the ship on the inclined planes, or take the weight in part off the blocks.

To keep the cradle in the proper direction while the ship is descending, long strips of fir, from 5 to 6 inches square, are nailed on the sliding plank, without the builgeways, called ribbands; these are placed so as to be clear of the outside of the builgeways, at the upper end $\frac{1}{4}$ of an inch, and at the lower end 1 inch; and at the lower end of the ways $1\frac{1}{4}$ of an inch. These ribbands are well shored on each side, to prevent spreading. The upper piece of ribband is in general from 8 to 12 feet in length, and of oak, coaked to the sliding plank, as against its fore end, a shore, called the dog-shore, is fixed. The dog-shore abuts against this piece of ribband with one end, and against a cleat bolted to the side of the builgeways, called the dog-cleat, at the other : it has its fore end capped with iron.

In launching the ship, the shores against the body

are taken down, and the blocks (1) under her keel, that support her while building, are regularly split out and removed, beginning with the after one. The ship is then brought to bear on the cradle, and that on the inclined plane which is on each side; then being thus supported, she has a tendency, by the force of gravity, to descend; but is still kept, till the time appointed for launching, from approaching towards the water, by the dog-shore and two or three of the foremost blocks, which remain to keep the strain from the dog-shore; two or more of which are allowed to remain, and are upset as the ship descends. When to be launched, the dog-shores are knocked down, and if the force of gravity does not overcome the adhesion and the pressure on the blocks left under, the bed screws fixed against her gripe are hove till she moves; the ship will then descend with increased velocity, until she is borne by the water.

LAYING-OFF is the taking off from the draught and delineating upon a floor prepared for the purpose, in an extensive room called the mould loft floor, the different parts of the ship to the true size, so as to obtain the correct form of all the timbers that compose the frame (42) and other principal parts of the structure (see LAYING-OFF).

LEAK (Swedish, *läcka*; Danish, *læk, lække*; Dutch, *lek*; German, *leck*; French, *voia d'eau*; Italian, *falla*; Spanish, *un agua*; Portuguese, *veia de agna*), a passage for the water through shakes, holes, or breaches in the bottom, sides, or decks. At the commencement of the leak, the ship is said to have sprung a leak.

LEAN (see CLEAN).

LEDGES (Swedish, *ribbor*; Danish, *ræbber*; Dutch, *ribben*; German, *ribben zwischen den deckbalken*; French, *barrotins*; Italian, *catene*; Spanish, *barrotes*; Portuguese, *barrotes*), (278).

LIGHT WATER LINE (see DRAUGHT OF WATER).

LIGNUM VITÆ (Swedish, *porkenholt*; Danish, *pok-holt*; Dutch, *pok-hout*; German, *pock-holz*; French, *gayac ou gaïäc*; Italian, *legno santo*; Spanish, *palo santo*; Portuguese, *páo santo*), guaiacum or pockwood. The officinale, or common lignum vitæ, is that which is used in the mechanical arts, and for ships. The shives of blocks, rolls, and sometimes circular coaks, &c. are made of this wood.

LIMBER BOARDS (119).

LIMBERS, or LIMBER HOLES, (Swedish, *våghäl*; Danish, *lemme gater*; Dutch, *lokgaten*; German, *müstergaten*; French, *lumières, anguillères*; Italian, *bugi delle matere*; Spanish, *grueras de las varengas*; Portuguese, *boerias*), holes cut in the lower parts of bulkheads, lower parts of riders, &c. for a passage for the water.

LIMBER STRAKE (117).

LIPS OF THE SCARPHS, the end or thin part of the scarph.

LOAD WATER LINE (see DRAUGHT OF WATER).

LOCKERS, compartments built in general with 1¼ inch deal, in cabins and store-rooms.

SHOT-LOCKERS (Swedish, *kulbackar*; Danish, *kuglebakker paa dæcket*; Dutch, *kogelbakken op't dek*; German, *kugel-backen, auf dem deck*; French, *petits parquets pour les boulets, sur le pont*; Italian, *parchetti per le palle sopra la coperta*; Spanish, *cajas o ronnadas por las balas*; Portuguese, *arcadas ou chaleiras pregadas nas cubertas para conter as balas*), lockers placed between riding bitts under the cross-pieces, round the mast, &c. for placing shots ready for use.

LONG BOAT (see BOATS).

LOOVERED BATTENS, battens, fitted in frames, or between the stanchions, to different partitions, at such an angle as to admit air, and yet to prevent dirt from entering, or the apartment being exposed.

LUFF OR LOOF, the roundest part of the bow (see BOW).

LUGGER (Swedish, *lugger*; Danish, *logger*; Dutch, *logger*; German, *logger*; French, *lougre*; Italian, *bastimento chiamato, loggre*; Spanish, *logger*; Portuguese, *logger*), a vessel having three masts for carrying lugsails; the yards are lateen, but hang nearly at right angles to the mast when hoisted.

MAGAZINE (Swedish, *krutdurkar*; Danish, *krudkammer*; Dutch, *kruid-kaamer*; German, *pulverkammer*; French, *soute à poudre*; Italian, *camera della polvera*; Spanish, *pannol de polvera*; Portuguese, *paiol da polvera*),

an apartment formed in large ships forward, and small
ships aft, called the grand magazine. The larger class of
ships have a small one aft, called the after magazine or
powder-room.

MANGER (Swedish, *vatubacken fram i bogen*; Danish,
*vandbakken, pissebakken*; Dutch, *pisbak, waterbak*; German, *pisback, wasser-back*; French, *gatte*; Italian, *cassa
delle cobie*; Spanish, *caja delle agua*; Portuguese, *tanque
das pellas*), a part separated across the bow, inside, upon
the working deck, with one or more heights of plank, to
interrupt the passage of the water, that may come into the
hawse holes, when heaving in the cable, or at other times.
The separation is formed by planks, called manger boards,
that are placed immediately within the hawse holes, or sufficiently forward that the bow chase gun may be worked.
The boards are from 3 to 4 inches in thickness, and if
more than one in height, they are rabbetted together; to
receive their side ends, a chock is bolted to the bow, called the manger chock, and has a groove taken out of it,
of a triangular form, for that purpose. When the manger
boards are not fitted to extend from side to side, nor to fix
in the bowsprit bitts, two stanchions are fixed for that
purpose, called manger stanchions, equally on each side
of the middle, and apart sufficiently for the bowsprit to
pass between them. The manger boards are not permanently fastened, but have a stop placed over their upper
edge, in the groove taken out of the chocks and stanchions,
that they may be readily taken away when the flat of the
deck wants caulking. Their edges are caulked, and a
cant is fixed upon the deck against their after edge, called
the manger cant.

*Manger Scuppers*, scuppers placed in the after part
of the manger, through the side of the ship, for carrying
off the water into the sea that comes in at the hawse holes.

MARGIN, a line at a parallel distance down from the
upper edge of the wing transom, forming the lower part of
a surface for seating the tuck rail; it terminates the ends
of the exterior planking, or what is called the tuck.

MAST (Swedish, *mast*; Danish, *mast*; Dutch, *mast*;
German, *mast*; French, *mât*; Italian, *albero*; Spanish,
*palo*; Portuguese *mastro*) (see MAST MAKING).

Y

Masts are distinguished into the *Main* (Swedish,
*stormasten*; Danish, *stormasten*; Dutch, *de groot mast*;
German, *der grosse mast*; French, *grand mât*; Italian,
*albero maestro*; Spanish, *palo mayor*; Portuguese, *mastro
real, mastro grande*), *Fore* (Swedish, *focke masten*;
Danish, *fokke masten*; Dutch, *de fokke mast*; German,
*der fock-mast*; French, *mât de misaine*; Italian, *albero di
trinchetto*; Spanish, *palo de trinquete*; Portuguese, *mastro
real do traquete*), and *Mizen Masts* (Swedish, *mesans-
masten*; Danish, *besans-masten*; Dutch, *de besaans-mast*;
German, *der besahn-mast*; French, *mât d'artimon*; Italian,
*albero de mezzana*; Spanish, *palo de mezena*; Portuguese,
*masto real da gata ou da mazena*). These masts are *Made*
(Swedish, *mast som är gjord af mer än et trä*; Danish,
*mast som er giort af meere end et træe*; Dutch, *een mast
van veel in malkandere ingevoegde stukken*; German, *ein
zusammengesetzter oder aus mehrern strücken gemachter
mast*; French, *mât composé*; Italian, *albero composto*;
Spanish, *palo compuesto*; Portuguese, *mastro composto*),
or of a *Single Tree* (Swedish, *mast af et stycke*; Danish,
*mast af eet stykke*; Dutch, *mast die vane en stuk is*; German, *ein aus einem stück gemachter mast*; French, *mât
d'un brin ou d'une pièce*; Italian, *pidro*; Spanish, *palo
macho*; Portuguese, *placa*) (see Mast Making).

Top-Masts, are the *Main* (Swedish, *stor stängen*;
Danish, *store stængen*; Dutch, *de groote steng*; German,
*die grosse stenge, order grosse mars-stenge*; French,
*grand mât de hune*; Italian, *albero di gabbia*; Spanish,
*mastelero mayor*; Portuguese, *mastareo grande ou de
gavia grande*), *Fore* (Swedish, *förstängen*; Danish, *for-
stængen*; Dutch, *de voor-steng, fok-steng*; German, *die
vor stenge, vormars-stenge*; French, *petit mât de hune*;
Italian, *albero di parrochetto*; Spanish, *mastelero de proa
ó de velacho*; Portuguese, *mastareo de velacho, do traqucte
ou da gavia menor*), and *Mizen* (Swedish, *kryss-stangen*;
Danish, *kryds-stængen*; Dutch, *kruis-steng*; German,
*kreuz-stenge*; French, *mât de perroquet de fougue*; Italian, *albero di contramezzana*; Spanish, *mastelero de
mezana*; Portuguese, *mastareo da gata*).

*Lengthened Top-mast* (see Mast Making).

*Top-gallant Mast*: the *Main* (Swedish, *stor brams-*

*stängen*; Danish, *stóre bram-stœngen*; Dutch, *de groole bram-steng*; German, *die grosse bram-stenge*; French, *grand mât de perroquet*; Italian, *albero di pappafico*; Spanish, *mastelero de juanete mayor, ó de juanete grande*; Portuguese, *mastareo do joanete grande*), Fore (Swedish, *for bramstängen*; Danish, *for bram-stœngen*; Dutch, *de voor-bram-steng*; German, *vorbram-stenge*; French, *petit mât de perroquet*; Italian, *albero di pappafico di parrochetto*; Spanish, *mastelero del juanete de velacho ó del juanete de proa*; Portuguese, *mastareo do joanete de proa*), and *Mixen* (Swedish, *kryss bramstang*; Danish, *kryds bram-stœgen*; Dutch, *de kruis-bram-steng*; German, *kreuzbram-stenge*; French, *mât de perruche*; Italian, *albero di cacaro o del belvedere*; Spanish, *mastelerito de periquito*; Portuguese, *mastareo da sobregata*).

MAST CARLING, large carlings fixed or let down on each side of the mast; they are placed at an equal distance from the middle line, and apart the diameter of the mast, and sufficient for wedging on each side; they score and face into the beams, before and abaft the mast, and lap on them about two-thirds the breadth of the beam, and are bolted with two bolts in each end.

MAST PARTNERS, commonly called cross partners, pieces placed before and abaft the mast for wedging against; they let into a double rabbet taken out of the mast carlings, and are bolted through these, with two or three bolts in the end of each piece.

MIDSHIPS (see AMIDSHIPS).

MIDSHIP BEND or FRAME (Swedish, *nollspant*; Danish, *middel-spant*; Dutch, *hoofd-spant, middel-spant*; German, *haupt-span, mittel-spann, lehr-spann*; French, *maître couple*; Italian, *quaderno maestro*; Spanish, *cuaderna maestra*; Portuguese, *baliza ou casa mestra*) called dead flat (see FLATS).

MITER or MITRE, the mode of joining two solid pieces, by bringing together two sections by which they are cut obliquely, or that, when together, the joint may form an angle equal to both.

MORTISE or MORTOISE, a hole of a certain depth, cut in any piece of timber, to receive the end, or what is called the tenon of another piece.

MOULD (Swedish, *mall*; Danish, *skabelon*; Dutch, *mal*; German, *mall*; French, *gabarit*; Italian, *garbo, festo*; Spanish, *galibo, grua de tablas, plantilla*; Portuguese, *forma*), a piece of thin deal or board made to any intended shape for giving the form of a timber.

MOULDED, formed to the mould: also the dimensions, size, or scantling of any timber. The way in which it is formed by the mould, as the in-and-out dimensions of the timbers of the frame (65), is the moulding, while the breadth is called the siding. In the same manner, the up-and-down dimensions of the beam are called the mouldings, because they are formed by the mould that way, while their breadth is likewise called the siding.

MOULDINGS, parts that project for ornament, as the rails of the stern and head, or the mouldings worked on the angles of different timbers and brought on the face, or worked in the panels of bulkheads. They are flat, round, hollow, or inflected; and consist of the fillet, list or annulet, the astragal or bead, the cyma reversa or ogee, the cyma recta, the cavetto or hollow, the ovolo or quarter-round, the scotia, and the torus. The rails are formed by an assemblage of these mouldings, with straight and curved ones alternately, applied, as to disposition and proportion, to produce the best effect. On the angles of different timbers, they are in general worked singly, and mostly the ovolo or quarter-round; and on the bulkhead, to give relief, and in the panels, the ogee, ovolo, and astragal are generally used.

MOULDING (Swedish, *bemalla*; Danish, *bemalle*; Dutch, *bemallen*; German, *bemallen, ein stük holz*; French, *garbarier une pièce*; Italian, *modellare, festare*; Spanish, *galibar*; Portuguese, *galivar*), forming any timber by a mould.

MUNIONS or MUNTONS, are pieces placed up-and-down to divide the panels in framed bulkheads, to give them the proper porportions; and to divide the lights in the stern and quarter-galleries.

NAILS (Swedish, *spik*; Danish, *spiger*; Dutch, *spykers*; German, *spiker*; French, *clous*; Italian, *chiodi*; Spanish, *clavos*; Portuguese, *cravas*), pins of iron used for fastening plank, board, iron-work, &c. They are of various descriptions, according to the purposes they are for; as the *Deck Nails*, which are double and single. Double deck nails are from 6 to 12 inches, and single from 4 to 5 inches in length; they have a small head, and are used for fastening planks and the flat of the decks. *Weight Nails* are similar to deck nails, but have a square and larger head; they are used for purposes where it is not necessary to have their heads driven within the wood, as any temporary fastening, as the cleats over the heads of shores, &c. *Ribband Nails*; these nails have large round heads, that they may be easily drawn, and have round points tapering; they are used for fastening the ribbands, &c. *Timber Nails* are slight nails, used for nailing thin pieces edgeways; they are in general from 7 to 14 inches in length. *Nails of Sorts* are called 2, 3, 4, 6, 10, 20, 24, 30, and 40-penny nails, all of different lengths, the 40-penny being next below the single deck; they are used for nailing thin plank, board, &c. *Clamp Nails* are a short stout nail, with large heads, used for fastening iron clamps, &c. *Port Nails* are similar to clamp nails, but are double and single; they are used for fastening iron work. *Rudder Nails* are likewise similar; they are used principally for fastening the pintles and braces. *Sheathing Nails*, when used, are for fastening the sheathing on the bottom. *Filling Nails* were a cast-iron nail driven into the sheathing, very thick, when copper sheathing was not used. *Lead Nails* are round-headed and small nails for fastening lead. *Scupper Nails* are short broad-headed nails, used for nailing the leather flaps over the scuppers, &c. *Flat Heads* or flat nails, are small nails sharp pointed, with flat heads, for nailing lead and paper under the copper, &c. *Boat Nails* are nails of various sorts, both of copper and iron, used in building boats; they are in general rose-headed and square at the point.

*Copper Nails*, used in boat-work, are distinguished by numbers from 1 to 12, and are from seven-eighths of an inch to $3\frac{1}{2}$ inches in length; and others, distinguished by their lengths, for knees and other purposes that require a slight nail, from $3\frac{1}{2}$ inches to 6 inches, above which common copper spikes are used. For common purposes, the copper nails are distinguished by No. 2', 3', 4', 7', and 9', and from 3-inch to 9-inch spikes; 2' are 1¼ inch long, and 9', 3½ inches long; 7' are the nails in common use for lining magazines. The copper nails used for fastening sheets are called counter-sunk nails.

NAVAL HOODS (see BOLSTERS OF HAWSE).

NECKING (see COVE).

NOG, a short treenail that projects, to keep any timber in its place (2), to place shores against, or that is driven in to fasten the heels of shores, &c.

NUT (see ANCHOR).

OAK (Swedish, *ek*; Danish, *leg*; Dutch, *eike*; German, *eiche*; French, *chêne*; Italian, *quercia*; Spanish, *roble*; Portuguese, *carvalho*), a timber from which ships are principally built. There are various sorts used in ship-building, The most common species used for building British ships are the English, Dantzic or North Country, American, and of late Adriatic and Italian Oaks. The *English Oak* is the *quercus fœmina* and *quercus robur*; the former is considered the best, and grows principally in Sussex and Kent. The latter, which is called the common English oak, grows in most parts of the kingdom and in Wales, in woods, forests, and in hedge-rows; this timber is used for all the principal parts of the structure, and for planking as low as the light water line. The *Dantzic or North Country Oak*, which is cut in Poland, is used for the flat of decks, where oak is used, and for the bottom below the light water line. The *American Oak* is of two sorts, the *quercus rubra* and *quercus alba*, or the Canada red and white. This timber is the most inferior to any of those from the other countries; it is used for some of the purposes for which the Dantzic oak is used. The *Adriatic* and *Italian Oaks* are considered preferable to any of the foreign oaks, and is employed for many purposes where the British oak is used.

OAKHAM or OAKUM (Swedish, *dref*; Danish, *wœrk*; Dutch, *werk*; German, *werg oder werk*; French, *étoupe*; Italian, *stoppa*; Spanish, *estopa*; Portuguese, *estopa*), a substance reduced from old ropes when untwisted; it is called black or white oakum, according as it is formed from tarred or untarred ropes, and sometimes of flax.

OARS (Swedish, *åra*; Danish, *aare*; Dutch, *riem*;

German, *riem*; French, *rame, aviron.*; Italian, *rèmo*; Spanish, *remo*; Portuguese, *remo*), instruments used for impelling boats, &c.

ORLOP (see DECK).

OUTBOARD, on the outside of the ship.

PALLETTING, a platform, formerly at a small dis‑ tance above the magazine, flat, to keep the powder from getting damp. Beams were laid about two feet apart across the magazine, called palletting beams, and between them carlings at the same distance apart, called palletting carl‑ ings; these beams were nailed to the flat, and had a rabbet taken out of their upper edges, to receive scuttles, which were called palletting scuttles.

PAUL or PALLS (see CAPSTAN).

PAUL BITTS (see BITTS).

PANEL (see BULKHEADS).

PARTNERS OF THE MAST (see MAST).

PARTNERS OF THE CAPSTAN (see CAPSTAN).

PAUNCH (see MAST MAKING).

PILASTERS, a square flat pillar, placed against thick stiles or munions of bulkheads, and sometimes on the mu‑ nions of the stern and quarters, for ornament; they seldom, in naval architecture, project more than from $\frac{1}{4}$ of an inch to $1\frac{1}{4}$ inch, as to project more would expose them to be knocked off. They in general have their faces receded or fluted, and have moulded caps and bases (see BULK‑ HEADS).

PILLARS (Swedish, *dack-stöttar*; Danish, *dæk-stöt‑ ter*; Dutch, *dek-stutten*; German, *deck-stutzen*; French, *épontilles*; Italian, *pontali delle coperte*; Spanish, *pun‑ tales de lãs cubiertas*; Portuguese, *pontaletes das cubertas*), pieces of timber erected vertically under the middle of the beams, for supporting the decks; their ends tenon into the beams above, and into the flat of the deck or keelson be‑ low; above the lower deck they are in general turned, but those on the orlop and in the hold have only a champher taken off their angles.

PINK (Swedish, *pink eller pinque*; Danish, *pink*; Dutch, *pink*; German, *pinke*; French, *pinque*; Italian, *pinco*; Spanish, *londro, pinque*; Portuguese, *pinque*), a vessel navigated in the Mediterranean, with two masts and two lateen sails, and a very small mizen. Likewise a ship with a very narrow stern; whence all vessels with sterns fashioned in like manner are called pink-sterned.

PINNACE (Swedish, *pinnasse*; Danish, *pinnasse*; Dutch, *pinas*; German, *pinasse oder pinnasse*; French, *le second canot d'un vaisseau de guerre, sorte de chaloupe mâtée en goëlette*; Italian, *la segunda lancetta d'un basti-mento di guerra, sorte di goeletta*; Spanish, *el segundo bote de un navio de guerra, sorte de goeleta*; Portuguese, *pinaca*), (see BOATS).

PINTLES (Swedish, *roder-haker*; Danish, *roer-hager*; Dutch, *roer-haaken*; German, *ruder haken*; French, *éguillots du gouvernail*; Italian, *maschj del timone*; Span-ish, *machos del timon*; Portuguese, *machos do leme*), (see GOOGINGS).

PLANKS (Swedish, *planker*; Danish, *planker*; Dutch, *planken*; German, *planken*; French, *bordages*; Italian, *bordaggi*; Spanish, *tablas*; Portuguese, *pranchas, taboas*), all timber from 1½ inch to 4 inches in thickness has this name given it, except fir, which frequently, to 3 inches in thickness, is called deal.

PLANKING (95).

PLANKSHEER (see GUNWALE).

POLACRE (Swedish, *polacker*; Danish, *polakker*; Dutch, *polaka, polaak*; German, *polacker*; French, *po-lacre*; Italian, *polacre*; Spanish, *polacra*; Portuguese, *polacre*), a ship navigated in the Levant and other parts of the Mediterranean. They have three masts, commonly formed with the standing mast, top-mast, and top-gallant mast in one; and in general carry square sails upon the main, and lateen upon the fore and mizen masts; though some polacres carry square sails on all three masts. The top-gallant and top-sail yards lower down, so as to furl and reef on the yards below, as they have no horses upon them.

POOP or ROUNDHOUSE (see DECK).

POPPETS (see LAUNCH).

PORT, a name given to the larboard side (see LAR-BOARD).

PORT (Swedish, *portar*; Danish, *kanon-porter*; Dutch, *poorten*; German, *pforten, stuck-pforten, pfort-gaten*; French, *sabords*; Italian, *potelli*; Spanish, *portas*;

Portuguese, *portas*), the holes or embrasures in the sides of ships of war, for pointing the guns through, on the different decks or batteries. The ports are formed on the sides by the timbers of the frame\*, and on the upper and lower parts by pieces lying after the sheer, called port sills (Fig. 12 and 15); they are distinguished by the upper (*m*) and lower (*n*) port sills; the upper is tailed into the timber, and the lower billed.

PORT HOOKS, iron hooks for fixing the port hinge upon, and upon which the port-lid revolves. One arm of the hook is driven through the side, at a proper height above the port, and is clenched on the inside.

PORT LIDS, lids or shutters fixed to the middle and gun decks of ships of the line. They are made of fir, in two thicknesses; the inner thickness is called the lining, and is placed with the range of fibre up and down, and of about 2 inches in thickness, with its inner part bedding or faying close to the back stops. The outer thickness, called the outside stuff, lies fore and aft, so as to cross the lining, and is of a substance sufficient to be well with the outer part of the outside planking, at the thinnest part. The lining is fastened to the outside stuff by nails, about 2¼ inches apart. These lids are hung with two hinges, which have in their lower end one shackle in each, outside, for the port ropes, and one in each, inside, for the port fastening. These shackles in general forelock. The hinges are fastened, in addition to the shackles, which form part of the fastening, with one saucer-headed bolt, as close up to the upper part as to be just below the upper stop, which is driven on the inside and forelocked on the out; and one or two saucer-headed bolts in each breadth of outside stuff is driven from the outside, and clenched upon the lining. In the port lid is cut a scuttle, to be opened for air when the lid is shut in; and one illuminator is fixed in the lid, to give light, when the badness of the weather compels the scuttle to be shut in. The port lids are made to fit very close to the back stops, but to come out and shut in easy. After the ports are eased in, which is not done, for the last

---

\* The timbers that form the sides of the ports are called port timbers, and in general have an excess of siding over the other timbers.

Z

time, till all the guns and stores are on board, the back
stops are lined over with fearnought or kersey; and likewise the back stops of the scuttle.

PORT SILLS (Swedish, *portrympel, tröskel*; Danish,
*bossebænken*; Dutch, *drampel*; German, *drempel*; French,
*seuillets*; Italian, *mezzanili*; Spanish, *batiportes*; Portuguese, *batentes*), (see PORT).

PORT STOPS, are the ends and edges of the planks left
round the ports, from 1½ to 2½ inches from the sides of the
timbers and upper and lower parts of the sills, to receive
the port lids and half-ports.

POST, STERNPOST (Swedish, *ackterstäf*; Danish,
*agterstævn*; Dutch, *steven, agter-steven*; German, *steven,
hintersteven*; French, *étambot*; Italian, *asta di poppa*;
Spanish, *codaste*; Portuguese, *cadaste*), (20).

SAMSON's-POST (Swedish, *stöttar med klampar*;
Danish, *stötter under storlugens bielker med klamper*;
Dutch, *stutten met klampen om af, of op te klimmen*;
German, *deck-stutzen mit lippen*; French, *étances d
manche*; Italian, *pontali della stiva con tachj*; Spanish,
*pies de carnero*; Portuguese, *pés de carneiro*), a post or
stanchion extending from one deck to the other, fixed
against the side of the beam of the deck above, and tenoned
into the flat of the deck below, for bringing a strap or leading block to, when hoisting in the boats, &c. It has a
notch formed in the middle, for the strops of the block, and
a strong cleat on each side of its head, nailed to the beam
above, to prevent its coming out of its place when in use.
The samson's-post is now frequently formed in the fore
bulkhead of the great cabin; its foreside shews a pilaster,
and its after side is formed to a semicircle; to fasten the
purchase, an eye-bolt is driven through it.

PREVENTER BOLTS (see CHAIN BOLTS).

PREVENTER PLATES (see CHAIN BOLTS).

PROFILE (see DRAUGHT).

PROVISIONS (see Table 2).

PUMP (Swedish, *pump*; Danish, *pompe*; Dutch,
*pomp*; German, *pumpe*; French, *pompe*; Italian, *tromba*;
Spanish, *bomba*; Portuguese, *bomba*), a machine used for
discharging water from the hold of the ship into the sea.
Pumps used generally on board of ships are of two sorts,
called the hand-pump (Swedish, *stekpump*; Danish, *steeg-*

*pompe*; Dutch, *steek-pomp*; German, *steek-pump*; French, *pompe à bâton, pompe à main*; Italian, *tromba da mano*; Spanish, *sacabuche*; Portuguese, *bomba de maom*), and chain-pump (Swedish, *storm-pump, kiettings-pump*; Danish, *storm-pompe, kiede-pompe*; Dutch, *ketting-pomp*; German, *ketten-pumpe*; French, *pompe à chapelet*; Italian, *tromba a catene*; Spanish, *bomba de cadena, ó de rosario*; Portuguese, *bomba de roda*). The *Hand-pump* is formed by a wooden tube, that extends from the limbers (or from a cistern in the well, if for washing decks) to the deck upon which it is to be worked, with a part in the bore, or hollow of the tube, to a certain distance down, called the chamber, at the lower part of which is fixed a plug, called the lower box ; and placed at the upper part is an iron stanchion, fixed to the pump by means of a hoop and a staple, that it may be unfixed, for forming the fulcrum for the handle or brake ; and to the end of the brake is attached an iron rod, called the spear, with a piston fixed to its lower end, called the upper box. The brake, which is fixed by a bolt between two cheeks in the stanchions, is made to act as a lever on the spear, to produce the motion on the upper box. At the lower end of the pump or tube in the limbers is fixed what is called a basket, to prevent any thing that may stop the action of the valves in the boxes from ascending. These pumps are used principally in small vessels, and only for secondary purposes in the larger class of ships. The *Chain-pumps* are formed by a mixed metal chamber at the lower part, let sufficiently down into the timbers, below the limbers, for the water to drain to its lower part, having a tube connected with it for the water to be conveyed up by means of a chain, that passes over a wheel, called the sprocket wheel, fixed on the gun and upper or middle deck, according to the place where they are to be worked, formed of a number of similar links, that in the event of one being broken, it may be readily replaced, connected together at their joints by pins, and having fixed to every sixth link a saucer for bringing the water up, called the saucer link. This chain has no end ; the links are connected all round, and made to pass over the wheel and through the chamber below, bringing up on one side, as the wheel turns, a column of water with it, and returning on the other through a trunk, called the back casing. The tube and back casing is fixed, and the circumference of the wheel over them, so that the saucers pass up one and down the other without striking. The wheel has an axle connected with it, upon which winches are fixed for turning it. The winches in general revolve on rhodens attached to the topsail sheet and jeer bitts, and to the pillars, or else in cranks suspended to the beams for the purpose; and the axle works on rhodens fixed to the cistern, which receive the water as it is thrown up. The cisterns are two on each side; they are made of oak plank, the bottom and ends 4 inches and the sides 3 inches in thickness; the bottom and ends have a double rabbet taken out of them, to receive the sides, and have two or three strengthening bolts driven through them. These cisterns are caulked, and are fixed over what is called the poppets, or short pieces of the tube and back casing, to continue them above the deck; they are let down into the mast carling or partners, and are hooped. As the pump dale is only fixed to one cistern on each side, conductors are attached to the cistern, that the water may have a free communication with the whole of them.

QUARTER-DECK (see DECK).

QUARTER-GALLERIES (see GALLERIES).

QUARTER-PIECES, pieces that form the boundary of the stern on each side, and the after part of the quarter-gallery.

QUARTER-RAILS (see GALLERIES).

QUICK-WORK (144).

RABBET (Swedish, *spunning*; Danish, *spunning*; Dutch, *sponning*; German, *sponning*; French, *rablure*; Italian, *battidura*, *appuntadore*; Spanish, *alefris*; Portuguese, *alefris*), a groove or channel cut longitudinally in any timber, or in the edge of any plank or board, to form into a similar channel or groove in any other piece; or for receiving the edge of any plank, as the rabbet of the keel (8); to receive the edge of the garboard strake, or the ends of any planks, as the rabbet of the stem (10) and stern post (22), to receive the hooding ends.

RAG BOLT (see BOLT).

RAILS, strips of timber brought on different parts of

the ship, to form a protection ; as the *Roughtree Rails*
(Swedish, *finkenäts-relingar* ; Danish, *reilinger, reilings-
lister* ; Dutch, *regelinger van het vinkenet* ; German,
*regelingen des finkenetzes* ; French, *lisses de bastingage,
lises de batayoles* ; Italian, *battagliuola* ; Spanish, *ba-
tayola* ; Portuguese, *corrimaom das trincheiras*), which
are mortised on the heads of the roughtree timbers (see
HEADS OF THE TIMBERS), on the roundhouse, or forecastle in small vessels ; *Breast Rails*, which form the rails
of the breast-work (see BREAST-WORK) and fife-rails (92) ;
or rails for ornament, as the *Waist Rail* (Swedish, *răhult* ;
Danish, *raaholt* ; Dutch, *haahout* ; German, *raaholz,
raaleiste* ; French, *lisse de vibord ;* Italian, *cao da banda* ;
Spanish, *galon da borda* ; Portuguese, *verdugo da borda*),
a rail that formerly extended the length of the ship on the
topside, and was placed in midships, about halfway up the
upper deck ports, and carried parallel to the sheer ; *Sheer
Rail*, a rail formerly extending the length of the ship, in
a line with the channels ; *Drift Rails*, rails placed on the
topside, parallel to the sheer, and formed with the drifts ;
*Rails of the Head, Stern, and Quarter* (see HEAD, STERN,
and QUARTER, for their different names) ; and *Land Rail*,
a rail or moulding brought on the landing strake of boats,
which forms a moulding and fender.

RAKE, to incline, as what the stem is inclined forward
from a vertical line, or a line perpendicular to the keel, it
is said to rake more or less ; or according as the stern post
and counter timber or stern are inclined aft, they are said
to rake aft.

RANGES (see CLEATS).

RATE, the denomination of the different class of ships,
or the order into which ships of war are divided according
to their force.   The rates of ships formerly were, those of
100 guns and upwards, *first rates* ; those of 98 and 90
guns, *second rates* ; 80, 74, and 64 guns, *third rates* ; 60
and 50 guns, *fourth rates* ; 40, 38, 36, and 32 guns, *fifth
rates* ; and all under, *sixth rates*.  Fire ships and hospital
ships were rated as fifth rates.  Now, ships of 120, 112,
110, 108, 106, and 104 guns, are rated as *first rates* ; of
84, 82, and 80 guns, *second rates* ;  78, 76, and 74 guns,
*third rates* ;  60, 58, and 50 guns, *fourth rates* ;  48, 46,

44, and 48 guns, *fifth rates*; and ships of 34, 32, 28, 26, and 24 guns, as *sixth rates*.

RENDS, are large splits or shakes in timber or plank, most common to planks.

REPAIRS are the replacing any defective part, or the operation of amending injuries sustained in tempestuous weather, in battle, by taking the ground, or by any other means. Repairs are considered under two general classes, *Casual* and *Thorough*. Casual, when visible damages and defects are made good; thorough, when all defects are searched for, and such parts removed as may prevent the discovery of defects, and the whole replaced. This repair is divided into several classes, according to the state of the ship (see *Apendix*, No. I).

RHODENS or RHODINGS, a kind of brass cleats used as the bearings, for the axles and winches of the chain-pumps to work in (see PUMPS); also fixed in the steering wheel stanchions, for the axle of the steering wheel, &c.

RIBBANDS (Swedish, *senlor*; Danish, *sœnter*; Dutch, *centen of senten*; German, *senten*; French, *lisses*; Italian, *forme, maestre*; Spanish, *maestras, vagaras*; Portuguese, *armudouras*), (53) (see HARPINS).

RIDERS (Swedish, *kattspâr*; Danish, *katspor*; Dutch, *kattespooren*; German, *katspuhren, katsporen*; French, *porque*; Italian, *porche*; Spanish, *bularcamas*; Portuguese, *prodigos do poraom*). Those in the hold were called *Floor* (Swedish, *katsporets, bälnstäckar*; Danish, *katsporets, bundstokker*; Dutch, *buikstukken van de kattespooren*; German, *bauchstucke der katspuhren*; French, *varangues de porques*; Italian, *matere delle porche*: Spanish, *planes de las bularcamas*; Portuguese, *cavernas dos prodigas do poraom*), and *Futtock Riders* (Swedish, *katsporrets uplanger*; Danish, *katsporenes oplanger*; Dutch, *de oplanger van de kätspooren stainders*; German, *auflanger der katspuhren*; French, *allonges de porques*; Italian, *alamenati delle porche*; Venetian, *forcameli dei raisoni*; Spanish, *jenoles de las bularcamas*; Portuguese, *bracos dos prodigos do poraom*): and those above, *Breadth* and *Top Riders* (142 to 149).

RIM RAILS or RIMS (see QUARTERS).

RING BOLTS (see BOLTS).

Rings, circles of iron, copper, or mixed metal, upon which the points of bolts are clenched or rivetted. Also rings that pass round the mast hole, for fixing the mast coat to, &c.

Rising Floor (see Floor).

Rising-wood or Deadwood (see Deadwood) (35).

Rollers (Swedish, *rullar*; Danish, *ruller*; Dutch, *rollen*; German, *rollen*; French, *rouleaux*; Italian, *rotoli*; Spanish, *polines*; Portuguese, *rolos*), cylindrical pieces of oak, or some hard wood, with a hoop at each extremity, and with pins, or what are called sprigs, to form an axle for them to revolve on, driven into each end. These rollers are fixed wherever any hawser, &c. is worked, or where it would chafe hard against any part of the ship, in transporting, unmooring, &c. as against the jeer and topsail sheet bitts. Those for the use of the royal or messenger, are called messenger rolls; two or more vertical, and one or more horizontal, are placed close forward on the hawse hook, when there is one, for passing the bight of the messenger when heaving the cable in.

Room and Space, or what is sometimes called timber and space, is the distance from the joint or middle, between the two assemblages of timbers of the frame, to the joint of the filling frame; therefore while the scantling or siding of the timber is constant, the greater the room and space, the less the quantity of timber in the frame.

Rough-tree Rails (see Rails).

Roundhouse (see Deck); likewise places of convenience formerly fixed for the officers at the fore part of the beakhead bulkhead.

Round-aft, the segment of a circle, of which the stern is formed above the wing transom.

Round Stern (see Stern).

Round-up, the segment of a circle of which the upper surfaces of the deck, filling, and wing transoms, beams, transoms, and hooks to the different decks, and the upper part of the different rails of the stern, are formed.

Row Port (Swedish, *ro-porter*; Danish, *roe-porter*; Dutch, *roey-poorten*; German, *roje pforten*; French, *sabords des avirons*; Italian, *portelli dei remi*; Spanish, *portas de los remos*; Portuguese, *portas dos remos*), large scuttles in small vessels, through the side, between the gun ports, to work the sweeps for impelling them in calm and light winds.

ROWLOCKS (Swedish, *år-klampar*; Danish, *klamper paa tollegangen, aar klamper*; Dutch, *roejklampen, velden*; German, *roje-klampen*; French, *taquets de nage, dames, tolletières*; Italian, *scarmi al modo di norte*; Spanish, *toletes al modo de norte, tojinos de remos*; Portuguese, *toleteras*), the spaces between pieces fixed in the gunwale of boats, called tholes, which are for forming the fulcrum for the oars when rowing, and to prevent them sliding forward.

RUDDER (see HELM).

RUDDER, or ROTHER (Fig. 11), a machine attached to the stern post by pintles and braces (googings), for steering, or directing the course of the ship. It is formed of several pieces coaked and bolted together; the principal piece is called the main piece (*E*), and forms the head; it is of oak. The other pieces (*F*) make up the breadth at the lower part. Those on the aft side are in general of fir, and those on the foreside of elm: a plank is frequently brought on the aft side, called the back, and a piece on the lower end, called the sole. The fore edge of the rudder is formed to an angle at the middle line, called the bearding, to allow the rudder to go sufficiently over. Formerly the whole of the bearding was taken off the rudder, but now it is taken equally off the rudder and stern post.

RUDDER CHOCKS, chocks made to fill up on each side the rudder in the rudder hole, to keep the rudder from motion while a tiller is refixing, in the event of its being carried away, &c. They are made of fir, with a projection at the upper part, to keep them up, and a ring bolt driven through them, for the convenience of getting them in and out of their places.

RUDDER IRONS, a name sometimes given to the pintles.

RUN (Swedish, *piken*; Danish, *piggen*; Dutch, *piek*; German, *piek*; French, *les ailes, extremités de la cale vers les façons de l'arrière*; Italian, *pajolo nel taglio di poppa*;

Spanish, *panol de los delgados de popa*; Portuguese, *paiol do delgado arré*), the narrowing of the after part of the ship; thus a ship is said to have a full, fine, or clean run.

RUNG or WRUNG HEAD, a name sometimes given to the upper ends of the floor timbers (see FLOOR HEAD).

SADDLE, a piece, formerly, sometimes brought on the upper part of the lacing of the figure, for securing the fore end of the main head rails.

*Saddle for the Jib Boom* (see MAST MAKING).

SAGGING, a bending down; an effect produced on the structure contrary to hogging (see Note to p. 7), and mostly takes place in the neighbourhood of the main mast; to prevent which an additional keelson has lately been introduced on each side, under the step of the mast.

SAMPSON'S POST (see POST).

SAP OF TIMBER (Swedish, *spint*; Danish, *spint, gejle*; Dutch, *spind of spint*; German, *spint*; French, *aubour, aubier*; Italian, *alburno*; Spanish, *albono*; Portuguese, *alvura interior da madeira*), sap-wood or alburnum, the outer and softest part of the wood, or intermediate portion of the caudex, which is always removed, except from elm, before the timber is employed in the ship.

SCANTLING, the dimensions that are given for the different timbers, planks, &c.

SCARPHING, the uniting of two pieces together, by lapping one piece on the other, and letting them in at the thin ends or lips, so as to bring them almost to appear as one solid, and with even surfaces.

SCARPHS (Swedish, *lask eller skarf*; Danish, *lask*; Dutch, *lasch*; German, *scherbe*; French, *ècart*; Italian, *giunta, paella*; Spanish, *junta, escarba, escarpe*; Portuguese, *escarba*). Scarphs are called side, when their surfaces are parallel to the sides, as the scarphs of the keel (4) and beams (170); and flat, when their surfaces are opposite, as the scarphs of stem (11), deadwood (37), and keelson (70). They are called coak scarphs when they have coaks in them; hook and butt scarphs, when they are formed with a hook or projection, for one part to form into the other, as the scarphs of the string (152) and clamps (131); and key scarphs, when their lips are made to form tail, and are set close by wedge-like keys at the hook.

A A

SCHOONER (Swedish, *scooner*; Danish, *skooner*; Dutch, *schoener*; German, *schuner oder schooner*; French, *goëlette*; Italian, *goletta, scuna*; Spanish, *goeleta*; Portuguese, *scuna*), vessels with two or three masts, with fore and aft sails, suspended from gaffs.

SCREEN BULKHEAD (see GALLERY).

SCUPPERS (Swedish, *spygattor*; Danish, *spyegatter*; Dutch, *spy-gaten*; French, *dalots*; Italian, *brunali*, *imbrunali*; Spanish, *embornales*; Portuguese, *embornaes*), holes cut through the side, with leaden pipes in them, for conveying the water from the different decks into the sea. The scuppers are now in general formed in two parts, to prevent the inner lap from being broken by the working of the ship.

SCUTTLES, openings through the deck, in general, for passing different articles from deck to deck (see HATCHES); likewise holes through the side into the officers' cabins, and through the port lids, for the admission of air and light.

SEAMS (Swedish, *näter*; Danish, *naader*; Dutch, *naaden*; German, *nathan*; French, *coutures*; Italian, *incomenti*; Spanish, *costuras*; Portuguese, *costuras*), the space between the edges of the different planks when worked (see CAULKING).

SEAT or SEATING, a surface trimmed out for a chock or any timber to fay to; likewise the part of the floor which fays on the deadwood, and the transom which fays to the stern or inner post.

SEAT TRANSOM, a transom fayed and bolted to the counter timbers, above the deck, in general at the height of the port sills.

SHACKLES, small ring bolts fixed in the port lids and scuttles, for fixing them in, &c.

SHAKEN, or SHAKEY, a defect in timber and plank, when it is full of splits or clefts. It is said to be quaggy, and is produced in general while growing, by lightnings, powerful winds and frosts. They are commonly called cup shakes when the concentric, and heart shakes when the divergent layers are separated.

SHALLOP, a large boat with two masts, generally rigged as a schooner.

SHANK (see ANCHOR).

SHANK PAINTER (Swedish, *rustlina* ; Danish, *röst-linie* ; Dutch, *rust-lyn, russeling* ; German, *rustlien* ; French, *serre-bosse* ; Italian, *serra-boza delle patte* ; Spanish, *boza de la unna* ; Portuguese, *bôca das unhas*), a chain fixed at one end by a spansbackle, or bolted to the topside, for hanging the shank and fluke of the anchor, while the ring and stock are hung up by the stopper to the cathead.

SHEATHING ( Swedish, *förhunding* ; Danish, *forhudning* ; Dutch, *verdubbeling* ; German, *spiker-haupt* ; French, *doublage* ; Italian, *dobblaggio, buombordo* ; Spanish, *embon, forro* ; Portuguese, *forro*), a thin doubling of fir board, formerly brought on the bottoms of ships, to protect the plank from worms, &c., between which and the bottom were inserted tar and hair, and sometimes brown paper dipt in tar and oil. Now the bottom is covered with copper sheathing of 18, 28, and 32 oz. to the foot square. Mostly on large ships 32 oz. is used at the water line and bows, and the 28 oz. in the other parts ; 18 oz. is used on the bottom of small vessels. It is laid on in sheets 28 and 32 oz. of 14 inches by 4 feet, and 18 oz. of 20 inches by 4 feet. The sheets are placed for the after end of one sheet to lap over the fore end of the other, and the upper edge to lap over the lower.

SHIVE or SHEAVE (Swedish, *skifua* ; Danish, *skiven* ; Dutch, *schyf* ; German, *scheibe* ; French, *rouet* ; Italian, *poleggia* ; Spanish, *roldana* ; Portuguese, *roldana ou roda*), a pulley or small wheel that revolves upon an iron pin for its axis, in a channel or groove of a block, or in channels cut in different parts of the ship, as in the fixed blocks, catheads, &c.

SHIVE-HOLE (Swedish, *skifgattlet* ; Danish, *skivgattet* ; Dutch, *schyfgat* ; German, *scheibengat* ; French, *mortaise, clan* ; Italian, *occhio d'un bozzello* ; Spanish, *mortaja, cajera* ; Portuguese, *o gorne*), a mortise or channel for the shive to work in.

SHEER (Swedish, *skabnaden of et skepp* ; Danish, *skibets skabning* ; Dutch, *strooking, strook* ; German, *stroking oder strook des schiffs* ; French, *fabrique d'un vaisseau* ; Italian, *l'arcato* ; Spanish, *trazo* ; Portuguese, *tozamento*), (85).

SHEER DRAUGHT (see DRAUGHT).

SHEER RAILS (see RAILS).

SHEER STRAKES (102).

SHEER WALES (100).

SHIFT, to shift, the disposing or placing different timbers and planks in relation to each other, so as for them, by their combination, to give the most strength; as the shift of the different planking (154), shift of deadwood (37), and apron (12).

SHIP (Swedish, *skepp*; Danish, *skib*; Dutch, *schip*; German, *sckiff*; French, *vaisseau*; Italian, *vascello*; Spanish, *navio*; Portuguese, *navio*), a general name given to all vessels, but particularly applied to those equipped with three masts, having lower masts, topmast, and topgallant masts. Ships of war are distinguished from each other by their classes and force (see RATES).

SHOLES (251).

SHORE (Swedish, *stöttar*; Danish, *stötter*; Dutch, *stutten, schooren*; German, *stutzen*; French, *acores, épontilles*; Italian, *pontali*; Spanish, *escoras, puntales*; Portuguese, *esbirros, escoras*). Shores are props placed under the ribbands, and at different parts of the frame, or against the sides and bottom, to support the ship while building.

SHOT LOCKERS (see GARLANDS).

SIDE COUNTER TIMBER (66).

SIDED, is the size or dimensions of any timber from side to side, or the breadth. It is a dimension given the contrary way to the moulding (see MOULDING).

SILLS (see PORT).

SKEG, the after end of the keel, or that part upon which the stern-post steps.

SKEG SHORES, shores placed under the after end of the keel, for steadying the after part of the ship, while supported by the cradle, before she descends. They are placed perpendicular to the ways, and are in general made of 4-inch plank, with the upper end rounded.

SLEEPERS, timbers inside for giving strength to the buttocks, and for combining the stern frame to the frame (42). Their after ends lie upon the transoms, through which they are bolted with two bolts in each; and they extend to some distance forward, so as to bolt through several of the adjoining timbers of the frame.

SLICES, pieces about 12 inches wide, and from 2 to 3 feet in length, according to the purpose they are for, formed like wedges of small angles (see LAUNCH).

SLIDING PLANKS (see LAUNCH).

SLIP (1).

SLOOP (Swedish, *enmastad fartyg* ; Danish, *eenmastig fartöj* ; Dutch, *eenmastig vaartuig, een vaartuig met eene mast* ; German, *einmastiges fahrzeug* ; French, *bâtiment à un mât* ; Italian, *bastimento che ha un salo albero* ; Spanish, *balandra* ; Portuguese, *chalupa*), a vessel with one mast, with the principal sail, which is abaft the mast, attached to a gaff, called the main sail, and two sails before, called the foresail and jib ; they have, likewise, sometimes sails attached to the yards, called the square sail and square topsail.

SNAPE, to bevel off the end of any timber, so that it may fay to an inclined surface, or be inclined to any surface.

SNOW (Swedish, *snau*; Danish, *snau*; Dutch, *snauw*; German, *schnau* ; French, *sénau* ; Italian, *checia, senau* ; Spanish, *paquebote* ; Portuguese, *paquebote, senau*), a large brig, with a main trysail mast.

SNYING (81).

SOLE (see RUDDER and BUILGEWAYS).

SPALLING, keeping the frames (51) of the ship to their proper breadth (see CROSS-SPALLS).

SPANSHACKLE, a bolt with a swivel, such as the bolt used, in general, for securing the shank painter to the side, &c.

SPARS (Swedish, *spirar eller bommar* ; Danish, *spirer*; Dutch, *spieren*; German, *spieren oder sparren* ; French, *espars*; Italian, *percie, bastoni* ; Spanish, *perchas, bordones* ; Portuguese, *perchas, vergontas*). Spars or sticks from six hands downwards, are distinguished into cant, barling, boom, middling, and small. *Cant* spars are from 5 to 6 hands, at 3 feet 4 inches from the butt; *Barling* from 4 to 5, at 2 feet 8 inches; *Boom* from 3 to 4, at 2 feet; *Middling* from 2 to 3, at 2 feet; and *Small*, from 1 to 2 hands in circumference, at 2 feet from the butt.

These spars are in length, cant from 33 to 35 feet, barling
from 28 to 30, boom from 20 to 24, middling from 16 to 20,
and small from 11 to 16 feet; whereas sticks not hewn,
but in their round state, from 6 to 25 hands in circumference, are called hand masts; they are from 36 to 93 feet
in length; but sticks that are hewn are called inch masts,
yards, &c.

SPECIFIC GRAVITY is the relative weight of any
body, when compared with an equal bulk of any other
body. Bodies are said to be specifically heavier than
other bodies when they contain a greater weight under the
same bulk; and when of less weight they are said to be
specifically lighter.

### Table of Specific Gravities.

| | | | |
|---|---|---|---|
| Lead, molten | 11,352 | to | 11,445 |
| —— Ore | 7,587 | | |
| Copper, fine | 9,000 | | |
| —— cast | 7,788 | | |
| Brass, according to the proportion of the substances of which it is composed | 7,600 | to | 8,800 |
| Copper, hammered or wire drawn | 8,878 | | |
| Iron, cast | 7,207 | to | 7,425 |
| —— Bar and wrought | 7,645 | to | 7,788 |
| Roman Cement, with Half Sand when formed in a solid state | 1,792 | to | 1,820 |
| Sand | 1,516 | to | 1,560 |
| Tar | 1,016 | | |
| Pitch | 1,150 | | |
| Rosin | 1,100 | | |
| Bees' Wax | 965 | | |
| Fish Oil | 923 | | |
| Linseed Oil | 932 | | |
| Water, Rain | 1,000 | | |
| —— Spring | 1,009 | | |
| —— Sea | 1,026 | to | 1,030 |
| Wood—Oak, English .. dry | 745 | | |
| —— —— Canada | 714 | | |
| —— —— Dantzic | 704 | | |
| —— Beech | 706 | | |
| —— Elm | 600 | | |
| —— Fir, Riga | 616 | | |
| —— —— Red Pine | 591 | | |
| —— —— Norway | 514 | | |
| —— Yellow Pine | 451 | | |
| —— Lignum Vitæ | 1,330 | | |
| —— Ash | 800 | | |
| —— Cork | 240 | | |

SPILES (Swedish, *spik-pinnar*; Danish, *spiger-plygger eller spiger-pinder*; Dutch, *spyker-pinnen*; French, *épiles*, Italian, *spiccie*; Spanish, *espiches*; Portuguese, *bujoes*), wooden pins which are driven into nail holes to prevent their leaking. Those for bolts, and formed cylindrical or somewhat conical, are called plugs.

SPINDLE (see CAPSTAN).

SPINDLE OF A MAST (see MAST MAKING).

SPIRKETTING (Swedish, *sättvägare*; Danish, *satgangen*; Dutch, *set weeger*; German, *setzweger*; French, *feuilles bretonnes*; Italian, *serrette fulli trincanili*; Spanish, *cerretas ó varengas sobre los trancaniles*; Portuguese, *cusseiras* (141)

SPLA BOARDS, boards fixed obliquely to allow the light to diverge, as those fixed formerly to the magazine lights; or to break the sea off, as those fixed under the hammock board in the waist, &c.

SPRIGS (Swedish, *dykar*; Danish, *dyker*; Dutch, *duikers*; German, *dukers*; French, *petits clous sans tête*; Italian, *piccoli chiodi senza testa*; Spanish, *clavos sin cabeza*; Portuguese, *pequenos cravos sem cabeca*), an iron pin cylindrical at one end, and sharp-pointed, and in general jagged at the other, as those driven into the ends of rollers, &c. (see ROLLERS).

SPRUNG, a term signifying that a mast or any timber has been over strained, consequently has a disruption, or has some of its fibre broken off. To spring is likewise to raise or quicken the sheer.

SPURN WATER or SPUN WATER, a hollow channel left above at the ends of a deck, to turn the course of the water to the side of the ship, or to prevent its flowing over.

SQUARE FRAMES (42).

STABILITY, the resistance the body opposes to inclination. If the body inclines more, when compared with other ships under the same sail, she is said to be crank or to want stability; and when the body becomes less inclined, to be stiff or have greater stability. The measure of stability is the perpendicular distance at which the mean direction of the water, acting upwards, passes from the center of gravity of the ship at any inclination, and the moment is this distance multiplied into the displacement or whole weight of the ship. Having therefore the moment of stability of any ship that has been proved and known to stand up well under canvass and of any plan, the moment of sails may then be adjusted in the ratio of the two stabilities, with safety. The meta-center is a theorem established by several French and other authors, and is sometimes taken as the measure of stability, but cannot be relied on for ascertaining the requisite stability of vessels except in cases in which the angles of inclination or heeling are very small (see Architectura Navalis Mercatoria, by Frederick Henry De Chapman; Translated by the Rev. J. Inman, D. D., Chap. II.)

STANDARDS (see KNEES).

STANCHIONS or STANTIONS, the upright pieces attached to different bulkheads, for forming and securing them. There are likewise iron stanchions (Swedish, *sceptor*; Danish, *scepter*; Dutch, *scepters*; German, *zepter*; French, *chandelières de fer*; Italian, *candelieri di ferro*; Spanish, *candeleros*; Portuguese, *balaustes de ferro*), placed in different parts for fixing rails in, &c. (see HAMMOCK STANCHIONS).

STAPLES (Swedish, *krampa*; Danish, *krampe*; Dutch, *kram*; German, *krampe*; French, *crampe*; Italian, *crampa*; Spanish, *crampon*; Portuguese, *tisoura*), a bent fastening of metal, formed as a loop, and driven in at both ends, for securing two pieces; as the keel staples, which are of copper, for securing the false to the main keel. These staples have the two parts that are driven in, jagged.

STARBOARD (Swedish, *styrbord*; Danish, *styrbord*; Dutch, *stuurboord*; German, *steurbord oder sturbord*; French, *tribord*; Italian, *bordo a dritta*; Spanish, *estribor*; Portuguese, *estibord*). The side of the ship that is on the right hand when looking forward, is called the starboard side.

STEELER (82).

STEERING WHEEL (Swedish, *drill*; Danish, *rattet*; Dutch, *stuur-rad*; German, *steurrad*; French, *roue de gouvernail*; Italian, *routa del timone*; Spanish, *reuda de timon*; Portuguese, *roda do leme*), (see WHEEL).

STEM (Swedish, *forstäf*; Danish, *forstævn*; Dutch,

*steven, voor-steven*; German, *steven vorsteven*; French, *étrave*; Italian, *astella, asta di proa*; Spanish, *branque*; Portuguese, *roda de proa*), (9).

STEMSON (73).

STEPPING, a rabbet taken out of the deadwood, for the heels of the timbers to step on. The line that forms its lower part is called the bearding line ; it is up to this line that the deadwood partakes of the form of the body (38).

STEPS OF THE MAST (Swedish, *mastespär* ; Danish, *mast-spor* ; Dutch, *mast-spoor* ; German, *spuhr der masten, mast-spuhr*; French, *carlingue du mât* ; Italian, *micla d'un albero* ; Spanish, *carlinga de palo* ; Portuguese, *carlinga dos mastros*), pieces of timber for fixing the heels of the masts in. The main and fore steps are fixed across the keelson ; the *Main* is made to shift forward and aft, according as it may be desirable to rake the mast ; the *Fore* is bolted through the bottom. The mizen step is in general fixed on the lower deck beams. The mortises taken out of them are according to the heeling of the mast.

STEP FOR THE CAPSTAN (see CAPSTAN).

STEPS OF THE SIDE (Swedish, *trapp-klampar*; Danish, *trappe-klamper* ; Dutch, *trap-klampen* ; German, *trepp-klampen* ; French, *taquet d'échelle, ou échelon* ; Italian, *tacchj per la scala* ; Spanish, *passos de escalera* ; Portuguese, *cunhos do portaló*), pieces worked with mouldings, and fastened on the ship's side, at the gangway, for the convenience of ascending and descending.

STERN, the part from the wing transom upward, or the posterior face of the ship, or that part which would be presented to view, when behind or astern of the ship, in a line with the keel, and looking forward. The upper part of the stern is called the taffrail, and the boundary or outline of the taffrail is formed by a rail called the taffrail rail. The basis of the stern is the wing transom, at the upper part of which is placed a rail, called the tuck rail ; above the tuck rail is the lower counter, which is bounded at the upper part by a rail, called the lower counter rail ; above this rail is the upper counter, which is likewise bounded by a rail at the upper part, called the upper counter rail. This rail forms a basis for the lower tier of lights, which communicates with the ward-room of two and three-deck ships, and the captain's cabin in frigates; above these lights, in two and three-deck ships, is the balcony; if a three-deck ship, it is the one connected with the admiral's cabin, and is called the lower balcony, middle gallery, or middle walk of the stern, while the one above is called the upper balcony, &c. and is connected with the captain's cabin. In two-deck ships it is called the balcony, stern gallery, or stern walk. Above the upper or stern gallery or lights, in frigates, is an arched moulding, called the cove, which forms the lower part of the taffrail. The stern, from the lower balcony upwards, is formed at the sides by pieces, called quarter-pieces, formerly carved with different figures, but now bounded by a moulding (see GALLERY, COVE, TAFFRAIL, and QUARTER-PIECES).

*Round Stern.* When the after part of the ship is constructed with a curvilineal form, for the guns to have the greatest advantage in their training, and to prevent, as in the square or common sterns, there being in the amplitude of the bearing of the broadside and right aft guns, any part, within the range of shot, on which the guns cannot be brought to bear. To give increased strength to the body, and for the after extremity to be protected from small shot.

In forming the round stern, the timbers of the frame (Fig. 16) have their disposition so as to give the best place for the ports (see *Laying-off*, Art. 138), and that the lights may produce a proper effect as to appearance (58), by the timbers that form them being in the same plane with the middle timber, in an athwartship projection, and their sides, in a fore-and-aft projection, when produced meeting at the same height in the middle line above the stern.

The planking (Fig. 19), both the exterior and interior, have the strakes to continue round, that they may as much as possible combine in preserving the connexion of the two sides, which connexion is likewise aided by the hooks, ekeing, &c. of the different decks (Fig. 30, *b*).

The exterior of the stern is formed by several stools, one in the range of each deck; the lower stool which is in the range of the middle deck in three-deck ships, and upper deck in all others, is made to enclose the rudder head, and of a curve (Fig. 30, *r r*), so that at the embrasure of the right aft gun it may project as little as possible, and to be of a form to have a water-closet in each quarter. Below this stool a finishing is formed; and at a certain distance above it a rail is placed, between which and the rail that is placed upon the stool, it is birthed in to give it the appearance of the upper counter in the square stern.

The stools above, corresponding with the upper and quarter-deck in three-deck ships, and quarter-deck in two-deck ships, are for forming balconies or stern walks, and for placing the water-closets for the cabins which communicate with them. There is likewise a stool corresponding with the quarter-deck of frigates, and round-house of large ships. Above this stool, and coinciding with its after edge, is a close birthing, upon the after side of which is formed the taffrail. Some part of this birthing is made of solid pieces, firmly bolted to the stool, and secured by iron standards or knees, for hanging the other part of the birthing, as doors, which swing forward, and form the embrasures of the quarter-deck or round-house guns when they are used: these solid pieces aid likewise in supporting the iron davits for the boats, and spiders or outriggers, for the main brace; and to the middle part is affixed the clasp and tumbler for supporting the ensign staff.

The stool for the lower balcony is first formed (Fig. 30, *o o*), to give the space required and to give the best appearance*; from this the other stools take the form of their after edges, the same as the breast rail is obtained from the foot space in the common stern with balconies (see *Laying-off*, Art. 172), that is, all lines intersecting the after edge of this stool, and coinciding with the after edge of the others above, must be in the same plane with the rake of the stern at the middle line, on an athwartship projection, while they tend to the same point above the stern in a fore-and-aft projection.

The stools are formed of several pieces, as shewn by Fig. 30, *ppp*, and are bolted, as shewn by the dotted lines. The lower stool has likewise additional support from iron knees, brought on under it; and the stools above are supported by iron stanchions, continuing the support from the lower stool.

* These stools must not be carried so far aft as to prevent the guns being sufficiently depressed.

The water-closets are formed by birthing, placed up and down, affixed to circular cants, or let into the stools and supported by thick stiles (Fig. 30, *sss*). These stiles are placed, as to their direction, with regard to the rake and falling-home, the same as explained for the timbers that form the lights, and as just explained for obtaining the form of the upper stools, that the lights and mock lights may produce a good effect both on an athwartship and fore-and-aft view.

The stern is finished with cornices and headings under the stools, and pilasters on the stiles. The balconies are protected by iron stanchions and railing.

STERN FRAME (19).

STERN POST (see POST).

STILES (see BULKHEAD).

STIVE, the angle upwards that any timber, &c. makes with the horizon, or what it is elevated above a horizontal line, as the stive of the cathead, bowsprit, &c.

STOOLS (see QUARTERS).

STOPPINGS-UP (see LAUNCH).

STOPPER BOLTS, large ring bolts, driven through the deck and beam, for stoppering the cable to.

STRAKES (Swedish, *gäng af plankor*; Danish, *gang af planker*; Dutch, *gang van planken*; German, *gang von planken*; French, *virure de bordages*; Italian, *filaro de tavole*; Spanish, *hilada*; Portuguese, *fiada ou carreira de taboas*), a breadth of plank, either within or without board, that ranges from one end of the ship to the other.

*Side-binding Strakes* or *Letting-down Strakes* (228).

STRING (152).

SUPPORTERS (see CATHEADS).

SURGE (see CAPSTAN WELPS).

SYPHERED or CYPHERED (see HARRIS-EDGED).

TABLING (see COAKING).

TAFFRAIL or TAFFAREL (Swedish, *hackebräde*; Danish, *hakkebret*; Dutch, *hakkebord*; German, *hackbord oder hackebord*; French, *coronnement*; Italian, *coronamento*; Spanish, *coronamiento*; Portuguese, *grinalda*), that part of the ship's stern above the cove; it was formerly made of solid fir, and ornamented with carved figures, &c. but now a birthing or planking rabetted is brought on the aft side of the stern timbers, called the backing, from the head of the lights to the upper part of the quarter-deck barricading; and the outline of the taffrail is formed by a moulding, which makes a fair curve with the outline of the quarter-piece.

TAIL or DOVETAIL, the letting in or forming of one piece or timber into another, in a wedge-like form, to prevent their separating.

TANKS (see Table III.).

TARE (see Table II. and III.).

TENON (Swedish, *tapp, pinne*; Danish, *tap, pind*; Dutch, *pen*; German, *pinne*; French, *tenon*; Italian, *dente, anima*; Spanish, *peon*; Portuguese, *dento, macho, piaom*), the end of one piece diminished, to form shoulders, to fix in the hole of another piece, called the mortise, for uniting and fastening them together.

TERM PIECES or TRUSSES, a kind of cartouzes or pieces of carved work, placed under each end of the cove or lower part of the taffrail. They are placed on the side counter timber, and extend down to the breast or foot space rail of the balcony.

THOLES (Swedish, *tullene*; Danish, *tollene*; Dutch, *dollen*; German, *dullen*; French, *toulets*; Italian, *scarmi*; Spanish, *toletes*; Portuguese, *toletes*), pieces fixed in the gunwales of boats to form the rowlocks.

THROAT, the hollow of any piece, or curved part, that connects the two arms of any knee timber, as the inside at the middle of the transoms, the upper part at the middle of the floors, &c. The hollow of the jaws of the gaff is called the throat of the gaff.

THWARTS (Swedish, *toftar*; Danish, *tofter*; Dutch, *doften, dogten*; German, *duchten oder duften in dem boot in der schlupe*; French, *bancs d'une chaloupe*; Italian, *banchi*; Spanish, *bancos de la lancha*; Portuguese, *bancos*), seats or benches in boats for the rowers, &c.

THWARTSHIPS (see ATHWART).

TILLER or TILLAR (Swedish, *roder pinnen*; Danish, *roerpinden*; Dutch, *roerpen*; German, *ruderpinne*; French, *barre du gouvernail*; Italian, *angola, manovella, ribolla*; Spanish, *canna del timon*; Portuguese, *cana do leme*), a lever fixed in the head of the rudder, for turning it when steering.

TIMBER (Swedish, *timmer*; Danish, *tommer*; Dutch, *hout*; German, *holz*; French, *bois*; Italian, *legno*; Spanish, *madera*; Portuguese, *madeira*), is the body of the root, stem, and branches of trees, which is in general designated by the appellation of wood. Timber is in general distinguished into rough, square, or hewn, sided, and converted timber. *Rough Timber* is the timber to the full size, as it is felled, with the lop, top, and bark taken off; *Hewn Timber* is timber squared, as rough timber is squared for measurement, &c. *Sided Timber* is the tree having the full size one way as it is felled; but with the slabs taken off two of its sides, or made straight; the other, so that at the middle of the tree it must be ⅛ of its depth or siding, more than its siding between the wanes. *Converted Timber* is timber cut for different purposes; it is distinguished into thick stuff, plank, board, carling, and scantling. *Thick Stuff* is from 4½ to 12 inches, *Plank* from 1½ to 4 inches, and *Board* below 1½ inch in thickness; *Carling* is timber cut to a rectangular form, and above 4½ inches the smallest way; *Scantling*, commonly called quarter or ledges, is the same as carling, but has one of its dimensions below 4½ inches. Fir, from 3 inches in thickness, downward, is commonly called deal, when sent into the service with the edges taken off, to certain breadths; but if narrow, they are called battens: Fir, when cut from timber in the service, in general takes the name of plank, board, &c. according to its thickness.

Timber of various sorts is used in the construction of the hull, and for the different species of furniture. Principally for the hull, oak, fir, beech, and elm, with now various species of foreign woods; these, with ash and lignum vitæ, are commonly used for the furniture (see ASH, BEECH, ELM, LIGNUM VITÆ, and OAK).

TIMBER HEADS, timbers that are left for lashing the anchor, stopper, shank painter, &c.

TIMBER (Swedish, *inhult*; Danish, *indtömmer*; Dutch, *inhouten*; German, *inholzer*; French, *membres d'un vaisseau*; Italian, *membri d'un vascello*; Spanish, *maderas de la ligazon*; Portuguese, *membros do navio*), a general name given to timbers that compose the frame (42).

TIMBER and ROOM (see ROOM and SPACE).

TIMBERS OF THE HEAD (see HEAD).
TIMBERS OF THE TRUSS FRAME (263).

TONNAGE. The tonnage of a ship is the capacity the body has for carrying a cargo or weights, or the burthen computed according to any established rule.

The common rule for finding the burthen of ships, or what is called the builder's tonnage, is to multiply the extreme breadth into the length, and that product, by half the extreme breadth, and the whole product, divided by 94, is the tonnage according to the rule.

The *Length*, or the length for tonnage, is got by making certain deductions, in proportion to the breadth and height of the wing transom, for the rake of the stem and stern post; that is, from the distance between two perpendiculars to the keel, one drawn passing through the fore part of the stem at the height of the hawse holes, except flush-deck vessels, when it is to be at the height of the upper deck; and the other through the after part of the stern post at the height of the wing transom; subtract 3-5ths of the extreme breadth for the rake of the stem; and, as many feet as the upper side of the wing transom, at the middle line, is above the upper edge of the keel, deduct so many $2\frac{1}{2}$ inches for the rake of the post, and the remainder is the length of the keel for tonnage; but if the stern post rakes more than $2\frac{1}{2}$ inches in a foot, the perpendiculars are then drawn for the first length, through the fore part of the stem at the height of the upper deck and the aft side of the main post at the upper edge of the keel, and a deduction only of 3-5ths of the extreme breadth taken out, for the rake of the stem, neglecting the rake of the post. This last rule for the length of the keel for tonnage is likewise observed, in measuring all ships for tonnage duties, without regarding the rake of the post. The *Breadth* is the breadth to the outside of the timber, with the thickness of the plank of the bottom added on each side.

The foregoing rule gives to all bodies, whatever their capacity, while their length and simple breadth are equal, the same tonnage; to the fullest merchant ship the same as the sharpest cutter.

To give an exact rule for determining the capacity of a ship, can only be such as will give the difference of the load and light displacement, or the capacity of the body between the load and light water line ; but to obtain this would be attended with considerable difficulty, and n suited for general applicatiou, since in foreign ships a ships in the merchants' service, the light water line is seldom known, and the load water line seldom fixed.

If the bodies of ships were regular solids, similar, or varied according to some general law, there would be but little difficulty in forming a common rule, that would be correct and answer for general purposes ; but since this is not the case, and it is only by regularly cubing the body that the exact tonnage can be obtained ; all that can be done is to give a rule, that will be sufficiently near for the purpose, and at the same time give the least errors from a few simple elements, of easy application : and since the measurement must take place under different circumstances, they should be such as can be obtained with the lading in as well as out.

To form a rule, that when applied to different formed bodies, the computed tonnage will vary in some degree with the capacity of the vessel, requires some measurement to be taken, as an element, that changes the most with the form of the body, according to its sharpness or fullness, since the principal dimensions may be the same in bodies of very different capacities.

The girth of the midship section appears to be a measurement that varies most with the form, and that can be easily obtained under the ordinary modes in which ships are measured ; this, probably, if combined in a formula with certain quantities of the length, breadth, and depth, may form a rule of easy application, and be more exact than the one in common use.

TOP AND BUTT (80).

TOPMAST and TOP-GALLANT MAST (see MAST MAKING).

TOPSIDE, that part of the ship above the main wales.

TOP TIMBERS, the timbers in the frame that give the form of the topside (45).

TOP TIMBER LINE. The top side is the upper extremity of the timbers of the frame, before the fore drift, and abaft the main drift. The line that bounds the heads of the timbers between the drifts, or the uppermost line that can be carried the whole length of the ship, parallel to the sheer, without being broken off by the drifts, is ᴛᴇᴅ the top timber line ; this line terminates the frame ween the drifts.

Tʀᴀɪʟ Bᴏᴀʀᴅs, the carved work placed between the cheeks, from the lower part of the figure, on the knee of the head.

Tʀᴀɴsᴏᴍs (Swedish, *nedra häktbjalkarne* ; Danish, *varpen* ; Dutch, *worpen* ; German, *worpen des platten spiegels* ; French, *barres d'arcasse* ; Italian, *gue* ; Spanish, *puercas, cochinatas* ; Portuguese, *gio segundo, terceiro, &c.*) (25).

*Deck Transom* (see Dᴇᴄᴋ Tʀᴀɴsᴏᴍ).

*Helm-Port Transom* (see Hᴇʟᴍ-Pᴏʀᴛ Tʀᴀɴsᴏᴍ).

*Wing Transom* (Swedish, *häckbalk* ; Danish, *hæk-bielke* ; Dutch, *hekbalk* ; German, *heck-balken* ; French, *lisse d'hourdie ou la grande barre d'arcasse* ; Italian, *triganto* ; Venetian, *crose* ; Spanish, *yugo de la popa, yugo principal* ; Portuguese, *gio grande*), (25).

*Filling Transom* (25).

Tʀᴀɴsᴏᴍ Kɴᴇᴇs (see Kɴᴇᴇs).

Tʀᴀɴsᴘᴏʀᴛɪɴɢ Bʟᴏᴄᴋs (see Bʟᴏᴄᴋs).

Tʀᴇᴇɴᴀɪʟs (Swedish, *naglar* ; Danish, *naagler eller nagler* ; Dutch, *naagels, nagels* ; German, *nagel, hölzerne nagel, nai-nagel* ; French, *gournables* ; Italian, *caviglie* ; Spanish, *cabillas* ; Portuguese, *cavilhas*), pins of a cylindrical form, in general of oak of the best quality ; they are used for fastening chocks on different timbers, or for slightly fastening different timbers together, but they are principally used for fastening the different planking to the timbers. Treenails vary from 1 inch to 1¼ of an inch in diameter, and the different gradations from the smallest to the largest diameters are distinguished by particular marks, and are called by the workmen, one, two, three, four, and five edlars cross, cross, broad arrow, round O, and round O and spot.

Tʀᴇsᴛʟᴇᴛʀᴇᴇs (Swedish, *längsalningar* ; Danish, *lang-salinger* ; Dutch, *lang-zaalingen* ; German, *lang-sahlingen* ; French, *longis, barres maitresses de hune* ; Italian, *bai* ; Spanish, *baos* ; Portuguese, *vaos*), (see Mᴀsᴛ Mᴀᴋɪɴɢ).

Tricing Battens, battens for tricing the hammocks up to; they are nailed between the beams under the decks.

Truss (see Terms).

Trussed Frame (262) (see Timber and Truss-pieces).

*Trussed Frame*, the resistance it opposes (269).

Truss-Pieces to the Diagonal or Trussed Frame (268).

Trysail Gaff (see Mast Making).

Trysail Mast (see Mast Making).

Tuck, where the after extremities of the exterior planking end, either on the wing transom or against the tuck timber.

*Round-aft* or *Square Tuck* (30).

Tuck Rail (see Rails and Stern).

Tumbling-home, or Falling-home, what the topside is inclined inwards, from a vertical line drawn through the main breadth, or what it is within a perpendicular to the transverse axis.

Upper Deck (see Deck).

Upper Works (see Hull).

Waist (Swedish, *keulen*; Danish, *kulen*; Dutch, *kuil*; German, *kuhl des schiffes*; French, *coursive*; Italian, *pozzo*; Spanish, *plaza de armas*; Portuguese, *couves*), that part of the topside between the main and fore drifts (90) that is above the upper deck.

Waist Rails (see Rails).

Wales (Swedish, *berghulterna*; Danish, *berkholter*; Dutch, *berghouten*; German, *berghölzer*; French, *preceintes, cintes, carreaux*; Italian, *cinte*; Spanish, *cintas*; Portuguese, *cintas*), (85).

*Main Wales* (Swedish, *stora eller understa berghultet*; Danish, *store bergholtet*; Dutch, *het groote berghout*; German, *das grosse bergholz*; French, *grande preceinte*; Italian, *cinta della prima coperta, cinta della boca*; Spanish, *cinta de la manga, cinta primera*; Portuguese, *cinta grande, cinta do grasso*), (96).

*Middle Wales*, or *Sheer Wales* (100).

*Channel Wale* (98).

Wash Boards under the Cheeks (Swedish, *bräder under gallionsknän at for hindra störtningen af sjon*; Danish, *gallion braeder*; Dutch, *blaasbalk*; German, *blasebalken*; French, *tambour d'éperon, mouchoir ou remplissage sous les jottereaux*; Italian, *battimare*; Spanish, *badidero*; Portuguese, *chapuzes das curvas do beque*), solid pieces brought under the lower part of the cheeks of the head, with their outer parts lying obliquely, from the outer part of the cheek to the bow, for breaking the sea off from the under side of the cheek when the ship pitches. Wash-boards, sometimes called weather-boards, are likewise shifting strakes made to fix into the gunwale or topside of small vessels or boats occasionally to keep the sea out.

WATER (see Table III).

WATERWAYS (Swedish, *vaterbordsplankar*; Danish, *livholter*; Dutch, *waater-borden, waatergangen*; German, *leibhölzer*; French, *gouttières*; Italian, *trincanili*; Spanish, *trancaniles*; Portuguese, *toboas dos trincanizes*) (219).

*Thin Waterways* (287).

*Thick Waterways* (220 and 222).

WEDGES OF THE MAST (Swedish, *mastkilar*; Danish, *mastkiler*; Dutch, *vystingen, mastkeggen*; German, *masten-kiele*; French, *coins des mâts*; Italian, *conj degli alberi*; Spanish, *cunnas del palo*; Portuguese, *cunhos dos mastros*), wedges of fir driven between the mast and the partners; they circumscribe the mast, and are from 10 to 14 inches above the partners; at their head or upper end, they are in general from 1 inch to 1¼ inch larger than at the partners; and are caulked.

WELPS or WHELPS (see CAPSTAN).

WHEEL, or STEERING WHEEL, a wheel for obtaining the power on the tiller when steering.

WINCH (Swedish, *dräyare*; Danish, *drejer*; Dutch, *draajer, hand-vat*; German, *dreher*; French, *manivelle*; Italian, *manubrio*; Spanish, *ciguenna*; Portuguese, *manivella, manubrio*), a machine used for more powerfully applying different ropes, in general in cutters and small vessels; it is formed of two conical pieces of wood, united to an iron spindle, which forms its axis, and works in two rhodens or gudgeons; the power is applied by two cranks.

WINDLASS (Swedish, *brädspel*; Danish, *bradspil*; Ducth, *braadspil*; German, *bratspill*; French, *vindas, virevant*; Italian, *mulinello*; Spanish, *molinete*; Portuguese, *molinete, ou bolinete*), a machine used in small vessels, instead of a capstan, for heaving up the anchor, &c. The windlass is fixed between the carrick bitts; it is in general formed of one large piece of oak of an octagonal form, which has an iron spindle driven into each end, with their centers very accurately in a right line so as to form the axis; these spindles are kept in their places by a bolt in each, that passes through them and the barrel. At the middle and sometimes at each end is fixed a plate or hoop with teeth, called the ratchet or paul plate, or hoop for the pauls, which is of iron, and fixed to the paul bitts; and sometimes carrick bitts, to catch in to prevent the return when heaving a heavy strain, or charged with the effort of the cable. The spindles work in brass rhodens or gudgeons, fixed to the carrick bitts, and the common way of obtaining the power is by handspikes, which are fixed in holes or mortises cut through the barrel for the purpose. The power is obtained sometimes by a tooth-wheel and pinion, and applied upon a crank attached to the pinion.

WING TRANSOM (see TRANSOM).

WOODS (see TIMBER).

WOODLOCK, a chock put in the throating or score of the pintle, above the load water line, or as near to it as possible; to prevent the rudder from rising, one end abuts under the lower side of the brace, and the other against the score. The woodlock is in general coppered over.

WRUNG HEADS, a name given formerly to the floor heads at that part of the body beside the keel, which is in contact with the supporting surface when the body takes the ground (see FLOOR HEADS).

XEBEC (Swedish, *chebeque*; Danish, *schierbek*; Dutch, *schebeck*; German, *schebecke*; French, *chébec*; Italian, *sciambecco*; Spanish, *jabeque*; Portuguese, *zabeco*), a small vessel with three masts, with the sails mostly similar to those of the polacre, but furnished with lateen as well as square yards, which are used according to the point of sailing, and the state of the weather. These vessels are navigated on the coasts of Spain, Portugal, and Barbary.

YACHTS, vessels of state or accommodation.

YARD (Swedish, *rä*; Danish, *raa eller ræ*; Dutch, *raa of ree*; German, *rah oder raa*; French, *vergue*;

Italian, *pennone*; Spanish, *verga*; Portuguese, *verga*), (see MAST MAKING).

*Lower Yards.* Main Yard (Swedish, *stor rän*; Danish, *store raaen*; Dutch, *de groote raa*; German, *die grosse raa*; French, *la grande vergue*; Italian, *pennone di maestra*; Spanish, *verga mayor*; Portuguese, *verga grande*) and *Fore Yard* (Swedish, *fock ran*; Danish, *fok raæn*; Dutch, *de fokke raa*; German, *die fock-raa*; French, *la vergue de misaine*; Italian, *pennone di trinchetto*; Spanish, *verga de trinquete*; Portuguese, *verga do traquete*).

*Topsail Yards.* Main (Swedish, *stormärs-ran*; Danish, *store mærs-raaen*; Dutch, *de groote mars-raa*; German, *die grosse mars-raa*; French, *la vergue de grande hunier*; Italian, *pennone di gabbia*; Spanish, *verga de gabia*; Portuguese, *verga de gabia*), *Fore* (Swedish, *for mäs-rän*; Danish, *for mærs-raaen*; Dutch, *de voor mars raa*; German, *die vor-mars-raa*; French, *la vergue du petit hunier*; Italian, *pennone di parrochetto*; Spanish, *verga de velacho*; Portuguese, *verga do velacho*), and *Mixen* (Swedish, *kryss ran*; Danish, *kryds-raaen*; Dutch, *de kruis-raa*; German, *die kreuz-raa*; French, *vergue de perroquet de fouge*; Italian, *pennone di contramezzana*; Spanish, *verga de sobre-mesana*; Portuguese, *verga da gata*).

*Top-gallant Yards.* Main (Swedish, *stor-brämrän*; Danish, *store-bram-raaen*; Dutch, *de groote bramraa*; German, *die grosse bramm-raa*; French, *la vergue de grand perroquet*; Italian, *pennone di pappafico di maestra*; Spanish, *verga de juanete mayor*; Portuguese, *verga do joanete grande*), *Fore* (Swedish, *för bram rän*; Danish, *for-bram raaen*; Dutch, *de voor-bram-raa*; German, *die vor-bram-raa*; French, *la vergue de petit perroquet*; Italian, *pennone di pappafico di parrochetto*; Spanish, *verga del juanete de velacho*; Portuguese, *verga do joanete de proa*), and *Mixen* (Swedish, *krys-bram-ran*; Danish, *boven-kryds-raaen*; Dutch, *de boven-kruis-raa*; German, *die kreuz-bram-raa*; French, *vergue de perruche*; Italian, *ponnone del belvedere*; Spanish, *verga de periquito*; Portuguese, *verga da sobregata*).

*Royal Yards.* Main (Swedish, *stor bofven-bramran*; Danish, *store-boven-bram-raaen*; Dutch, *de groote boven-bram-raa*; German, *die grosse ober bram-raa*; French, *la vergue de grand perroquet volant*; Italian, *pennone di contra pappafico di maestra*; Spanish, *verga de sobre-juanete mayor*; Portuguese, *verga do sobrejoanete grande*), and *Fore* (Swedish, *för-bofven-bram-răn*; Danish, *for-boven-bram-raaen*; Dutch, *de voor-boven-bram-raa*; German, *die vor-ober-bram-raa*; French, *la vergue du petit perroquet volant*; Italian, *pennone di contrapappafico di parrochetto*; Spanish, *verga del sobrejuanete de velacho*; Portuguese, *vergilha do sobrejoanete de proa*).

*Cross-Jack Yard* (Swedish, *begine răn*; Danish, *beginne-raaen*; Dutch, *de bagyn-raa*; German, *die bagien-raa*; French, *vergue seche, vergue barrée, vergue de fougue*; Italian, *pennone di fuoco*; Spanish, *verga seca, verga de gata*; Portuguese, *verga seca*).

*Spritsail Yard* (Swedish, *blind-ran*; Danish, *blinde raaen*; Dutch, *de blinde raa*; German, *die blinde-raa*; French, *vergue de civadière*; Italian, *pennone di civada*; Spanish, *verga de cebadera*; Portuguese, *verga da cevadeira*).

*Studding-sail Yards* (Swedish, *läseglets răn*; Danish, *læ-sejls-raaen*; Dutch, *lee-zeils-raa*; German, *leesegel-raa*; French, *vergue des bonnettes*; Italian, *pennone di cortelazzo*; Spanish, *verga de ala*; Portuguese, *verga do cutello* (see MAST MAKING.)

YAWL (Swedish, *julle*; Danish, *jolle*; Dutch, *jol*; German, *jolle*; French, *canot*; Italian, *barca*; Spanish, *barca*; Portuguese, *hum bote* (see BOAT).

THE END.

CPSIA information can be obtained
at www.ICGtesting.com
Printed in the USA
BVHW030416020822
643544BV00013B/1191

9 781166 463953